The Age

The Ages of the Justice League

Essays on America's Greatest Superheroes in Changing Times

Edited by JOSEPH J. DAROWSKI

McFarland & Company, Inc., Publishers

Jefferson, North Carolina

LIBRARY OF CONGRESS CATALOGUING-IN-PUBLICATION DATA

Names: Darowski, Joseph J., editor.
Title: The ages of the Justice League : essays on America's greatest
superheroes in changing times / edited by Joseph J. Darowski.
Description: Jefferson, North Carolina : McFarland & Company, Inc.,
Publishers, 2017. | Includes bibliographical references and index.
Identifiers: LCCN 2016044303 | ISBN 9781476662251
(softcover : acid free paper) ∞
Subjects: LCSH: Justice League of America (Fictitious characters) | Justice
League of America (Comic strip) | Comic books, strips, etc.—History and
criticism. | Superheroes in literature. | Literature and society—United States.
Classification: LCC PN6728.J87 A37 2017 | DDC 741.5/973—dc23
LC record available at https://lccn.loc.gov/2016044303

BRITISH LIBRARY CATALOGUING DATA ARE AVAILABLE

ISBN (print) 978-1-4766-6225-1
ISBN (ebook) 978-1-4766-2707-6

Front cover illustration © 2017 DigitalVision

Printed in the United States of America

McFarland & Company, Inc., Publishers
Box 611, Jefferson, North Carolina 28640
www.mcfarlandpub.com

To Trixie Smith—
thanks for helping me figure out
this essay collection thing.

Table of Contents

Preface

The Justice League of America. The Justice League. JLA. Justice League International. Justice League Europe. Justice League Dark. Justice League: Task Force. Young Justice. Super Friends. Justice League Unlimited.

Without a doubt, DC Comics' Justice League is one of the most important properties in popular culture history. There is the undeniable staying power of the initial concept of uniting DC Comics' most powerful characters into a single team, but there is also the fact that imitation from competitors is at least partially responsible for the rise of Marvel Comics' superhero universe. Comic books, television cartoons, live action series, blockbuster films, and huge amounts of merchandise all owe a debt to the Silver Age launch of the Justice League. In a world where our popular landscape includes film universes and television series with intersecting characters, the Justice League is a key part of our entertainment industry's legacy and future.

The comic book industry saw a boom period that has come to be called the Golden Age of Comics when Superman and other costumed heroes found huge audiences in the late 1930s and 1940s. Eventually, several of these characters joined together as a team called the Justice Society of America. In the latter half of the 1940s other genres rose in popularity as interest in superheroes waned, and most comic book series featuring the crime fighting adventures of superpowered characters were phased out by publishers.

Legendary DC Comics editor Julius Schwartz launched the Silver Age of Comic Books when his company reintroduced Golden Age characters with the same superhero names but new origins and secret identities, starting with the Flash in 1956. After seeing readers respond favorably to new versions of individual characters, it was a natural extension of the strategy to re-imagine and reintroduce the first superhero team in American comic books. In updating a 1940s series for the 1960s, the name was changed from the formal-sounding Justice Society to the bolder Justice League. Writer Gardner Fox and artist Mike Sekowsky launched the team in 1960, and the franchise has been one of the mainstays for DC Comics ever since.

As with any decades-long property that has had dozens of creators and editors guiding the stories, there have been many different interpretations of the Justice League. This essay collection features 17 essays by scholars who have performed close readings of comic book stories from different eras of the Justice League. The goal of this book is to demonstrate connections between the time period when these stories were being produced and the themes found in the comic books. These themes can be found in the types of villains being fought, the characteristics of members of the team, the messages found in the stories, or the general tone of the tales. Many talented writers, artists, colorists, letterers, and editors were involved in the creation of these comic books, and their work is naturally a product of their times. Highlighting the relationship between a society and the entertainment that is produced and consumed in a given era illuminates the enduring significance of these popular culture products.

The first essay in the collection considers some of the very earliest stories of the Justice League, before the team even had their own comic book title. In "The Brave and Bold Beginning of the Silver Age Superteam" John Darowski looks at several Justice League stories that appeared in *The Brave and the Bold*. He identifies several threats to the Cold War American identities that are explored in the Justice League's battles, including issues involving atomic weapons, scientists, and the nuclear family.

Louie Dean Valencia-García explores the manner in which the Justice League begins to act as a surrogate family for its members. "A League of Orphans and Single Parents: Making a Family in an Era of *Father Knows Best*" presents the argument that family dynamics on display are subtly subversive to the idealized "nuclear family" that was generally promoted in the culture of the time.

"The Caged Bird Sings: *The Justice League of America* and the Domestic Containment of Black Canary" explores the history of the Black Canary. However, in order to fully appreciate the complexity of the transformation the character undergoes, and to illuminate the multiple influences on those changes, Thomas C. Donaldson contrasts the Golden Age version of Black Canary with one that is pulled into the Silver Age Justice League comic books.

W.C. Bamberger and Gene Phillips both explore the influence of 1960s social issues on the superhero team. In "Social Justice and Silver Age Superheroes" Bamberger looks at the evolving attitudes towards morality and the Vietnam War that found their way into *The Justice League of America* comic books from that era. Phillips looks at a pair of comic books from the same era that contain moral messages aimed at the juvenile target audience. While some elements have not aged well, "Relevance in Wonderland: The Mixed Success of Gardner Fox's Message Comic Books" praises the intent behind storylines that address disabilities and racial prejudice.

Peter W. Lee looks at story from the 1970s as the Justice League is joined by the Golden Age Justice Society of America in a journey to another parallel Earth where heroes are still fighting Nazis because World War II never ended in this dimension. "A Crisis of Infinite Dearth: Winning Vietnam via the Never-Ending War on Earth-X" argues that this story has a blend of nostalgia for a simpler past, critique of America's place in the contemporary world, and hope for a role the country could take.

Jason Sacks takes a close look at Steve Englehart's ten-issue run on *Justice League of America*. Sacks highlights Englehart's unique take on DC's premier team, which blends an honoring of the character's histories with a revolutionary interpretation of the icons. "The Benefits of Doubts: Steve Englehart's Radical Take on Tradition" highlights how a writer can honor tradition in order to advance narrative complexity and improve characterization.

Similarly, Ruth McClelland-Nugent in "The Not-So-Golden Age: Gender, Race and Nostalgia in *All-Star Squadron* 1981–1987" examines how Roy Thomas considers the Golden Age history of DC Comics (and many of its competitors in the field) while modernizing the stories and characters in *All-Star Squadron*. Thomas walked a line between nostalgia for the Golden Age, and recognition that by the 1980s many aspects of American society had improved considerably from their status four decades earlier.

Charles Henebry and Brian Cogan each examine one of the most famous eras of the Justice League, when the comic was written by Keith Giffen and J.M. DeMatteis and drawn by Kevin Maguire. In "Gritty Levity: The Giffen/ DeMatteis Era of the Justice League" Henebry argues that this run, noted for its light-hearted use of jokes, actually shares more thematic relationship with other 1980s comics, such as *Watchmen* and *The Dark Knight* than it appears at first. Brian Cogan's "'I'm Batman! Bwah ha ha!' Comedy in the Grim 'n' Gritty Eighties" concludes that this version of the series grounds the team in reality far more than its earlier incarnations because it leaves behind the A-list, godlike characters and also the combination of light-heartedness with heavy drama is more realistic than the grim 'n' gritty style prevalent in other DC comics of the era.

Fernando Gabriel Pagnoni Berns and Leonardo Acosta Lando take a close look at the European branch of the Justice League. "Lacking Leadership: The Justice League Europe's Place in the DC Universe" considers how the relationship between the established Justice League and its newly formed European branch mirrors many of the geopolitical relationships of the era when the comic book was being published.

In "Extreme Transitions: Trends and Trepidations from 1992 to 1996" D.R. Hammontree considers an era between the more humorous Giffen/ DeMatteis run and Grant Morrison's famous relaunch of the series with the *JLA*. This era saw several attempts to redefine and establish a bold new identity for the iconic franchise that are very reflective of the early 1990s comic book industry.

Nicole Freim considers a story written by Mark Waid and drawn by Howard Porter and Steve Scott in "What We've Got Here Is Failure to Communicate: Trust, Technology and Fear in 'The Tower of Babel.'" The storyline sees the Justice League torn apart by a series of plans Batman prepared in order to take down each member in the event they turned bad. Freim considers the environmental concerns expressed by the villain as well as the role technology, and the fear of its abuse, plays in the plot.

Joseph J. Darowski's "'Whether we fear we do too much—or not enough': *JLA/Avengers* and the Cross-Universe Causes of Conflict" considers the last crossover between the two largest American comic book companies. While it is easy to dismiss the mini-series as either a cash grab by the companies or superfluous fan service, Darowski argues that the series is distinctly a post–9/11 artifact of popular entertainment.

Jennifer Swartz-Levine analyzes Darwyn Cooke's *The New Frontier*, a mini-series published in 2004 but set in the early days of the Cold War. "Madwomen: Sexism as Nostalgia, or Feminism in *The New Frontier*" examines how the representation of the female characters simultaneously represents and subverts attitudes from an earlier era of American history.

"Absolute Secrets Kept Absolutely: Public Memory and Forgetting in *Identity Crisis*" looks at the role of trauma and memory in the formation of identity. Daniel J. O'Rourke positions the mini-series by Brad Meltzer as a story that explores a heinous event in a superhero universe that had long-lasting effects on fictional characters and as a story with particular resonance for a readership that had passed through a national renegotiation of identity following the terrorist attacks of 9/11.

Cathy Leogrande looks at the Justice League comic books that were produced following a massive, company wide continuity reboot. "The Good, the Bad and the Reboot: *Justice League* in the *New 52*" considers fan and critical reaction to the new series, particularly in light of issues of race and gender.

The Justice League has an important place in American popular culture, and the essays in this collection represent a fraction of the scholarship that can and should be done to better understand the relationships between our popular entertainment and the evolution of American society. Considering the iconic figures of the American entertainment industry and how they evolve to remain relevant for changing tastes and times leads to insights into how and why certain characters and stories can endure in popularity across generations.

The Brave and Bold Beginning of the Silver Age Superteam

JOHN DAROWSKI

On July 24, 1959, Vice President Richard Nixon and Soviet Premier Nikita Khrushchev engaged in a lively, impromptu debate over the merits of the American way of life at the U.S. Exhibition in Moscow. The display of groceries, clothes, cars, and houses, representing the everyday life in the United States during the affluent 1950s, was part of a 1958 agreement to exchange expositions of science, technology, and culture (Marling 242, 250). Due to the political leaders' discussion taking place at the centerpiece of the exhibit, a model of a suburban home, it was subsequently dubbed the Kitchen Debate. Nixon argued that the domestic technology offered a freedom from drudgery and that the multiplicity of consumer options reflected the democratic freedom of choice. Khrushchev, who claimed that that the USSR would catch up to this U.S. technology within a few years, wondered why so many choices were needed when the focus should be on function and, more importantly, why there were no scientific displays to equal Sputnik (242). Underlying this debate was each country's relationship with technology at the height of the Cold War. This concern over technology and its centrality in the space race, the arms race, and American lifestyle would frame the earliest adventures of the Justice League of America in the pages of *The Brave and the Bold* in 1960.

Hope and anxiety over technology abounded throughout the 1950s as American culture projected its role into the future to either create a utopia of leisure or a devastating apocalypse. During the decade, luxuries which had once been reserved for the wealthy became easily accessible to the growing middle class (Marling 21). But the same science that was creating the conditions for

5

economic prosperity and abundance was also responsible for producing the atom and hydrogen bombs (Costello 54). This was not so much a concern as long as the United States held a monopoly on the secrets for these weapons. In their national hubris, it was thought that communist countries could not challenge democratic countries in the sciences, where the free competition of ideas created progress (Boorstin 591). But once the USSR claimed to hold the same power over the atom or, more terrifyingly, moved ahead with Sputnik, the potential for the technology which provided security and comfort to be utilized to take away freedom or simply destroy became quite real (Maguire, "Supervillains" 18). National security became a race for more and better means of destruction.

The race for technological superiority was one of the centerpieces of the Cold War. Political and popular culture rhetoric circumscribed this complex geopolitical conflict into a simple binary. In the discourse from the West, the United States, valuing freedom, individualism, and private property, was democratic and good. Inversely, the Soviet Union was totalitarian, atheistic, and evil (Doherty 2). This moral dichotomy was reinforced by political action such as the creation of the North Atlantic Treaty Organization (NATO) in 1949, a mutual defense alliance of Western European nations and the United States, and the Warsaw Pact in 1955, a similar alliance between the Soviet Union and Eastern European satellite countries, as well as the construction of the Berlin Wall in 1961. The duel between the free world and those behind the Iron Curtain did not allow for nuance between different types of communism. The Chinese Communist Revolution of 1949 caused the People's Republic of China to be viewed as a puppet state of the USSR, despite their differences (MacDonald 79). The Korean War (1950–53) was then interpreted as an effort by the Sino-Soviet monolith to extend its influence into the Pacific (Doherty 7). The Cold War came to be viewed as a battle between two superpowers over the fate of the world.

This rise of the United States as a global superpower was not merely a matter of international policy, but of national security. Following the Great Depression and World War II, America had learned that neglecting international affairs threatened their political and economic prosperity (Costello 33). Additionally, citizens desired stability after the previous decade and a half of trials (Johnson 70). These ideals of prosperity and stability became enshrined in the middle class family. By the end of the 1950s, the rising standard of living and increasing equality which supported the nuclear family became evidence of America's virtuous society, a view advocated by the Cold War dichotomy (Costello 49–50). However, this international duality also led to essentialism. Consensus became the norm and any dissent from this ideological hegemony was viewed as un–American (39). The House Un-American Activities Committee (HUAC), the "witch hunts" of Senator Joseph

McCarthy, the blacklist, and loyalty oaths were all paranoid measures to police society for undesirable influences.

American popular culture reflected this consensus hegemony as adventure stories became political morality plays. Whether they featured cowboys, spies, or superheroes, heroes were pitted against villains, usually thinly-veiled stand-ins for communists, bent on world domination, destroying the American way of life, or just plain destruction. This value-laden symbolism of individual do-gooders triumphing over evil helped perpetuate the image of the United States as a virtuous, democratic system that would overcome its totalitarian foes. However, as much of this content was realized in serialized form through radio, television, and comic books, the ongoing narratives necessitated the continuation of the conflict between good and evil through new enemies that always arose, highlighting the ongoing nature of the Cold War.

For superheroes to actively participate in this consensus ideology, some change in their characterization was necessary. During the golden age (1939–55), beginning with the introduction of Superman, superheroes had crusaded for change as embodiments of the New Deal and World War II. But after those victories had been won, superheroes had lost direction and relevancy and declined in popularity (Wright 59). New genres, such as crime and horror, became popular. But these did not adhere to consensus values of society and came to be viewed as a threat. It was only through the adoption of the Comics Code, a self-censoring set of content guidelines, that the industry was able to endure. The Code was modeled after the Hollywood Production Code and the Television Code and served much the same purpose: to avoid government censorship, placate moral guardians, and lend respectability to a disreputable medium (Doherty 68). It also paved the way for the return of the superhero, as they morphed from agents of change into agents of the state (Johnson 73).

DC Comics led the Silver Age revival by revamping older characters such as the Flash and Green Lantern with a science fiction twist beginning in 1956. Titles like *Showcase* and *The Brave and the Bold* became a place to try out concepts before, if they proved successful, giving them their own title. In 1959, editor Julius Schwartz felt it was time revive the superhero team. With writer Gardner Fox, creator of the original Justice Society of America in 1940, and artist Mike Sedowsky, Schwartz brought together headliners Superman, Batman, and Wonder Woman, new versions of the Flash and Green Lantern, and back-page characters Aquaman and Martian Manhunter (Wells 16). But Schwartz felt the team needed a new name: "To me, 'Society' meant something you found on Park Avenue. I felt that 'League' was a stronger word, one that readers could identify with because of *baseball leagues* [and] I decided to use it in the revival" (qtd. in Wells 16–17).

The newly christened Justice League of America received its tryout in

The Brave and the Bold #28–30, before receiving its own title in late 1960. Bringing together a team of superheroes during the height of the Cold War could have been a superheroic representation of the United Nations or NATO, individuals coming together for a common purpose. But as the superhero team's name is the Justice League of America, the team is an explicit American endeavor despite a roster that includes a Martian, a Kryptonian, an Amazon, and an Atlantean. Despite the comraderie suggested by the name "Justice League," the members did not necessarily fight as a single unit. These initial issues established a chapter format, bringing the team together in the first and then separating them for individual or team-up missions for subsequent chapters before bringing them back together again at the end. Additionally, Superman editor Mort Weisinger and Batman editor Jack Schiff didn't want their heroes' appearances to detract from their own titles, so Superman and Batman would not participate in any meaningful way during the initial years. They may appear briefly at the beginning and end of the stories, and never on the covers (Wells 17).

The first appearance of the Justice League of America was in *The Brave and the Bold* #28 (February-March 1960) in a tale entitled "Starro the Conqueror!" Rather than an origin story, the League is already formed and ready to combat the titular Starro, a giant starfish from outer space. Starro's plan for the conquest of Earth involves stealing atomic energy, kidnapping scientists, and brainwashing a suburban community—topics rife with national phobic pressure points built around themes of science and technology.

As Starro does not travel in a spaceship, his link to the threat of technology may not be immediately evident. However, this comes after a few years of the Soviet Union leading the way in the space race, beginning with the launch of the satellite Sputnik I in October 1957. This was followed by Sputnik II, carrying the dog Laika, in November 1957 and Sputnik III in May 1958. In 1959, the USSR launched satellites to the moon with Luna I and Luna III. This was followed two years later by the first man in space, Yuri Gagarin, in April 1961 (Maguire, "Wonder Woman" 42).

The U.S. government countered the Soviet efforts with the formation of the National Aeronautic and Space Administration (NASA) in 1958. While the goal was to show that America was not behind in the new space race, results were not immediately forthcoming. Vanguard I, the first American attempt to launch a satellite, failed in December 1957, as did the subsequent launch in February 1958. Explorer I achieved success in January 1958, but that seems to be an exception in these years, as the program continued to be plagued with failures and rocket explosions (Maguire, "Wonder Woman" 42). This is not to say the Soviets did not have their share of catastrophes, but their successes were more monumental in comparison. Malfunctioning technology magnified the American unease that hostile powers were technologically ahead and that the nation could not adequately defend itself (49). While the United States already feared invasion, whether full-scale or more subtly through subversive agents, the space race added a new direction for infiltration and science fiction stories exploited the idea of alien invaders coming to destroy the world.

However, in a nation that celebrated individualism, if the government cannot adequately protect the populus, citizens such as superheroes will step in to fill the gap. Such is the role of the Justice League, as seen in *The Brave and the Bold* #28, even with a storyline that appears quaint by modern storytelling standards. The issue begins with Aquaman, while patrolling the Atlantic coast, receiving a warning: "My friend Peter ... the puffer fish ... is calling me and—Great Neptune! What an incredible tale it is thought-beaming at me!" (8). Starro has descended into the ocean and deputized three starfish, granting them a portion of his power, to help him in his goal to conquer the planet. Aquaman immediately summons the Justice League to their headquarters, though Superman is busy preventing meteors from hitting Earth and Batman is closing in on his archenemies in Gotham City. Flash, as chairman, quickly divides the rest of the team for individual missions, though exactly how they know where Starro will strike is unclear.

Green Lantern is sent to Rocky Mountain National Park to prevent Starro's minion from stealing an atom bomb from an Air Force plane. Upon seeing the alien, one of the plane's crewmembers exclaims: "A starfish.... Gigantic.... Flying..." The pilot orders: "Hold your fire! Maybe it'll just fly past us!" (12). It does not. Though Green Lantern and the pilots fight valiantly, they cannot stop the giant starfish from escaping with the bomb. When Green Lantern give chase, the starfish detonates the bomb and absorbs the energy before transmitting it to Starro.

While Starro's intention in stealing an atomic bomb is unknown, the threat of nuclear power was quite clear. After the first and only military uses of atomic bombs to end World War II, it was hoped that fear of this superior power would prevent future conflicts (Pagnoni Berns and Marino 36). It was thus quite a disturbing blow when the Soviet Union detonated their own atomic bomb in September 1949. America was quick to develop the more destructive hydrogen bomb, only to have Soviet Premier Georgi Malenkov announce to the world in 1952 that the United States no longer held a monopoly on that technology either (MacDonald 47). For the first time in history, the nations of the world feared not just military or political defeat, but literal annihilation.

The public was quite aware of this potential devastation through the new medium of television. Cultural historian Thomas Doherty writes: "The cultural fallout from the Bomb settled all over American culture, but a series of made-for-television events sent out particularly intense shockwaves" (8).

Live broadcasts of bomb tests began in 1951. Especially relevant was the broadcast by all networks on March 17, 1953, when the Atomic Energy Commission and Civil Defense Administration utilized "Doom Town," a fabricated two-household community complete with mannequins to represent the family, to simulate the impact of an atomic explosion on the average home (10). Networks also produced "fictionalized documentaries," hosted by respected newsmen, postulating on what would happen after an enemy attack on U.S. cities (MacDonald 44–45). Fears of destruction may have been alleviated somewhat in 1958 when the U.S., the UK, and the USSR agreed to a moratorium on testing, though no permanent agreement was reached and escalating tensions ended the moratorium in 1961 (Maguire, "American Military" 51). Anxiety over the bomb lay just beneath the cultural surface throughout the 50s.

That Starro was able to steal an atomic bomb from a plane in American airspace was not an outrageous fiction. Nuclear weaponry was often transported this way and this resulted in some near disasters. On February 5, 1958, a B-47 bomber dropped a nuclear bomb in the waters off Tybee Island, Georgia, after a collision with Air Force jet ("For Fifty"). On March 11, 1958, a B-47E bomber on its way to England for exercises accidently dropped its bomb on Mars Bluff, South Carolina. Fortunately, the nuclear core had been stored separately, though the bomb did land on two little girls' playhouse (Lamar). And on January 24, 1961, a B-52 bomber broke up in midair over Goldboro, North Carolina, releasing two nuclear bombs which nearly detonated. Of the incident, Secretary of Defense Robert McNamara stated: "By the slightest margin of chance, literally the failure of two wires to cross, a nuclear explosion was averted" (Lacey-Bordeaux).

Fear of destruction was coupled with concern over the environmental impact of the radioactive fallout. Films such as *Godzilla* (1954) and *Them!* (1954) featured creatures mutated by radiation as one possible catastrophic outcome. This was also reflected on the cover of *The Brave and the Bold* #28 where the Justice League wrestled a giant starfish on a beach. The metropolitan city in the background reveals what is at stake should the League fail to in their battle with Starro.

Returning to the issue, the second of Starro's deputies has lifted the Hall of Science into the sky above Science City. It states: "My mission is to rob the brainpower of the scientists inside this building!" (17). Wonder Woman and the Martian Manhunter battle to save the scientists and subdue the creature, which is now able to unleash atomic rays. With the help of her invisible jet, Wonder Woman is able to bring the building down for a safe landing, though it is unclear if the Starro's warrior had been successful or not in stealing the scientists "mind knowledge" (12).

This vignette illustrates the importance of scientists but also the potential for the subversion of scientific knowledge through spying. American society had some ambivalence over the role of scientists after World War II, seeing them as both the cause of and solution to many of their problems. While the technology they created increased productivity and created commodities that resulted in more leisure time, they had also created the atomic bomb. His-torian Daniel Boorstin explains: "But many American were haunted by fear that in the mushroom cloud over Hiroshima they had conjured a fifth rider of the Apocalypse. Along with Pestilence and War and Famine and Death, was there now a horse reserved for Science?" (586). Historian Richard Hof-stadter sees this fear as creating an attitude of anti-intellectualism in Amer-ican life in the early 1950s. But Sputnik shocked the nation into realizing that this suspicion of the life of the mind had become a hazard to survival (5). The United States reevaluated its education system, especially through com-parison with the Soviet system, and enacted the National Defense Education Act (NDEA) to increase funding to educational institutions. However, this resulted in intellect being regarded as a resource for creating rockets and bombs rather than actually increasing individual intelligence (5).

Coupled with this renewed emphasis on education and scientific devel-opment was the potential for new knowledge and discoveries to be stolen and then subverted by the enemy through spying. This had already occurred in 1949 when the FBI, investigating how the Soviets had developed their own atomic bomb so quickly, discovered that Julius and Ethel Rosenberg had been stealing secrets for the Russians (Doherty 7). The trial and execution of the Rosenbergs was one of the most sensational events of the Cold War and high-lighted the need for constant vigilance against domestic subversion.

This comes into play in the third chapter, as the Flash races to face the next of Starro's servants in the suburb of Happy Harbor. Using the newly gained atomic power and scientific knowledge, this agent learns to control human minds, placing the entire community under its thrall with the excep-tion of the teenager "Snapper" Carr. The teen, finishing his lawn work, observes his family: "Mom! Dad! Sis! You look like you're in Tranceville.… Wha' hoppen?" (24). Seeing that one person is not under his control, the starfish prepares to destroy Snapper, only for Carr to be rescued by the Flash. When the starfish tries to hide in a nearby lake, the Flash uses supersonic vibrations to defeat it.

Starro's brainwashing of Happy Harbor struck at the very core of Amer-ican consensus values through the middle-class suburban family. The family had come to represent the lynchpin of American culture and was essential to maintaining the status quo, which was key to domestic security. Matthew J. Costello writes: "The rhetoric of the government and anticommunist experts—that the family was the bulwark of American values and thus the greatest weapon against the communist—linked the popular fear of the communist to fears about the breakdown of the family" (51). One symbol of familial success was newly constructed suburbs, such as Levittown, New York. The ability to not only afford a home but also an automobile or two for transportation to work was a sign of economic prosperity. So, while Starro's third attack was not of strategic military, political, or scientific significance, it was an attack at the heart of America.

Part of the consensus rhetoric concerning the family was that each of its members assumed gendered roles within a patriarchal status quo. These essentialist roles included the father as breadwinner and mother as housewife was well as serving as role models for developing children (Ormrod 54). Following World War II, this necessitated women returning from the workforce to the home. This dynamic was frequently reinforced in superhero stories by featuring female characters as love interests and to help balance a group (Sheppard 30). Wonder Woman is an oft-cited exception to this rule, but even she is not immune to the domestic pull. As she explains in this issue to her love interest, Steve Trevor: "As I told you before, Steve Trevor, I can't marry you until my services are no longer needed to battle crime and injustice…" (9). However, among the Justice League, she does not fulfill the female role of a mother/wife/girlfriend, but is treated as an equal.

Snapper Carr represents a new wrinkle to the family dynamic in the 50s: the teenager. This age group, with disposable time and money, had not existed in previous generations. As such, any actions by them that did not adhere to the perceived norms was viewed with suspicion. This paranoia led to the belief that there was an epidemic of juvenile delinquency, with blame being laid at the feet of mass media. One result of this was the Comics Code Authority. DC executive Whitney Ellsworth insisted that the Justice League include a hip-talking character based on teen idols to appeal to young readers (Wells 17). By portraying Snapper as hip yet responsible, becoming an honorary member of the team by the end of the issue, the comic book showed that the perceived threat of juvenile delinquency was a non-issue and that the rising generation could be trusted with the security of the future.

Starro's use of mind control was yet another Cold War weapon attributed to Communists. After World War II, some U.S. allies lost their colonies to Communist uprisings. As America viewed democracy and capitalism as the logically superior systems, rather than try to understand why communism may appeal the developing nations, it was assumed that they were manipulated by a non-rational appeal. This was seemingly confirmed by the "brainwashing" of captured troops during the Korean War (Marling 186). Fear of this was further promulgated in 1957 when ad executives experimented with subliminal pitches—words like "Drink Coca-Cola!" and "Hungry: Eat Popcorn!"—that were flashed over movie images for one three-hundredth of a second. While concession sales were reported to have gone up by 50 percent at the theaters at that time, increasing the belief in the power of suggestion, the results were ultimately discredited (186). While brainwashing was disproven, it became fodder for numerous science fiction stories in the era.

Starro and its world-conquering "technologies" are defeated through hard work and science. The reunited Justice League discovers that the reason Snapper was not affected by the mind control is that he had been spreading lime on his yard. Green Lantern observes: "Oyster men use quicklime to fight starfish who prey on oysters at sea!" (31). Once Starro is coated in lime, it is imprisoned in an unbreakable shell.

Subsequent adventures of the Justice League also address areas of unease in Cold War America, albeit in not so wide-ranging a manner. In *The Brave and the Bold* #29 (April–May 1960), "Challenge of the Weapons Master!," the arch-criminal Xotar in the year 11,960 is about to be captured by the intersolar police. Based on a note in a ten-thousand-year-old book, Xotar travels back in time to confront the Justice League and discover which of his four weapons will allow him to escape the police. Taking Snapper hostage, Xotar challenges to the members of the League to stop him from destroying various objects, including the Project Venus Rocket, which will help the United States pull ahead in the space race, the Panama Canal, and Mount Rushmore. Having defeated his first three weapons, the League reunites to confront Xotar at the Valley of Ten Thousand Smokes in Alaska. Overcoming his final weapon, Xotar is sent back to his own time, where he is promptly arrested. It is then revealed that the note, which Xotar thought guaranteed his success, was missing the crucial passage that revealed he was unsuccessful in the past.

That the Weapons Master used four different weapons to threaten locations of importance to the United States in the Americas points to this story as an allegory for the arms race. Ever since the Soviets claimed to have their own atomic bomb, each superpower raced to develop more powerful weapons and store them in more strategic locations. By 1957, distance didn't matter as much as rocket technology allowed the USSR to launch an intercontinental ballistic missile, with the claim from Moscow that they could now reach any part of the world (Boorstin 591). Communist propaganda helped fuel the arms race, but, through the secret U-2 spy plane, the U.S. government knew that the Soviet military strength was significantly less than they boasted, amounting to approximately one-tenth of American stockpiles (Maguire, "Wonder Woman" 44; Ormrod 55). In defeating the Weapons Master, the Justice League showed that it is not technology that would win the day, but American virtue and hard work.

In *The Brave and the Bold* #30 (June–July 1960), the League must solve "The Case of the Stolen Super Powers!" In the course of their normal, super-heroic activities, Flash, Green Lantern, Aquaman, Wonder Woman and

Martian Manhunter all briefly lose their powers. It is soon discovered they have been stolen by the android Amazo, who is now on the hunt for the longest-living members of the animal kingdom so his creator, Professor Ivo, can create an immortality serum. Amazo is able to defeat each member of the League when they confront him, keeping them sedated with chlorine gas. Professor Ivo succeeds in creating the elixir, steals all the League's powers for Amazo, and prepares to have his android wipe their minds using Green Lantern's powers. However, Green Lantern, knowing that his ring is powerless against the color yellow, uses the yellow chlorine gas to prevent his mind wipe. He then steals back the League's powers from Amazo, rendering the robot powerless and defeating Ivo. The captured Professor Ivo is sentenced to 500 years in jail while the powerless Amazo is put on display in the Justice League headquarters.

One way in which the Amazo story may be read is about the threat of malfunctioning technology. As already seen, the challenges of catching up to the Soviets in the space race was rife with problems. This implied that American technology could fail, whether through error or sabotage, and thus weakened faith in the national security (Maguire, "Wonder Woman" 46–47). The Justice League first had their powers malfunction and then turned against them. However, through Green Lantern's own "sabotage," he was able to cause Amazo to malfunction at a crucial moment.

This brings up a theme of over-reliance on technology within its ubiquity in the American lifestyle. In the years following World War II, returning soldiers searched for what sociologists termed "the standard consumer package": a girl, a car, a new home, and eventually a television set (Marling 134). But with new and improving technology, new appliances and conveniences would soon be added to the package, such as a refrigerator and oven. With continued abundance and prosperity, legitimate wants had been satisfied, but the capitalist system depended on perpetual consumption, even if the items were not really needed (Marling 252). Advertisers introduced the annual model, allowing citizens to update to the latest form of labor-saving device every year as a way to prove they were climbing the social and economic ladder (Boorstin 552). But this new style of consumerism also resulted a homogenized consumption with little room for individual expression (Costello 54). Within a consensus culture, such homogenization should be expected.

Of greater concern was the increased leisure time technology was providing. The Puritan work ethic ingrained into American culture saw idle time as a threat to public order (Marling 53). Coupled with the anxieties over the Cold War, laziness could be equated with a lack of preparation for the challenges facing the country. Presidential candidate John F. Kennedy would warn: "We have gone soft.... The slow corrosion of luxury is already beginning to show" (qtd. in Marling 252). This is perhaps what Premier Khrushchev saw when touring the U.S. exhibition.

The concern over laziness would have also been compounded with the shift from a blue-collar, production-oriented workplace before World War II to a white-collar, consumer-oriented one afterwards, resulting in a crisis of masculinity (Getner 963). In a sense, Professor Ivo embodies the negative aspects of this crisis. Rather than doing the work himself, Ivo put his faith in technology to overcome the natural power of the Justice League (Berger 202). The underlying message of such a story is that America's innate virtuous traits would still lead to victory over its enemies even if technology should fail.

The Justice League of America proved to be another success in DC Comics Silver Age revival. Editor Julius Schwartz stated: "Irwin Donenfeld used to get reports of how well the magazine was doing. He wouldn't give us the final figures, but he would say 'up six,' 'down three,' and so on. So all *The Brave and the Bold* 'Justice Leagues' had 'up,' 'very good,' and 'excellent.' When the final one came in, he didn't give me a number. You know what he gave me? […] An exclamation point!" (Wells 18). *The Justice League of America* would have its own title by the end of 1960.

For all the concern over them during the Cold War, science and technology should be considered neutral factors of society. It is a question of who is using it to what ends that determines whether it is beneficial or detrimental to society. Arthur Asa Berger writes: "The victories of the good guys express a fundamental American optimism and reflect an awareness of the potentialities for good and evil in machines and a belief in man's ability to control them. Thus, comic strips have a realistic awareness of the moral dilemma posed by science and technology" (203). The initial adventures of the Justice League of America in the pages of *The Brave and the Bold* built around this theme of technology as part of the ambient fears of the Cold War milieu. While embodying the superiority American's felt was inherent in their democratic and capitalist system, the heroes would continue to address concerns over the role of science as they fought alien invaders as an allegory for the space race, defeated new weapons a metaphor for the arms race, and protected the American way of life in their further adventures.

WORKS CITED

Berger, Arthur Asa. *The Comic-Stripped American: What Dick Tracy, Blondie, Daddy Warbucks, and Charlie Brown Tell Us About Ourselves.* New York: Walker and Company, 1973.

Boorstin, Daniel J. *The Americans: The Democratic Experience.* New York: Vintage, 1974.

Costello, Matthew J. *Secret Identity Crisis: Comic Books and the Unmasking of Cold War America.* New York: Continuum, 2009.

Doherty, Thomas Patrick. *Cold War, Cool Medium: Television, McCarthyism, and American Culture*. New York: Columbia University Press, 2003.

"For Fifty Years, Nuclear Bomb Lost in Watery Grave." NPR. 3 February 2008. Web. 12 April 2016. http://www.npr.org/templates/story/story.php?storyId=18587608.

Fox, Gardner (w), and Mike Sekowsky (p). "Starro the Conqueror!" *The Brave and the Bold* #28 (February-March 1960) in *The Justice League of America: The Silver Age Vol. 1*. Burbank: DC Comics, 2016.

_____. "Challenge of the Weapons Master!" *The Brave and the Bold* #29 (April-May 1960) in *The Justice League of America: The Silver Age Vol. 1*. Burbank: DC Comics, 2016.

_____. "Case of the Stolen Super Powers!" *The Brave and the Bold* #30 (June-July 1960) in *The Justice League of America: The Silver Age Vol. 1*. Burbank: DC Comics, 2016.

Getner, Robert. "'With Great Power Comes Great Responsibility': Cold War Culture and the Birth of Marvel Comics." *The Journal of Popular Culture* 40.6 (2007): 953-78.

Hofstadter, Richard. *Anti-Intellectualism in American Life*. New York: Knopf, 1963.

Johnson, Jeffrey K. *Super-History: Comic Book Superheroes and American Society*. Jefferson, NC: McFarland, 2012.

Lacey-Bordeaux, Emma. "Declassified Report: Two Nuclear Bombs Nearly Detonated in North Carolina." CNN. 12 June 2014. Web. 12 April 2016. http://www.cnn.com/2014/06/12/us/north-carolina-nuclear-bomb-drop/.

Lamar, Cyriaque. "In 1958, America Accidently Dropped a Nuclear Weapon on Two Little Girls' Playhouse." iO9. 24 April 2012. Web. 12 April 2016. http://io9.gizmodo.com/5904633/in-1958-america-accidentally-dropped-a-nuclear-weapon-on-two-little-girls-playhouse.

MacDonald, J. Fred. *Television and the Red Menace: The Video Road to Vietnam*. New York: Praeger, 1985.

Maguire, Lori. "The American Military in *The Incredible Hulk* During the Vietnam War." In *The Ages of the Incredible Hulk: Essays on the Green Goliath in Changing Times*. Ed. Joseph J. Darowski. Jefferson, NC: McFarland, 2016.

_____. "Supervillains and Cold War Tensions in the 1950s." In *The Ages of Superman: Essays on the Man of Steel in Changing Times*. Ed. Joseph J. Darowski. Jefferson, NC: McFarland, 2012.

_____. "Wonder Woman Comics and Military Technology After Sputnik." In *The Ages of Wonder Woman: Essays on the Amazon Princess in Changing Times*. Ed. Joseph J. Darowski. Jefferson, NC: McFarland, 2014.

Marling, Karal Ann. *As Seen on TV: The Visual Culture of Everyday Life in the 1950s*. Cambridge: Harvard University Press, 1994.

Ormrod, Joan. "Cold War Fantasies: Testing the Limits of the Familial Body." In *The Ages of Wonder Woman: Essays on the Amazon Princess in Changing Times*. Ed. Joseph J. Darowski. Jefferson, NC: McFarland, 2014.

Pagnoni Berns, Fernando Gabriel, and Cesar Alfonso Marino. "A Globe-Trotting Atomic Weapon: Illustrating the Cold War Arms Race." In *The Ages of the Incredible Hulk: Essays on the Green Goliath in Changing Times*. Ed. Joseph J. Darowski. Jefferson, NC: McFarland, 2016.

Sheppard, Natalie R. "'Gorgeous new menace': Black Widow, Gender Roles and the Subversion of Cold War Expectations of Domesticity." In *The Ages of Iron Man: Essays on the Armored Avenger in Changing Times*. Ed. Joseph J. Darowski. Jefferson, NC: McFarland, 2015.

Wells, John. *American Comic Book Chronicles. The 1960s: 1960–1964*. Raleigh: TwoMorrows Publishing, 2012.

Wright, Bradford W. *Comic Book Nation: The Transformation of Youth Culture in America*. Baltimore: Johns Hopkins University Press, 2001.

A League of Orphans and Single Parents

Making a Family in an Era of *Father Knows Best*

Louie Dean Valencia-García

In an era of television shows like *Father Knows Best* and *Leave It to Beaver*, the original members of the Justice League of America—Wonder Woman, Superman, Batman, Aquaman, Flash, Green Lantern, Martian Manhunter, and Snapper Carr—made for a sort of awkward "family." The Justice League first appeared in *The Brave and the Bold* #28 (March 1960), and were given their own title in October of that year, helmed by writer Gardner Fox. Just as Fox had worked with editor Julius Schwartz to reinvent characters such as Hawkman and the Atom, he also reinvented the Justice Society of America, a team he had originally created in 1940, as the modern Justice League of America (JLA). The JLA straddled its characters' inherent deviations from the American "nuclear family" popularly promoted during the mid–20th century and the need to adhere to stricter regulation that censored perceived threats to youth by the regulatory hand of the Comics Code Authority.

Curiously, with the exception of teenage sidekick Snapper Carr and the Flash, none of the original Justice League members belonged to the stereotypical sort of "nuclear families" popularly represented in American media of the 1960s (although there was some ambiguity as to Green Lantern's father throughout the period). Of the three most prominent members of the Justice League, Superman had been orphaned—twice; Batman was orphaned, raised by his butler (Alfred), and later raised his "ward," the also-orphaned Dick Grayson, along with Alfred; Wonder Woman was raised by her mother and an island of women. To be sure, none of the "big three" super-heroes fit the mold of what would be considered a "traditional" American family during the mid-century; these heroes belonged to the earlier half of the 20th century—the American Progressive Era. While the original Justice Society of America primarily provided a platform for which superheroes to team-up, the early Justice League of America operated much more as a family unit, and reflected a way National Periodical Publications was able to create a family structure for orphaned superheroes, moving the heroes closer to a post-war heteronormative ideal of a family unit, a model which was later repeated in super-hero teams such as Teen Titans and Marvel's X-Men. No longer were these heroes just orphans and single-parents, but they belonged to a family.

Social policy scholar Michelle Kahan describes the Progressive Era as "a time of child welfare reform, the rise of social work, beginnings of the family preservation movement, early efforts to regulate adoption, and Mothers' Pensions as a means to help worthy poor women take care of their children" (51). The Progressive Era's construction of family contrasted starkly with ideal of the postwar era, which coincided with both a baby boom and a rapid growth in the middle class (and its so-called family values). With this, even the reasons for adoption had also changed from the Progressive Era to the 1950s. Previously, poverty served as a significant motivation to place a child in an orphanage, while mid-century adoptions were motivated to avoid the stigma of having an illegitimate child (Kahan 62). In fact, the first national adoption conferences were held in the late 1940s and early 1950s by the coincidently-named "Child Welfare League of America," which intentionally attempted to expand the definition of who might be adoptable, reporting "any child ... who needs a family and who can develop in it, and for whom a family can be found that can accept the child with its physical or mental capacities" (Kahan 62, Carp 32). This expanded definition helped to bring orphans into heteronormative "nuclear families"; the nuclear family need not include "natural-born" children, but could also include adopted children as well. Nevertheless, as historian Robert O. Self has argued, the constructed "ideal nuclear family was never truly representative of how most Americans lived" (6). While the 1950s saw a shift in policy that promoted an idealized two-generation, single-family household wherein the "breadwinner" was the father, that model was largely new (and predominantly depicted as white), and hardly reflective of all American families during the period—American families were multigenerational, of the same gender, composed of multiple breadwinners, single-fathers, single-mothers, divorced couples, unmarried, remarried, and increasingly mixed-race families.

In the wake of the 1954 United States Senate Subcommittee on Juvenile Delinquency hearings on comic books, provoked by German-American psychiatrist Fredric Wertham's *Seduction of the Innocent*, published the previous year, and the subsequent creation of the Comics Code Authority, the Justice League comics of the 1960s demonstrated how editors and writers reconciled a necessity to keep their heroes unmarried for the purpose of storytelling (i.e., children might not tend to want to read about the domestic adventures of Wonder Woman or Superman), while still presenting the heroes as part of what could have been read as a more heteronormative familial structure. Comic book characters that had in the previous decade been read by the likes of Wertham as queer and deviant, were placed on a team together.[1]

Wertham was particularly afraid of comic books' impact on the family, citing a second-hand account told to him of a father, whose son told his mother (the father's wife) "if she'd take off her blouse she'd be as pretty as a comic-book girl!" In response to this threat to the family, the father burned all the comic books he found in the home (Wertham 51–52). Wertham's evidence played on fears of incest, and exemplified the perceived threat comic books had to the nuclear family. This fear would eventually play out in the self-regulatory "Comics Code Authority's General Standards." In its section on "Marriage and Sex" the code mandated:

1. Divorce shall not be treated humorously nor represented as desirable.

2. Illicit sex relations are neither to be hinted at or portrayed. Violent love scenes as well as sexual abnormalities are unacceptable.

3. Respect for parents, the moral code, and for honorable behavior shall be fostered. A sympathetic understanding of the problems of love is not a license for moral distortion.

4. The treatment of love-romance stories shall emphasize the value of the home and the sanctity of marriage.

5. Passion or romantic interest shall never be treated in such a way as to stimulate the lower and baser emotions.

6. Seduction and rape shall never be shown or suggested.

7. Sex perversion or any inference to same is strictly forbidden ["Code"].

By looking at the first decade of *Justice League of America* comics scholars can see how heteronormative constructions of the family unit, gender, and sexuality were subverted and reinforced during the early years of both the Comics Code Authority and the sexual revolution.

Moreover, we must ask whether or not the invention of the Justice League gave a sort of "legitimacy" to the proliferation of adopted superhero sidekicks who also starred in the pages of *Superman*, *Batman*, *Wonder Woman*, and *Aquaman*. Not only did the family structure of the Justice League solve the perceived problem of perpetually single superheroes raising sidekick heroes alone (usually of the same gender, with the exception of Superman/

Supergirl), but it created a diverse family structure from which the DC Universe would eventually be constructed.

Sociologist Jon Barnardes recognizes the difference between the concept of "family" and "The Family" in his seminal article "We Must Not Define 'The Family'!" Barnardes identifies "family" as a socially constructed idea, which is both malleable and defies definition. However, he, too, points out the construction of the European "Nuclear Family" as a concept that "does not exist except as a powerful image in the minds of most people" (23). Barnardes argues, "traditional views of 'The Family' have been conservative, racist, classist, and heterosexist" (23). While the Justice League indeed could be understood as a family, that family structure still allowed for a place for the queer, or the non-normative, family to still exist. The team had no leader, and instead had a "rotating chairman" position. In fact, Wonder Woman is prominently featured in the role early on as the team decides on admitting a new member (Fox, "Doom…"). Moreover, only one member could be invited to the team at a time, creating an exclusivity to the Justice League family. In practice, the JLA rejected patriarchal leadership, instead opting for a democratic, and even intentional, rule of governance.

Only Children, Orphans and Adopted Children

Before delving into the family dynamics of the JLA, it is first helpful to situate the characters' family life during the Silver Age. While many of these origins change over the ensuing decades, I will limit these character studies to their Silver Age 1960s incarnations, and specifically to Snapper Carr's time as an honorary member of the team. The Justice League of America members were primarily composed of orphans or were from families that would not be considered ideal, nuclear families by the heteronormative standards of the 1960s. Moreover, while all the characters have on-again-off-again relationships during this period, none of the original seven members were married.

Some "orphan" characters such as Superman, Batman and Wonder Woman inherited their stories from the Golden Age. Superman was an orphan twice over, first on Krypton, then with the passing of the Kents, yet again. Batman's parents were killed in front of him. Both characters are only children when they first become orphans. Another character who largely maintained her original origin story into the Silver Age, Wonder Woman, was made of clay, given life by the gods of Olympus, had no father, and was raised by a single-mother and an island full of Amazons. In the Silver Age, Wonder Woman is given a sister, Wonder Girl, who also comes from magical origins.[2] Aquaman was the son of Atlanna, a woman of mysterious origins, and Thomas Curry, an ex-sailor and lighthouse keeper (Bernstein). When Aquaman's mother dies as a young boy, he discovers she was Atlantean royalty and he was heir to the throne. After his mother dies, Aquaman's father remarries, and has a half-brother, who eventually becomes his enemy, Ocean Master.

The revamped Silver Age superheroes, Flash and Green Lantern, both had extended families surrounding them. Flash is the only child of Nora and Henry Allen (Broome, "The Doom…"). Flash's love interest, Iris Allen, is a reporter. Carol Ferris, Green Lantern's love interest, is his boss at Ferris Aircrafts. Like Lois Lane, both Iris and Carol are working women who challenge the heteronormative ideal of what it means to be a white, middle-class woman in the 1960s. While Green Lantern's parents are never mentioned in his early adventures, his two brothers appear in 1961 in *Green Lantern* issue #9 of the relaunched series. In that ongoing series references are made regularly to Hal's extended family, and the Jordan brothers are shown to actively engage in one another's lives (although no mention is made about his parents until well after the Silver Age). J'onn J'onzz, the Martian Manhunter, is a father who lost his family and planet, and is an orphan, but unlike Superman and Batman, only became one well into adulthood. Snapper is established as a popular teenager coming from a heteronormative, nuclear family and has a sister.

A later recruit, Green Arrow, is a playboy who survives on an desert island and adopts a Robin Hood inspired identity. Green Arrow is soon joined by Roy Harper, a child who is orphaned when his parents die in a plane crash. A later addition to the Justice League, Hawkman, is married to Hawkgirl, and the two have no children. In the Silver Age reinterpretation of the Golden Age characters, the two are space police from the planet Thanagar. While Hawkman joins the Justice League in issue #31, Hawkgirl is not invited as per Justice League rules disallowing multiple members to join at once. Another 1960s recruit, the Atom, dated Jean Loring, a defense attorney, who was not particularly interested in becoming a housewife. Black Canary, a refugee from the Golden Age world of Earth-Two, only joined the Justice League once her prospects of a heteronormative family were dashed when her husband, Larry Lance, was killed in an early Justice League/Justice Society adventure (O'Neil).

While sidekicks did have the effect of producing an "extended family" of sorts, the hero-helpers were almost always of the same gender as their mentor. At the time of the Justice League's first adventure, March of 1960, original members Superman, Batman, Flash, and Aquaman all had sidekicks. Kid Flash had joined Flash in an issue cover dated January 1960 (Broome, "Meet…"); Aquaman only got Aqualad the previous month of the same year (Bernstein); Wonder Woman only gets Wonder Girl in 1965 (Haney, "The Amazing…"). Supergirl, Kara Zor-El, first appeared in Action Comics #252 (May 1959), but was kept a secret, and often had her own solo adventures within Superman comics. While Superman's "pal" Jimmy Olsen, who was a default sidekick to Superman, had been a prominent character since 1954, it was not until late in the 1960s that Olsen was established as an orphan (Dorfman). The constant application of this generic trope left only Martian Manhunter and Green Lantern without sidekicks. Of the later additions to the team in the 1960s, only Green Arrow has a sidekick, Speedy.

As a team, the Justice League in essence adopts Snapper Carr as an honorary member early on, giving young readers a character through which they could mediate and interpret the adventures of the JLA (Fox, "Justice…"). Curiously, despite being a teenager, Snapper is given agency by Fox, demonstrated in his ability to vote on the team's decisions. In fact, Snapper is placed on equal footing with Batman and Superman in determining Green Arrow's complicity in helping two villains escape, although the teen is often found staying behind and not actively engaging in the adventures of the team (Fox, "When…"). As both Superman and Batman, in a sense, already had "families" of their own, they often were left tending to business in Metropolis and Gotham. Up until issue #25, each issue featured the whole team, after which point the cast tended to rotate.

Team Dynamics of the World's Greatest (Unmarried) Heroes

There were three prominent superhero teams published by National Periodicals prior to *Justice League of America* with which to compare the family/team dynamics, most famously the exploits of Golden Age Justice Society of America, which stopped publication in 1951 with a declining interest in the superhero genre. More contemporary teams included the Challengers of the Unknown, which first appeared in 1957 (Wood), and the Legion of Super-Heroes, which premiered in 1958 (Binder). In the early Silver Age the JLA, Challengers, and Legion all shared a common diversity in that the members were not related by blood or marriage—with only a few exceptions, like siblings Lightning Lad and Lightning Lass. The Metal Men, artificially intelligent robots, appear in as a team in 1962 (Kanigher). The Doom Patrol appears in 1963 (Drake). The earliest incarnation of the Teen Titans, not yet called that, debuted in 1964 (Haney, "The Thousand…"). Despite the potential for romantic relationships, only the Legion prominently featured romantic entanglements between its members in the 1960s, primarily because the members of the Legion did not have their own individual titles with which to explore romantic relationships. Other groups, such as the JLA, the Challengers, and the Teen Titans suffered a severe gender imbalance, limiting the possible relationships between the members given the heteronormativity of the period.

Moreover, the characters featured in *Justice League of America* and *Teen Titans* shared many of the characters which were featured across various titles.

To understand the familial relationship of the Justice League of America, first it is helpful to understand the characters' romantic relationships in their individual comic book titles at the time. While characters like Batman and Robin were given romantic interests in 1956, Kathy and Betty Kane (Batwoman and Batgirl), in order to counter Wetham's claims that queer undertones belied the comic,[3] Wonder Woman and Superman were stuck in interminable relationships, with Steve Trevor and Lois Lane, respectfully, that could not end with a heterosexual marriage without running the risk of forcing the heroes to "settle down"—which in turn would run the risk of narrowing storytelling possibilities.

In fact, in Wonder Woman's first Justice League appearance, she is shown reiterating that sentiment to her paramour, pulling away from him as he attempts to put his arm around her, "As I told you before, Steve Trevor, I can't marry you until my services are no longer needed to battle crime and injustice." Noting a call from her teammates, she thinks to herself ,"Great Hera! A secret signal from the Justice League…!" (Fox, "Justice…"). Wonder Woman's claim that she cannot be married as long as she has to fight "injustice," only to be interrupted by the Justice League, creates a paradigm in which her *de facto* family in the patriarch's world became the JLA. Wonder Woman foregoes heteronormative marriage and having a child (as per the Comics Code Authority, and the norms of the period, she could not have sex, let alone a child, outside of marriage), instead dedicating herself to the Justice League.

Indeed, Superman was also left in a position where he too was not well-suited for marriage. For example, despite the title of Lois Lane's comic series, *Superman's Girl Friend, Lois Lane,* when Lois was not investigating a story, most of the star-reporter's interactions with the Man of Steel in the 1960s primarily depicted attempts to find out Superman's secret identity, woo him, or her fears of other women nabbing his attention.[4] Indeed, Superman and Wonder Woman were not the only heroes who resisted marriage, or were single. J'onn J'onzz, the Martian Manhunter, was a widower from Mars. Flash was dating Iris West, and would eventually marry her in the 1970s, only to become a widower himself after her death, then remarrying again later. Although Green Lantern and Green Arrow both had romantic relationships, they were also consummate bachelors—who would solidify their "bromance" with a cross-country road trip in the early 1970s.

Like Batman, Superman's cast also considerably grew through the 1950s with Supergirl, the miniature (but populated) Kryptonian city of Kandor, and Jimmy Olsen—all of whom ostensibly made up the "Superman Family." Both the Dark Knight and the Man of Steel even received their own comic book titles focused on their families by the mid–1970s—demonstrating a long-term effort to create an extended family for the characters. And while having younger sidekicks gave young audiences characters with whom to relate, none of the superheroes had kids themselves (which would have been impossible given the stigma associated with children from unmarried couple in the era). In effect, the Justice League of America created a group of superheroes, and also had the unintended effect of creating a queer family of characters who did not belong to a nuclear family.

Home Sweet Cave

When the Justice League was first introduced in *Brave and the Bold* #28 the reader is not given an origin story, but is placed *in medias res* as the heroes are called to their cavernous secret headquarters. Superman and Batman are both absent, tending to their own cases, as the league gathers together for the first time. In fact, the cave is often referred to narratively as both a "headquarters" and "sanctuary" as early as *Brave and the Bold* #29. By calling the space a sanctuary, the writers signaled to their readers that this is not just a place to meet, but a place where the members find safety and a place to relax—a home.

The JLA's sanctuary is located in a cave, noted by the sides of the exposed walls, but also is remarkably homey. The heroes are situated around a wooden table, Wonder Woman's Invisible Jet parked behind them. Aesthetically, the clean lines, minimalist staircase, large screen, extensive bookshelves, and long sofa, and warm yellows, oranges, and greens evokes a level of comfort not seen in Batman's cave or Superman's Fortress of Solitude (Fox, "Justice…"). Although, both those locales do evoke a sense of nostalgia and sanctuary—Superman's headquarters recalls the lost world of Krypton, and Batman contains trophies from his adventures. The JLA sanctuary contains a "Keepsake Korner" for trophies, a notable difference indicating a more familial setting (Fox, "For Sale…"). A computer lab is located on the second floor, which features an open floor plan, allowing the reader to see both floors at once. In the early adventures, the hidden cave appears in nearly every issue—the circular wooden dinner table/conference table featured prominently. Remarkably, the artist, Mike Sekowsky, maintains consistency when depicting the space throughout the first issues. Moreover, the characters appear comfortable in the space; Green Lantern even sits on the surface of the table (Fox, "Challenge…").

At the end of the second adventure against Xotar, the Weapons Master, the team gathers around Wonder Woman on the sofa as she sits cross-legged writing down their adventure into a scrapbook. As opposed to Wonder Woman's infamously marginalized role as "secretary" of the Golden Age Justice Society, we see her acting in a technically similar role, but this time she is surrounded by Flash, Aquaman, Green Lantern, J'onn J'onzz, and Snapper looking on with careful attention. Her role seems less that of a token role designated for a woman, and more so as that of a storyteller and keeper of the League's history.

The cave is depicted as a place of refuge and provides the heroes a place to rest. As seen in the tale "Secret of the Sinister Sorcerers," the League comes together to solve a case in which "man-made" objects are made inert because a spell. While regrouping in the cave, an exhausted Flash is seen rubbing his sore feet while seated on a sofa, Green Lantern is seen in a sort of comfortable contrapposto stance, leaning against a sofa, while Superman sits with his legs completely extended in a relaxed position, leaning his chin against clasped hands, flummoxed attempting to think of a solution to their case. Wonder Woman suggests to the group that they go to their library, for a solution, claiming they have "all of Earth's knowledge" stored there. While Wonder Woman reads a book of ingredients to conjure a spell, Green Lantern and Flash stir the potion intended to call the Arthurian wizard, Merlin, for help— "helping in the kitchen," as it were (Fox, "Secret...").

Often, Snapper Carr is left out of direct action, and finds himself situated in the cave. One of his duties as a member of the Justice League is checking mail, an apt household duty for a teenager. This is first seen in *Justice League of America* #6 as an adventure is started by Snapper's trip to the post office, where he receives two letters from people in need (Fox, "The Wheel..."). While seemingly mundane, Snapper's role is that of a child left behind while the adults attend to the heroics often plays a crucial plot device.

In *Justice League of America* #9, after months of mystery, the first origin story of the JLA appears. The comic opens with Snapper driving to the JLA headquarters in Happy Harbor, Maryland. Upon arriving, Wonder Woman is found with a soap and rag at hand, wearing an apron, ordering Snapper to "take a pail and mop and get to work! We want the place spotlessly clean for the party!" (Fox, "The Origin..."). Green Lantern is seen lifting two chairs off of the floor, presumably to mop. As Snapper cleans the display cases in the souvenir room he notices a case filled with wooden splinters and shavings. Again assuming her role as storyteller, Wonder Woman explains to Snapper those wood chips as being the first souvenir the team had collected, from their first case. The Amazing Amazon tells them she will tell the story after they clean. Jumping into the conversation Aquaman states, "While we don't have a permanent chairman—when it comes to cleaning time, we all agree Wonder Woman is boss, so—back to work, everyone!" We see Superman and J'onn J'onzz scrubbing the wall, Flash dusting, Wonder Woman vacuuming, and Aquaman moving the table for cleaning. While Wonder Woman assumes the role of "mother," placing a heteronormative role on her, she is given agency and management over the home. Afterward, they pass out cake, celebrating the League's birthday, as the original members begin to tell the tale of their origins to Green Arrow and Snapper, who were not yet members (Fox, "The Origin…").

While Wonder Woman is depicted as being in charge of the cleaning, playing to gender roles of the time, the lack of a permanent chairperson also indicates that at times she is also included in the leadership of the team—a proto-feminist stance implicitly indicating that a woman can indeed occupy the role of head of the household in multiple arenas. Moreover, in the story, Wonder Woman is depicted as having in-depth knowledge of science, even quoting the boiling point of mercury as 356.9 degrees centigrade off the top of her head. Wonder Woman both assumes the gendered role of the head of the household and cleaning while still demonstrating that she is capable of leadership and of critical thinking. In that origin story, Wonder Woman plays a pivotal role in freeing the other team members once they are captured, using her lasso of truth to stop a creature who turned them into trees, freeing the other members. At the end of her tale, Wonder Woman picks up the dishes, while Snapper and Green Arrow sing "Happy Birthday" to the Justice League (Fox, "The Origin…"). The quotidian nature of many of the scenes in the story not only sets a standard for which to consider the Justice League a family unit, but they also play into the gendered stereotypes of women for the period—both being transgressive and normative simultaneously.

Breaking Up the Nuclear Family in the Atomic Age

Within the diegesis of the *Justice League of America* comics, there were often cross-overs where the heroes of the Justice League's Earth—what became known as "Earth-One" or the Silver Age Earth—and "Earth-Two"— the Golden Age Earth that existed in an alternate universe—regularly interacted with one another. In what would be Gardner Fox's last storyline for *Justice League of America*, the author reimagined the Golden Age character of Red Tornado as a robotic android who had the capability to think independently and express emotion. At the end of the adventure, the Red Tornado is nominated for full membership in the Earth-Two Justice Society, but rejects the offer, claiming, "I want to be somebody! I want a face … an identity I can call my own! I want a personality … emotions … a home! I want to put roots … to belong! Somewhere—in this wide, wide world—there has to be a place for me" (Fox, "T.O.…."). Not only does Red Tornado demonstrate what appears to be genuine emotion, and even an emotive face, but he eventually decides to leave Earth-Two to find a home with the Justice League. While seemingly just a plot device to reintroduce a Golden Age character, it is important to consider that not only was this Fox's last story on his *JLA* run, but it also indicated that for Red Tornado, the Justice Society was not a home, or at least the type of home where a scarlet android could feel at home. While eventually Red Tornado would find a home with the JLA, the ambiguous note leaves Fox's final story waiting for a conclusion that would not occur until several months later.

Toward the end of the decade, a great number of shifts occurred in the Justice League. Not only does writer Dennis O'Neil take over from Fox, but he sets up what becomes the closing chapter of the JLA's time in their cavernous sanctuary, and a period of great expansion in their numbers. Moreover, as Wonder Woman loses her powers in her own comic, she attempts to resign from the JLA. However, the team rejects her resignation, and instead grants a leave of absence. As Wonder Woman parts ways, the Flash has a moment of reflection to himself, thinking, "I've always felt that some day Superman might marry her ... now, they've lost each other! As Aquaman has lost his wife Mera ... and Green Lantern has lost Carol Ferris! Sometimes it seems that we're all getting old" (O'Neil, "A Matter..."). Not only does Flash depict a never-before-possibility of romance within the team, but it also demonstrates a loss for what he saw as the end of a household headed by Wonder Woman and Superman—and a chance for a heteronormative family. While the comic had previously discussed past adventures with a sort of nostalgia, for Flash, Wonder Woman's leave of absence marked an elegy to an era that was quickly changing. While new members had joined, some had disappeared for months at a time (namely Martian Manhunter and Aquaman), Wonder Woman's departure left a significant void in the team. Such a void, that O'Neil would quickly devise a way not only to fill the spot of the only woman on the team, Earth-Two's Black Canary, but would do so in a way that brought her replacement into the family. While previous attempts had tried to break-up the family, namely a United Nations attempt to disband the JLA with a temporary injunction (Fox, "The Case..."), this was the first significant change to the line-up to the original members.

Breaking Up the Family: A New Paradigm

In 1970, LGBT activist Carl Wittman first published *Refugees from Amerika: A Gay Manifesto*. In his manifesto he claims, "We have to define a new pluralistic, role free social structure for ourselves. It must contain both the freedom and physical space for people to live alone, live together for awhile, live together for a long time, either as couples or in larger numbers; and the ability to flow easily from one of these states to another as our needs change" (Wittman). Wittman, a former member of the national council of

Students for a Democratic Society (SDS) was born in 1943, might never have considered how his idea of a new pluralistic social structure might have affected a comic book like the Justice League, but by the late 1960s even the Justice League of America was reimagining itself, and tackling the need for pluralism by the time Dennis O'Neil took over.

During the early O'Neil era, the JLA began to not only consider broader social issues, but they tackled them head on. *Justice League of America #77* begins with an assault on Snapper Carr for being pals with "freaks," only to be saved by the mysterious new character "John Dough"—"Mr. Average," the most normal man in America (O'Neil, "Snapper..."). In the story, Dough convinces Snapper to turn on the League. A *Daily Planet* issue features a headline stating "Dough Gains Followers! 'Mr. Average' Vows a Return to 'Normalcy.'" As Green Lantern points out rather bluntly, "Well.... We're not very 'normal.'" As a team the heroes discuss people's fear of the "strange," Green Arrow responds, "Baloney! Look, the human race has progressed so far as it has because men and women were brave enough to accept the different." Such a debate not only acknowledges the queer nature of the superheroes, but also asserts the value of differences. Later, at a rally Snapper claims, "I contend that super-heroes are harmful! As Mr. Dough points out, we've become too dependent on them ... we've forgotten how to fight our own battles! We're convinced that any trait that isn't average is ultimately harmful to the human race" (O'Neil, "Snapper..."). In the scene, Black Canary is even called a "commie," evoking fear mongering of the McCarthy era. While not depicting LGBTQ characters, a queer reading of the stance allows for the possibility of difference to exist.

Meanwhile, in Washington, D.C., a freed Batman rushes to stop a Batman imposter from attending a United States Senate Subcommittee called to investigate the League's actions, echoing the comic book industry's own trial in the 1950s caused by a character not too dissimilar to Dough—Fredric Wertham. It is soon discovered that Dough used mind-control devices to turn people against the Justice League. However, in a twist, Snapper admits that he was not controlled, that he believed that the Justice League's difference was detrimental to society, to which Green Arrow replies: "Dough's Glorification of the average is sheer nonsense! The 'world's work' gets done because of what's different in individuals ... each person has a talent, a skill, a thing he does better than his fellows! Take enough of those talents, put them together, and you build a civilization! Deny them and you cancel everything that makes us human" (O'Neil, "Snapper..."). It is only then that Batman reveals that Dough is none other than his arch-nemesis, the Joker—thus equating the imposition of conformity as ultimately a form of evil.

A dense issue, the betrayal of Snapper Carr demarcates a definitive shift from the Justice League of America as a "queer" family conforming to a nuclear family standard to one in which new members are added with frequency, beginning an era in which the League moves its headquarters to space and diversifies its membership. While the first era of the Justice League does end rather abruptly, in a single issue, the comments made by the likes of Green Arrow valuing difference, the JLA, in a sense, comes into its own—with its members accepting their own differences, and, perhaps, their own, "strange" nature as a family that need not try to situate itself into a heteronormative mold created by a fear, rejecting "normalcy."

NOTES

1. Queer readings of Batman, Superman, and Wonder Woman have been published in Christopher York, "All in the Family: Homophobia and Batman Comics in the 1950s," *International Journal of Comic Art* 2 (2000): 100–10; Louie Dean Valencia-García, "Truth, Justice and the American Way in Franco's Spain," in *The Ages of Superman: Essays on the Man of Steel in Changing Times*, edited by Joseph J. Darowski (Jefferson, NC: McFarland, 2012) and Jill Lepore, *The Secret History of Wonder Woman* (New York: Vintage, 2015).

2. While much can be said about the origins of the Donna Troy character, and many series have tried to create a cohesive origin story, for the purpose of this essay, I will delimit this discussion to manageable proportions.

3. Christopher York argues that these queer fears initiated what was a near for a sort of "nuclear Bat-family" in Christopher York. "All in the Family: Homophobia and Batman Comics in the 1950s," *The International Journal of Comic Art* 2 (2000): 100–10.

4. Lois and Superman's nebulous relationship status even led censors in Spain to ban the comics because they interpreted the Man of Tomorrow as queer. See Louie Dean Valencia-García, "Truth, Justice and the American Way in Franco's Spain," in *The Ages of Superman: Essays on the Man of Steel in Changing Times*, edited by Joseph J. Darowski (Jefferson, NC: McFarland, 2012).

WORKS CITED

Bernardes, Jon. "We Must Not Define 'The Family'!" *Marriage & Family Review* 28.3–4 (1999): 21–41.

Bernstein, Robert (w), and Lee Elias (a). "The Kid from Atlantis!" *Adventure Comics* #269 (February 1960). New York: National Periodical Publications.

Bernstein, Robert (w), and Ramona Fradon (a). "How Aquaman Got His Powers!" *Adventure Comics* #260 (May 1959). New York: National Periodical Publications.

Binder, Otto (w), and Al Plastino (a). "The Legion of Super-Heroes." *Adventure Comics* #247 (April 1958). New York: National Periodical Publications.

Broome, John (w), and Carmine Infantino (a). "Meet the Kid Flash." *The Flash* #110 (January 1960). New York: National Periodical Publications.

_____. "The Doom of the Mirror Flash!" *The Flash* #126 (February 1962). New York: National Periodical Publications.

Carp, E. Wayne. *Family Matters: Secrecy and Disclosure in the History of Adoption.* Cambridge: Harvard University Press, 1998.

"Code of the Comics Magazine Association of America. Inc." *Comics Magazine Asso-*

ciation of America: Facts About Code-Approved Comics Magazines. New York: Comics Magazine Association of America, 1959.

Dorfman, Leo (w), and Curt Swan (a). "The Sacrifice of Jimmy Olsen!" *Superman's Pal, Jimmy Olsen* #123 (September 1969). New York: National Periodical Publications.

Drake, Arnold, Bob Haney (w), and Bruno Premiani (a). "The Flaming Doom" *My Greatest Adventure* #80 (June 1963). New York: National Periodical Publications.

Fox, Gardner (w), and Mike Sekowsky (a). "Justice League of America!" *The Brave and the Bold* #28 (March 1960). New York: National Periodical Publications.

_____. "Challenge of the Weapons Master!" *The Brave and the Bold* #29 (May 1960). New York: National Periodical Publications.

_____. "Secret of the Sinister Sorcerers." *Justice League of America* #2 (January 1961). New York: National Periodical Publications.

_____. "Doom of the Star Diamond!" *Justice League of America* #4 (May 1961). New York: National Periodical Publications.

_____. "When Gravity Went Wild!" *Justice League of America* #5 (July 1961). New York: National Periodical Publications.

_____. "The Wheel of Misfortune!" *Justice League of America* #6 (September 1961). New York: National Periodical Publications.

_____. "For Sale—The Justice League!" *Justice League of America* #8 (January 1962). New York: National Periodical Publications.

_____. "The Origin of the Justice League." *Justice League of America* #9 (February 1962). New York: National Periodical Publications.

_____. "The Case of the Forbidden Super-Powers!" *Justice League of America* #28 (June 1964). New York: National Periodical Publications.

_____. "T.O. Morrow Kills the Justice League—Today!" *Justice League of America* #65 (September 1968). New York: National Periodical Publications.

Haney, Bob (w), and Bruno Premiani (a). "The Thousand-and-One Dooms of Mr. Twister." *The Brave and the Bold* #54 (July 1964). New York: National Periodical Publications.

_____. "The Astounding Separated Man." *The Brave and the Bold* #60 (June-July 1965). New York: National Periodical Publications.

Kahan, Michelle. "Put Up on Platforms: A History of Twentieth Century Adoption Policy on the United States." *Journal of Sociology and Social Welfare* 3 (2006): 51–72.

Kanigher, Robert (w), and Ross Andru (a). "The Flaming Doom" *Showcase* #37 (April 1962). New York: National Periodical Publications.

Lepore, Jill. *The Secret History of Wonder Woman.* New York: Vintage, 2015.

Nyberg, Amy. *Seal of Approval: The History of the Comics Code.* Jackson: University of Mississippi Press, 1998.

O'Neil, Dennis (w), and Dick Dillin (a). "A Matter of Menace!" *Justice League of America* #69 (February 1969). New York: National Periodical Publications.

_____. "Where Death Fears to Tread!" *Justice League of America* #74 (September 1969). New York: National Periodical Publications.

_____. "Snapper Carr—Super-Traitor!" *Justice League of America* #77 (December 1969). New York: National Periodical Publications.

Self, Robert O. *All in the Family: The Realignment of American Democracy Since the 1960s.* New York: Hill and Wang, 2012.

Valencia-García, Louie Dean. "Truth, Justice and the American Way in Franco's

Spain." In *The Ages of Superman: Essays on the Man of Steel in Changing Times.* Ed. Joseph J. Darowski. Jefferson, NC: McFarland, 2012, 45–61.

Wertham, Fredric. *Seduction of the Innocent.* Port Washington, NY: Kennikat, 1972.

Wittman, Carl. "A Gay Manifesto." 1972. *Out of the Closets: Voices of Gay Liberation,* 1st ed. Ed. Karla Jay and Allen Young. New York: Douglas Book Corporation, 1972.

Wood, Dave (w), and Jack Kirby (a). "The Secret of the Sorcerer's Box!" *Showcase* #6 (February 1957). New York: National Periodical Publications.

Wright, Bradford W. *Comic Book Nation: The Transformation of Youth Culture in America.* Baltimore: Johns Hopkins University Press, 2001.

York, Christopher. "All in the Family: Homophobia and Batman Comics in the 1950s." *International Journal of Comic Art* 2 (2000): 100–10.

The Caged Bird Sings
The Justice League of America *and the Domestic Containment of Black Canary*

THOMAS C. DONALDSON

The superhero genre is one in which males characters have traditionally held a privileged position, reflecting the hegemonic position men have held in the wider American gender order. According to scholar Norma Pecora, the superhero genre has served throughout its history as socializing agent promoting hegemonic masculinity:

> Superheroes ... are the heart and soul of comic books ... [and] these characters have been important symbols of "maleness" since Superman was introduced in 1939. Over the years ... except for a notable few, they have been predominately male, and have consequently presented a particular ideal of masculinity to their readers. They functioned in world that is male and white, where the women are either young and buxom or old and frail—but never equals [61].

The publication history of DC Comics' Black Canary serves as a case study revealing that the comic industry and the genre have a more complicated relationship with American gender politics and feminism in particular than previous scholarship has revealed. DC originally developed Black Canary in the late 1940s, but, like many Golden Age characters, fell into disuse after World War II. DC would reintroduce the heroine late in the Silver Age revival of the genre, making 1960's *The Justice League of America* series the major vehicle for her appearances. In reviving Black Canary, DC made significant changes that transformed the heroine from an avatar of progressive to conservative femininity. It would be easy argue that this development supports Pecora's analysis, demonstrating the industry's commitment to patriarchal gender values as second wave feminism was on the rise. However, DC transformed Black Canary during a period when the industry was expanding female representation, symbolically empowering women, in response to media trends. Therefore, the evolution of Black Canary shows the shifting portrayal of female empowerment in superhero comics, and should be seen as demonstrating the fluid and contradictory reality of gender portrayal within the superhero genre.

DC created Black Canary in response to shifts in the market for comics in general, and superheroes in particular. The comic industry was experiencing declining sales in the superhero genre. The Second World War, which had helped fuel the superhero boom, also served to change consumer tastes once it ended, according to historian William Savage:

> By 1946 or 1947 readers, whether they were children or belonged to the older audience built by the war, were jaded by the redundant deeds of redundant heroes. The costumed types, pale copies of Superman and Batman to begin with, had exhausted the dramatic possibilities of the medium ... in four action-packed years, everything that anyone could imagine them doing ... and comic-book sales plummeted.... Any number of heroes fell by the way, unable to pull their weight on an issue-to-issue basis. The survivors retained a loyal following, but a small one by comparison to what once had been ... the medium did survive, and it did so by adapting to a new sociocultural climate with a radically different psychological construct. The war had brought current affairs into the comic pages, and there could scarcely be retreat from that, owing to the circumstances of war's end. Hiroshima and Nagasaki had rather emphatically illustrated the futility of the kind of escapist fantasy prevalent before 1940. Comic books, like other entertainment media, could not ignore what the world had become, nor could they effect a return to simpler times. Who needed a superman when we, with our atomic bombs, had become supermen? [Savage 16–18].

As Savage makes clear, the comic book market was in a state of flux after the war, with companies casting about for strategies to cope with the decline of the genre which has been central to its success.

While some companies invested in other genres, notably western, romance, true crime, and horror, others, including DC Comics and Marvel Comics, tried to stem the flagging interest in superheroes by creating a spate of new heroines, among which was Black Canary.[1] According to Les Daniels, in his official history of Marvel Comics, "these shapelier versions of the superheroes were evidently a part of an effort to attract adolescent ... girls" (37). Creators introduced Black Canary in *Flash Comics* #86 (August 1947), as a supporting character in the Johnny Thunder feature. (Kanigher, "The Black..."). The feature's creative team initially developed the character not as a sidekick, but as a reoccurring femme fatale, albeit a safe one as she was not a true outlaw, but a heroine who took on criminals by infiltrating their organizations. As such, creators used her as a love-interest for the dim-witted Johnny Thunder.

It is not possible to do an issue by issue breakdown of Black Canary's Golden Age appearances in an essay of this length, but creators at DC Comics during this period incorporated several structural features into the character during this period that allow her to be read as feminist, perhaps the most feminist superhero of the era besides Wonder Woman. After a brief stint as titular co-star (*Flash Comics* #90 and #91), the company replaced "Johnny Thunder," a series that had run within the *Flash Comics* anthology since its first issue at the beginning of 1940, with the "Black Canary" feature, starting in *Flash Comics* #92 (February 1948). While not unique to Black Canary, creators gave greater agency to the heroine than was given to many other female characters, who were most often used in supporting roles, by elevating her to leading character; in doing so, they allowed Black Canary to be the feature's decisive actor, meaning a woman stopped the villain, a woman rescued the bystanders, a woman saved the day. Beyond the agency garnered as a leading character, Black Canary can be read as feminist because the heroine essentially takes the job of the male superhero with which she co-starred. DC also added Black Canary as a member of the Justice Society of America, the company's leading superhero team feature, appearing in *All-Star Comics*, beginning in issue #38 (December 1947). The company essentially used the heroine to replace Johnny Thunder as a member, as the latter character was dropped from the team after *All-Star Comics* #39 (February 1948).

After DC transitioned Black Canary to being a lead character in the *Flash Comics* anthology, writer Robert Kanigher and artist Carmine Infantino fleshed out the heroine, by establishing her civilian identity, Dinah Drake. The creators made Black Canary a florist when not in costume, thereby enhancing the feminist content of the character by giving her a career. While the occupation itself did not challenge accepted norms with regard to gender and labor, the creative team name the floral shop in which she works "Dinah Drake Flower Shoppe." Thus, the creators make it clear that the character is the sole proprietor of the store, which was a very unusual work situation in which to cast a female superhero at the time; several female superheroes did not work at all, while many other Golden Age heroines worked in traditional female support staff roles, such as nurse or secretary.[2] So while Kanigher and Infantino portray Drake engaged in feminine work of floral arrangement, they also infer that she has all of the responsibilities of any independent entrepreneur, handling any and all transactions in which the store was involved, not only with customer purchases, but with the shop's suppliers as well. According to business administration scholar Helene J. Ahl, the traditional discourse on entrepreneurship frames it as

> a male gendered concept with implications not only for individual entrepreneurs but also for the organization of society. Entrepreneurship as described in economics and in business research requires a particular gendered division of labor where it is assumed that a woman does the unpaid, reproductive work associated with the private sphere [56].

Kanigher and Infantino label the shop as Drake's, while at the same time portraying her as completely independent woman, with no family or husband supporting her. Readers must conclude that Drake's floral activities are not a passing hobby, but the basis of a successful business, profitable enough to keep the doors to the shop open. In doing so, Kanigher and Infantino subtly blurred the distinctions between men's and women's work, and challenge male privilege in the world of business.

Of course, the feminine delicacy of floral arrangement overshadowed the character's masculine entrepreneurial qualities, because the creative team was using the career much in the same way that creator in DC's Superman franchise used Clark Kent's glasses; Drake's chosen career established her as so feminine that the male foil, private investigator Larry Lance, could not possibly believe that she lead an action-packed secret life as Black Canary. From the outset of the feature, Kanigher and Infantino establish that Lance was an avatar of competent masculinity, very different from the bumbling Johnny Thunder, by connecting the character to tropes associated with hard-boiled detectives that had been popularized in pulp fiction and film noir. When the character is first introduced to readers, he literally demands "more respect" from Dinah Drake in their first encounter: "You're looking at the private eye who's been assigned to find out why trucks keep disappearing on the Franklin Turnpike!" (Kanigher, "The Huntress..."). In one sentence, Kanigher let readers know that the major male figure of the story was tied to characters such as Dashiel Hammet's Sam Spade, Raymond Chandler's Philip Marlowe, and DC Comics' Slam Bradly. Further, he was worthy of their company, despite his supporting role status, in that he was involved with an important criminal investigation, presumably at the behest of either the companies being victimized or the authorities, seeking a fresh perspective on the case.

In terms of visualization, Infantino connected Lance to the hard-boiled private eye tropes through the character's clothing. He depicted Lance wearing suits, a fedora, and sometimes a trench coat. Infantino also regularly showed the character smoking a cigarette. Through these visual cues, the artist likened Lance to characters like Hammet's Sam Spade, particularly as portrayed by Humphrey Bogart in the 1941 production of *The Maltese Falcon*. Erin Smith, in her analysis of hard-boiled detective fiction, argues that the way that private eyes dressed served to reconcile the "celebration of proletarian worldviews" with "careful instructions in consumerist ways" (28). Therefore, the private eye's carefully selected outfit became associated with "manly artisan heroes" who were "continuously doing battle with employers and police to defend their right to carry out their investigations their way," which, because they were the heroes of the stories in which they appeared, was inevitably the right way of doing things (Smith 28).

In other comic stories, creators usually contrasted a male character's strength, ingenuity, and courage against a female character's beauty and delicacy as a means to demonstrate heroic virtue. In the "Black Canary" feature, Kanigher and Infantino instead juxtaposed the heroine's lead character status with Larry Lance's hard-boiled detective status to demonstrate her heroic qualities. Therefore, Black Canary had to be tougher, cleverer, braver than the "manly artisan hero" Lance is supposed to be. As the feature star, she did consistently save the day, her actions did bring resolution to any given plot of the feature (often rescuing Lance as well), the creators imbued Black Canary with feminist implications, suggesting that women were capable of doing the same tasks as the manliest of men.

The company maintained "Black Canary" as a feature in the *Flash Comics* anthology until its cancellation in February 1949, for a total of 13 issues. As with *Flash Comics*, creators would maintain Black Canary as a member of the Justice Society for the remainder of the team's existence as lead feature of *All-Star Comics* until issue #57 (February 1950), after which the series became a western anthology. Coinciding with the shift in consumer tastes that led to the decline of superhero comics was the success of the anti-comics movement. Dr. Fredric Wertham energized the movement in the late 1940s and early 1950s by associating comic readership with juvenile delinquency and the promotion of homosexuality. Specifically, Wertham associated Wonder Woman's strength, and independence—particularly from marriage—with lesbianism. The movement caught the attention of prominent politicians, most notably presidential hopeful Estes Kefauver, Democratic Representative from Tennessee, and the industry found itself under threat of government regulation. To forestall any regulatory action, several companies banded together to create the Comic Code in 1954, a set of industry-wide production values designed to insure that companies were producing socially acceptable content. Among the values mandated by the Comic Code were a prohibition on portraying sexually deviant behavior (i.e., homosexuality), a ban on provocative depictions of female sexuality, and the validation of marriage and domesticity, rules which restricted the manner in which female characters could be portrayed. With the codification of gender values that validated domestic containment of women, the comic industry embraced anti-feminism to an unprecedented degree as a result of Wertham's contributions to the anti-comics movement. Thereafter, creators tended to make characters like the Invisible Girl rather than Wonder Woman, and companies shied away from publishing female superheroes as lead characters suggesting that they lacked the strength and independence to carry their own feature or comic series.[3]

Following the development of the Comic Code, the superhero genre experienced a renaissance, known to fans as the Silver Age, prompting DC Comics to revitalize several of its lapsed characters. Among these characters was Black Canary, but the company relegated the heroine to low-level status at first. She appeared as the token female character on the Justice Society of America, on the periodic occasions when creators had that team work with the Justice League in the latter team's eponymous comic; in this capacity the character made four appearances in *The Justice League of America* from 1963 to 1965. In 1965, DC expanded the profile of the heroine with a pair of appearances in *The Brave and the Bold*, a series that the company had been using to stimulate market interest in character concepts such as the Justice League, the revised Hawkman, the Teen Titans, and Metamorpho. In issues #61 (September 1965) and #62 (October 1965), writer Gardner Fox and artist Murphy Anderson paired the heroine with fellow Golden Age hero/Justice Society member Starman. While Starman garnered top billing on the cover of both issues, the creative team showed Black Canary to be nearly as capable as her male counterpart; Starman had to snap Black Canary out of a hypnotic spell placed on her by the villain in issue #61, but the heroine save the hero from an ambush the antagonists featured in issue #62 (Fox, "Mastermind..." and "The Big..."). Also in issue #62, Fox and Anderson has Black Canary subdue a rampaging gorilla using her hand-to-hand combat skills, suggesting that she is a master martial artist. While the creators show Black Canary to be a competent heroine (more so than many female superheroes of the time) as well as maintaining her alter ego as a working woman, they also established that the character had married Larry Lance in the interim, beginning Black Canary's transformation into an avatar of domestic containment.

A few years later, writer Dennis O'Neil, along with artist Dick Dillin and editor Julius Schwartz incorporated Black Canary into *The Justice League of America* in issue #74 (September 1969) (O'Neil, "Where..."). The creative team inducted Black Canary into the Justice League during the "mod" phase of the Wonder Woman franchise. Beginning in *Wonder Woman* #179 (November 1968), Wonder Woman gave up her Amazonian abilities and star-spangled outfit, operating as a non-powered, non-costumed (though very fashionable) adventurer, relying on martial arts training from an elderly Asian male mentor when confronting her foes.[4] Dennis O'Neil, who was writing both series at the time, had the heroine take a leave absence from the League in *The Justice League of America* #69 (February 1969) due to the character's depowering.[5] DC's revival of Black Canary took place against the backdrop of the growing prominence of second wave feminism. Feminism had been energized in the 1960s by the success of the African American Civil Rights Movement, the development of the birth control pill, the publication of Betty Freidan's *The Feminine Mystique* in 1964, and the coming of age of the Baby Boom generation. Feminists had particularly garnered notoriety for their cause, dubbed the "Women's Liberation Movement" by the media, after the New York Radical Women in 1968 protested the Miss America pageant.

Coinciding with the growing presence of feminism, the television industry had aired a few shows that portrayed women as cable at being action adventurers as they were of being wives and mothers. Arguably, the most successful of these was the import from England, *The Avengers*, a show created to capitalize on the popularity of espionage fantasies (spy-fi) inspired by the James Bond films; at the height of its popularity, the show featured the female (co-)protagonist Emma Peel, played by Diana Rigg. Other shows included *Honey West* and *Girl from U.N.C.L.E.* (a spin-off of *Man from U.N.C.L.E.*). Also in this period, producers of the highly popular Batman television series introduced Batgirl to the program. The comic industry seemed to take notice of this action heroine trend. Gold Key Comics produced licensed adaptations of *Honey West, Girl from U.N.C.L.E.*, and *The Avengers* (retitled *John Steed/ Emma Peel*, to avoid confusion with the Marvel superhero comic of the same name). Gold Key also developed original concepts "Jet Dream and Her Stunt Girl Counterspies," an all female paramilitary unit similar to that of Golden Age hero Blackhawk, and Tiger-Girl, a superhero concept that also included some common 1960s era spy-fi tropes. In 1967, Charlton Comics published a few adventures of spy heroine Tiffany Sinn, and ran a Nightshade feature in *Captain Atom* which had spy-fi elements, much like Tiger-Girl. In 1969, DC started publishing a Batgirl backup feature in *Detective Comics* (issues #359 [February 1969]–424 [June 1972]), and made Supergirl the lead feature in *Adventure Comics* (issues #381 [June 1969]–423 [October 1972]). Artist Mike Sekowsky, who worked with Dennis O'Neil on the "mod" revision of Wonder Woman, as well as Jet Dream for Gold Key, drew inspiration from Emma Peel for his work on Wonder Woman during his tenure as artist and, later, writer. According Les Daniels, in his official history of the Wonder Woman character:

> Another vogue influencing the new Wonder Woman was the cult developing around an imported British television series called *The Avengers*. One of its stars, Diana Rigg, played a slim, athletic secret agent who engaged in bouts of hand-to-hand combat while dressed in provocative and progressive fashions.... Mike Sekowsky ... was definitely in. "We were all in love with Diana Rigg and that show she was on," he said. The influence helped turn Diana Prince into a globe-trotting, karate-kicking spy... [128–29].

This spate of concepts not only represented the most significant expansion of female lead characters since the era in which DC Comics created Black Canary.

These characters also embodied the strongest validation of feminism since the creation of the Comic Code. The following scene from the sole issue of *Tiger-Girl*, written by Jerry Siegel, and drawn by Jack Sparling, the exchange between the titular heroine and her male foil, Ed Savage, "top agent of the government bureau of W.A.A.V.,"[6] makes the most explicit reference that comic creators were responding to some degree to second wave feminism as well as the trends in espionage fiction:

Ed Savage: Thanks for saving my life—but...
Tiger Girl: My pleasure! Why the frown Mr. Savage?
Savage: Tangling with arch-villains is for pros like WAAV agents! You should be home scrambling eggs over a hot stove!
Tiger-Girl: Its conceited apes like YOU who keep women from achieving EQUAL RIGHTS! Why I bother rescuing you! (Internal monolog: Except you are so handsome!) Come, Kitten [Tiger-Girl's pet tiger]—his supposed male superiority is driving me back to the jungle!
Savage (internal monolog): What a sizzle-tempered cutie! [Siegel].

With regard to DC Comics' Batgirl, film and cultural studies scholar Will Brooker has stated that the character

brought a light form of feminism into the mythos from the start. The comic book Batman declares "from what I've seen, she doesn't have to take a back seat to anybody," while Adam West's Caped Crusader [from the television show] also approves. "Whoever she is behind that mask of hers, she helped us out of a dire dilemma."

In a move that Brooker describes as "fully consistent with the character's role at the time," the U.S. Department of Labor mobilized the television iteration of Batgirl for a public service announcement to educate viewers about the "Equal Pay for Equal Work" campaign, and encourage compliance with the Federal Equal Pay Act of 1963. Produced in 1971, the PSA was shot in the style of a Batman television episode, and had Yvonne Craig, Burt Ward, and William Dozier reprise their roles from the show as Batgirl, Robin, and the narrator (actor Dick Gautier replaced Adam West) (Brooker). In it, Batman and Robin are tied up, while a bomb ticks away, when Batgirl enters the scene:

Robin: Holy breaking and entering! It's Batgirl!
Batman: Quick, Batgirl! Untie us before it's too late!
Batgirl: It's already too late! I've worked for you a long time, and I'm paid less than Robin!
Robin: Holy discontent!
Batgirl: Same job, same employer means equal pay for men AND women.
Batman: No time for jokes, Batgirl!
Batgirl: It's no joke! It's the Federal Equal Pay Law.
Robin: Holy act of Congress!
Batman: Can we talk about this... later?
Narrator: Will Batgirl save the Dynamic Duo? Will she get equal pay? [U.S. Department of Labor].

Like the scene from *Tiger-Girl* #1, the PSA serves to demonstrate that the television action heroines were intertwined with second wave feminism. Both artifacts serve to validate the liberal branch of the movement, which stressed the improvement of opportunities for women in the public sphere, particularly in the workplace, rather than endorsing radical feminism, which stood for the revision of gendered social conventions, such as the Miss America pageant.

In the story arc in which they have the Black Canary leave the Justice Society for the Justice League, O'Neil, Dillin, and Schwartz also kill off Larry Lance. In doing so, they severed Black Canary's ties with the earlier stories presented in *The Brave and the Bold* stories, allowing the heroine to come out of "semi-retirement" and return to public sphere activity of crime-fighting, unimpeded by the domestic responsibilities of being a wife. Along with liberating Black Canary from her marriage, O'Neil and Dillin also enhance the power of the heroine. In *The Justice League of America* #75 (Nov. 1969), the creative team has Black Canary recount the debate which ensued among several male members as to whether she should be granted membership:

> (As a flashback, showing Black Canary in Justice League headquarters, with Superman, Hawkman, the Atom, and Batman)
> **Hawkman:** I yield to no one in my admiration for Black Canary's courage and virtue…. But I wonder if she's accustomed to our kind of mission—our kind of danger…. I know she's a judo expert—but judo simply isn't enough against the sort of foes we tackle!
> **The Atom:** How do you know? It seems to me that she should have a chance!
> **Batman:** Still, we have no right to endanger her needlessly!
> **Black Canary:** Please stop talking about me as if I weren't here! All of you—stop bickering…
> **Black Canary** (Narrative caption, recounting events to Green Arrow): Suddenly I felt an odd singing inside my head—like nothing I'd never felt before—EVER! It seemed to move outside—then, the noise-that-was-not-a-noise seemed to leap away from me with tremendous force—and the mighty Justice League was flung about like leaves in a hurricane! [O'Neil, "In Each…"].

Creators would later dub this new ability the "canary cry." While creators would generally have Black Canary rely on the fighting skills that had been an aspect of the character since her inception in future stories, the development of this superhuman ability served to terminate the debate regarding her worthiness to join the League. Thereafter, DC maintained Black Canary as a stalwart member of the League for over a decade.

During the Silver Age, companies producing superhero comics typically only maintained a single token female superhero on any team, thereby suggesting that women only deserve a marginal presence in the public sphere. Unlike when the creative team on *All-Star Comics* incorporated Black Canary into the Justice Society during the Golden Age, O'Neil and Dillin were not adding a female character to the Justice League, but replacing another superheroine, Wonder Woman, thereby reinforcing this pattern. Additionally companies tended to restrict the publication of female superheroes to team series; DC was the only company to maintain a couple of female superheroes, Wonder Woman and Supergirl, as lead characters throughout the Silver Age and

The Justice League of America the only team series to have a superheroine as a member that was also used as a lead character elsewhere. Therefore, when O'Neil and company eliminated Wonder Woman from the series, the Justice League became just like every other superhero team in circulation, with a superheroine as a member whose entire reason for being is to be the token female.[7] Aside from a few guest appearances, creators would not reincorporate Wonder Woman into *The Justice League of America* until issue #128 (March 1976), essentially making Black Canary the sole female on the team for over half a decade, on a team that had ten male heroes on its roster.[8]

Creators on the *Justice League of America* also call into question Black Canary's competence as a hero, another Silver Age trope of female portrayal which served to reinforce the notion of women's inferiority. In *The Justice League of America* #75, O'Neil had Hawkman give voice to the concern regarding the heroine's competence, and that Batman affirms the validity of the concern. Batman famously possesses no superhuman abilities, but is able to overcome superhuman foes through a combination of his unparalleled skill in martial arts and high-tech gadgets carried in his utility belt. The incarnation of Hawkman seen in this issue is an extraterrestrial being, but unlike fellow aliens Superman or Martian Manhunter, DC Comics showed this Hawkman to be little different from a normal human in terms of intrinsic superhuman attributes; the character can fly, as creators made his wings a technology from his home world. Given that both of these characters rely on fighting skill, courage, and virtue, to deal with the dangers faced on Justice League missions, O'Neil makes this debate an exercise in sexist condescension, as the only characteristic that distinguishes Black Canary from Hawkman or Batman is her gender.[9]

O'Neil and the writers who followed changed Black Canary from a heroine that displayed the traits of calmness, intuitive thinking, and decisiveness as she did in the Golden Age to a stereotypically feminine character whose emotions often got the better of her. For over a year, creators working with Black Canary made her mourning as important aspect of her characterization; in *The Justice League of America* #75, Black Canary recounts to teammate Green Arrow about how her "mind wandered," during a meeting of the League,

> [to] the terrible events of weeks past … when the Justice League teamed with the Justice Society against the star-creature Aquarius. With a shudder of horror, I recalled how Aquarius caused the death of my husband, Larry—and how Superman to [join the Justice League] where perhaps I could … forget… [O'Neil, "Destiny's…"].

At the end of issue #78 (March 1970), O'Neil has the heroine acknowledge that she is "still filled with memories … [of] my late husband" ("The Coming…"). O'Neil again has the heroine mourn in *Green Lantern/Green Arrow* #78 (July 1970).

Once more, she relives the hideous death of her husband, Larry Lance ... struck down by the deadly sphere of the star-creature Aquarius ... and his funeral attended by both the Justice League of Earth-One and the Justice Society of Earth-Two.[10] She feels the grief bite into her soul ... the grief that drove her away from Earth-Two, with the countless reminders of Larry to this twin world, this parallel universe... [O'Neil, "A Kind..."]

In *The Justice League of America* #84 (November 1970), Robert Kanigher, co-creator of both Black Canary and Larry Lance, has the heroine experience a moment of grief:

Black Canary (interior monolog): Work! That's what I need to forget! WORK!

Narrative Caption: Inside [Justice League headquarters], surrounded by banks of computerized monitors screening the world's woes ... yet oblivious to the heartache of a single human inches away...

Black Canary (interior monolog): "B-but ... how can I forget...? I'm just a lonely girl—still mourning the death of my husband... [Kanigher, "The Devil..."].

Mike Freidrich, who took over as regular writer of *The Justice League of America* in issue #86 (December 1970), has Black Canary reveal her sadness to a complete stranger in issue #89 (May 1971): "When my husband died, I was stranded ... cut loose! The hurt is taking so long to heal! In the quiet of the night, when I'm alone, the pain throbs dully, down deep!" (Freidrich, "The Most..."). To some degree, such scenes seem like a logical outgrowth of the decision to kill off Larry Lance.

Despite the logic, creators during the 1960s had typically used such expressions of emotion as demonstrations of femininity for female superheroes during the Silver Age, a means to show that such fictional characters were proper girls to readers. Further, creators usually showed these emotional outbursts in a negative light, presenting them as distractions in the process of resolving a given plot, or worse, using them to create an opportunity for a story antagonist to put the heroes or innocent bystanders in jeopardy. Creators tended to contrast female emotionalism with its portrayed negative consequences with masculine decisive rationality, which helped bring about plot resolution, thereby showing males to be more competent than females at getting things done. Freidrich and Dillin replicate this trope in *The Justice League of America* #89 with the scene where Black Canary shares her grief with a stranger, as they reveal soon thereafter that the man to whom she is talking is the story antagonist, using the encounter to set the story in motion. In essence, by sitting down with the stranger and sharing her pain, rather than suppressing her emotions as a heroic man would, Black Canary puts herself and her Justice League teammates in danger. O'Neil and Adams also use this trope in *Green Lantern/Green Arrow* #78, as the Charles Manson–esque villain, Joshua, uses Black Canary's moment of emotional weakness to hypnotize her into joining his murderous death cult (O'Neil, "My Kind…").

And DC creators did not limit themselves to making Black Canary's moments of grief the only manifestations of feminine emotion. Despite making mourning her lost husband a sub-plot within *The Justice League of America*, creators quickly have Black Canary develop romantic feelings for teammate Green Arrow. In doing so, they replicate another convention common to the domestic containment heroine archetype, the romantic heroine in need of a paramour. O'Neil initiates the romance in *The Justice League of America* #79 (March 1970), when he has Green Arrow admit his attraction for Black Canary (O'Neil, "Come…"). In *The Justice League of America* #81 (May 1970), O'Neil suggests that Black Canary reciprocated Green Arrow's affection, admitting to herself that she misses the hero, despite thinking him a "nuisance" early on (O'Neil, "Plague…"). Soon thereafter, O'Neil incorporated Black Canary into *Green Lantern/Green Arrow* as a member of the series' supporting cast, beginning with issue #78 (July 1970). Kanigher and Dillon create a love triangle among Black Canary, Green Arrow in *The Justice League of America* #84 (November 1970) after Black Canary kisses Batman following her reverie of mourning described above (Kanigher, "The Devil…"). Mike Freidrich quickly terminated this plot point in *The Justice League of America* #88 (March 1971), however, with the heroine asking Batman for advice on how to deal with her attraction for Green Arrow, "as the brother you are to me"; not only does this scene cause Batman a moment of heartache, but it makes Black Canary seem emotionally flighty, if not damaged (Friedrich, "The Last…").

While the love triangle was quickly forgotten, the romance between Black Canary and Green Arrow would be a move that would permanently define the heroine's characterization and publication history; from this point forward, DC would tether Black Canary as romantic interest, domestic partner, and superheroic companion to the hero in features starring Green Arrow, so much so, that the character was adapted into the recent television adaptation *Arrow* which began in 2012. As a member of Green Arrow's supporting cast, creators used Black Canary like a conventional sidekick, much like how Kanigher and Infantino used Larry Lance during the Golden Age, often getting threatened, knocked out, or captured to allow Green Arrow an opportunity to demonstrate his heroism by rescuing her. Despite the comic book character maintaining her floral career, creators made Black Canary into an avatar of domestic containment by having the heroine co-habitate with Green Arrow in the text of various stories, as well as making features starring the hero a major venue for the publication of her exploits.

By the time that the Equal Rights Amendment was sent to the states for ratification by Congress in March of 1972, a high point for second wave feminism, DC Comics had effectively excised most feminist content from Black Canary and contained the character within the male dominated realms of *The Justice League of America* and "Green Arrow" features, as well as her romantic relationship with Green Arrow. Creators then added to Black Canary's realignment as an embodiment of conservative femininity as the 1970s unfolded. In *Green Lantern/Green Arrow* #82 (February 1971), O'Neil and Adams have Black Canary defend the male heroes from a deadly rampage by harpies, amazons, and a medusa, all fearsome images of powerful females from Greek Mythology. In the story, Green Lantern's arch foe, Sinestro, dupes these avatars of empowered femininity into attacking his enemies, manipulating their irrational hatred of men to do his bidding (O'Neil, "How..."). In *Adventure Comics* #418 (April 1972) and #419 (May 1972), O'Neil with artist Alex Toth produced the only first new Black Canary solo feature since the Golden Age, in which the heroine confronts a gang of female criminals posing as a women's rights advocacy group. Along with fighting villainous feminist proxies, creators on *The Justice League of America* imbue Black Canary with domestic skill by having her design and sew new costumes for teammate Red Tornado and, oddly, the team's android antagonist, Amazo (Wein, "The Man..." and "War...").

If viewed solely against the background of second wave feminism coming to the peak of its influence, the manner in which DC Comics portrayed Black Canary seems problematic, if not reactionary. However, a broader investigation of the history of Black Canary shows the industry's willingness to validate female empowerment waxing and waning with respect to different times, economic conditions, and societal climates. In having Black Canary usurp the publication space of Johnny Thunder in *Flash Comics* and in other ways, the character can be read as feminist, in that she represented a move toward greater gender parity in American public life and the legitimization of female empowerment. Creators' revision of Black Canary into an overly emotional heroine who was bound to Larry Lance, then Green Arrow shows that domestic containment values had become a powerful feature of the gendered message projected by the genre and industry in the wake of Fredric Wertham and the peak of the anti-comics movement. Yet, these developments took place in contrast to the characters published in response to the television spy-fi heroine trend, making it clear that the industry's gender values were in some degree of flux due to changing social mores regarding the proper role of women. A broad, contextualized examination of female portrayal in the genre, particularly of the "notable few" female superheroes like Black Canary, reveals an industry attempting to negotiate the complexities of gender politics rather than promoting a particular gender ideology as Pecora's analysis suggests. While few creators seriously questioned the common sense that was hegemonic masculinity, they were not consistently committed to antifeminism, the deprivation of women's public agency, as a companion gender value. Creators involved in this negotiation process were attempting to craft marketable products that would attract broad audiences and garner sales, while at the same time avoiding any notoriety for the industry that might harm its commercial interests. This negotiation process certainly led to awkward contradictions which would be viewed as problematic by feminists. Creators on *The Justice League of America* produced one such problem as they fundamentally reversed the fortunes for Black Canary. Nevertheless, this development, when viewed in context, shows the superhero genre was not a simple-minded champion of a patriarchal gender order, as Pecora and other scholars have argued.

NOTES

1. In 1944, Holyoke Comics revitalized Miss Victory and Chesler Comics reintroduced Yankee Girl, two characters created in the spate of superheroines that prompted DC to develop Wonder Woman. In 1945, Fawcett Comics launched *Mary Marvel* (1945), and in 1946, Harvey Comics began publication of *Black Cat* (1946), the first eponymous comics named for female superheroes to last more than ten issues since DC's *Wonder Woman* (1942). Marvel changed *All-Select Comics*, an anthology title that had been one of the comics dedicated to presenting the adventures of Captain America and the Human Torch, to *Blonde Phantom Comics* with issue #12 (December 1946), named for the company's new heroine. In 1947, Marvel later partnered the company's major male heroes with female sidekicks: the Sub-Mariner met his female cousin, Namora, Golden Girl replaced Captain America's long-time sidekick Bucky, and the Human Torch traded Toro, a teen sidekick with similar superhuman abilities, for Sun Girl, who had none. Marvel also published Sun Girl and Namora in eponymous comics in the same month that the company released *Venus* #1 (August 1948), in which creators used the Roman goddess of love as a superheroine. Along with Black Canary, DC contributed to the trend in *Star-Spangled Comics* by using Merry, Girl of 100 Gimmicks to replace Stripesy, sidekick to the Star-Spangled Kid in issue #81 (June 1948); the company then replaced Star-Spangled Kid with Merry as a lead character in *Star-Spangled Comics* #87 (December 1948).

2. Female sidekicks Hawkgirl (DC), Owl Girl (Dell), and Bulletgirl (Fawcett) were simply girlfriends of their male partners; leading heroines Phantom Lady (Quality/Fox) and Miss Masque (Nedor) were debutante daughters of socially prominent families; Blonde Phantom (Marvel) and Miss Victory (Holyoke) were both secretaries, and War Nurse (Harvey) was a nurse, while Wonder Woman (DC) served both as nurse and secretary in her civilian identity.

3. See Thomas C. Donaldson, "Ineffectual Lass Among the Legions of Superheroes: The Marginalization and Domestication of Female Superheroes, 1955–1970," *Ages of Heroes, Eras of Men: Superheroes and the American Experience*, ed. Julian C. Chambliss, William Svitavsky, and Thomas C. Donaldson (Newcastle on the Tyne: Cambridge Scholars Press, 2003), 139–152.

4. Several essays in *The Ages of Wonder Woman: Essays on the Amazon Princess in Changing Times* address this era of *Wonder Woman* comic books. See "What a Woman Wonders: This Is Feminism?" by Jason LaTouche, "Wonder Woman's Lib: Feminism and the 'New' Amazing Amazon" by Paul R. Kohl, and "Not Quite Mod: The New Diana Prince, 1968–1973" for several different types of analyses on these stories.

5. This phase lasted until *Winder Woman* #203 (September 1972). DC restored her powers and costume in response to criticism from Gloria Steinem and the editors of *Ms.* magazine.

6. An acronym for "War Against Arch Villainy." With this, the creative team connected Tiger-Girl to popular espionage fiction, as such acronyms were a popular spy-fi trope in the 1960s. They were made popular by the SPECTRE of the James Bond film franchise, which stood for was the SPecial Executive for Counterintelligence, Terrorism, Revenge and Extortion.

7. A few examples include Invisible Girl in the Fantastic Four, Wasp in the Avengers, and Marvel Girl in the X-Men.

8. Additionally, creators did not add any further female superheroes to the team until the induction of Hawkgirl in *The Justice League of America* [1960] #146 (September 1977).

9. Making this scene even more problematic, in *The Justice League of America* #69, when O'Neil initially has Wonder Woman take leave of absence because the male members refuse to accept her original request to resign altogether; Wonder Woman's teammate, the Flash, tells her, "Loss of your super-powers doesn't change the fact that you are a friend!" With this statement, O'Neil suggests that the male members have a deep loyalty to Wonder Woman, that she deserves a place on the team, even though she now possessed abilities similar to those of Black Canary.

10. It is difficult to discuss DC Comic's development of Black Canary without mentioning one of the more confusing features of the company's superhero product line: the concept of multiple universes. The company developed the multiple universe concept as a means to explain where DC's superheroes of the Golden Age (several of whom, like Black Canary, were members of the Justice Society) had gone in the period between the cancellation of series featuring these characters, and the beginning of the Silver Age in 1956. Each universe included its own Earth, often inhabited by super powered beings, many of whom were variations of the company's major heroes. This essay, insofar as possible, tries to avoid references to the multiple universe/Earth concept, in order to avoid confusion for readers less fluent with the minutia of DC Comics' publication history. Here, Dennis O'Neil offers the briefest and simplest explanation of the concept, as well as explaining its relationship to Black Canary.

WORKS CITED

Ahl, Helene J. *The Making of the Female Entrepreneur: A Discourse Analysis of Research Texts on Women's Entrepreneurship*. Jonkoping: Jonkoping International Business School, 2002. Electronic. Accessed January 16, 2016.

Berger, Arthur Asa. *The Comic-Stripped American*. New York: Walker and Company, 1973.

Blythe, Hal, and Charlie Sweet. "Superhero: The Six Step Progression." In *The Hero in Transition*. Ed. Ray B. Browne and Marshall W. Fishwick. Bowling Green, OH: Bowling Green Popular Press, 1983, 180–87.

Brooker, Will. "Batgirl and Feminism: the 1972 Equal Pay Act PSA." *In Media Res: A Media Commons Project*. February 4, 2015. Accessed February 16, 2016.

Fishwick, Marshall W. Introduction. In *The Hero in Transition*. Ed. Ray B. Browne and Marshall W. Fishwick. Bowling Green, OH: Bowling Green Popular Press, 1983, 5–13.

Cornell, R. W. *Gender and Power: Society, the Person and Sexual Politics*. Cambridge: Blackwell, 1987.

Daniels, Les. *Marvel: Five Fabulous Decades of the World's Greatest Comics*. New York: Harry N. Abrams 1991.
_____. *Wonder Woman: The Complete History*. San Francisco: Chronicle Books, 2000.
Donaldson, Thomas C. "Ineffectual Lass Among the Legions of Superheroes: The Marginalization and Domestication of Female Superheroes, 1955–1970." In *Ages of Heroes, Eras of Men: Superheroes and the American Experience*. Ed. Julian C. Chambliss, William Svitavsky and Thomas C. Donaldson. Newcastle on the Tyne: Cambridge Scholars Press, 2013, 139–52.
_____. "The Inflexible Girls of Steel: Subverting Second Wave Feminism in the Extended Superman Franchise." In *The Ages of Superman: Essays on the Man of Steel in Changing Times*. Ed. Joseph J. Darowski. Jefferson, NC: McFarland, 2012, 62–77.
Edgar, Joanne. "Wonder Woman Revisited." *Ms.*, July 1972: 50–55.
Faludi, Susan. *Backlash: The Undeclared War Against American Women*. New York: Anchor Books, 1992.
Fox, Gardner (w), and Murphy Anderson (a). "Starman and Black Canary." *The Brave and the Bold* [1955] #61–62 (August–October 1965). New York: DC Comics.
Friedrich, Gary (w), Charles Nicholas, and Luis Domiguez (a). "Tiffany Sinn." *Career Girl Romances* [1967] #38–39 (February–April 1967). New York: Charlton Comics.
"Girl from U.N.C.L.E." Internet Movie Database (IMDB). Accessed February 15, 2016. http://www.imdb.com/title/tt0059988/.
Hollows, Joanne. *Feminism, Femininity, and Popular Culture*. Manchester: Manchester University Press, 2000.
"Honey West." Internet Movie Database (IMDB). Accessed February 15, 2016. http://www.imdb.com/title/tt0058814/.
Horn, Maurice. *Women in Comics*. New York: Chelsea House, 1977.
Innes, Sherrie A. *Tough Girls: Women Warriors and Wonder Women in Popular Culture*. Philadelphia: University of Pennsylvania Press, 1999.
Jeffords, Susan. *The Remasculinization of America: Gender and the Vietnam War*. Bloomington: Indiana University Press, 1989.
Jenkins, Tricia. "Nationalism and Gender: The 1970s, *The Six Million Dollar Man*, and *The Bionic Woman*." *Journal of Popular Culture* 44 (2011): 93–113.
Kaler, Dave (w), and Jim Aparo (a). "Nightshade." *Captain Atom* [1965] #87–89 (August–December 1967). New York: Charlton Comics.
_____. "Espionage: Muscle Beach Style (Tiffany Sinn)." *Secret Agent* [1967] #10 (October 1967). New York: Charlton Comics.
Kanigher, Robert (w), and Carmine Infantino (a). "Johnny Thunder." *Flash Comics* [1940] #86–91 (August 1947–January 1948). New York: DC Comics.
_____. "Black Canary." *Flash Comics* [1940] #92–104 (February 1948–February 1949). New York: DC Comics.
Kanigher, Robert, John Broome (w), and Alex Toth, et al. (a). "Justice Society of America." *All-Star Comics* [1940] #38–39 (December 1947–February 1948). New York: DC Comics.
Lee, Stan. *The Superhero Women*. New York: Simon & Schuster, 1977.
MacKinnon, Kenneth. *Representing Men: Maleness, Masculinity in the Media*. London: Arnold Publishers, 2003.
Margolis, Maxine. *Mothers and Such: Views of American Women and Why They Changed*. Berkley: University of California Press, 1984.
Newman, Paul S. (w), and Al McWilliams, et al. (a). *Girl from U.N.C.L.E.* [1967] #1–5 (January–October 1967). New York: Gold Key Comics.

Newman, Paul S. (w), and Jack Sparling (a). *Honey West* [1966] #1 (September 1966). New York: Gold Key Comics.
Nyberg, Amy Kiste, *Seal of Approval: The History of the Comics Code*. Jackson: University Press of Mississippi, 1998.
O'Neil, Dennis (w), and Neal Adams, et al. (a). *Green Lantern/Green Arrow* [1960] #76–122, (April 1970–November 1979). New York: DC Comics.
O'Neil, Dennis (w), and Alex Toth (a). "Black Canary (The Cat and the Canary)." *Adventure Comics* [1938] #418–419 (May-June 1972). New York: DC Comics.
O'Neil, Dennis, et al. (w), and Dick Dillin (a). *The Justice League of America* [1960] #69–146, (February 1961–September 1977). New York: DC Comics.
Pecora, Norma. "Superman/Superboys/Supermen: The Comic Book Hero as Socializing Agent." *Men, Masculinity, and the Media*. Ed. Steve Craig. Newbury Park, CA: Sage, 1992, 61–77.
Reiley, Sean. "Super Friends: Hawkman (page 2)." Seanbaby.com. Accessed February 13, 2016. http://www.seanbaby.com/superfriends/hawkmanb.htm.
Robbins, Trina. *The Great Women Superheroes*. Northampton, MA: Kitchen Sink Press, 1994.
Robinson, Lillian S. *Wonder Women: Feminisms and Superheroes*. New York: Taylor and Francis Group, 2005.
Savage, William. *Comic Books and America, 1945–1954*. Norman: University of Oklahoma Press, 1990.
Scott, Joan. *Gender and the Politics of History*. New York: Columbia University Press, 1999.
Seigel, Jerry (w), and Jack Sparling (a). *Tiger-Girl* [1968] #1 (September 1968). New York: Gold Key Comics.
Smith, Erin. "Dressed to Kill: Hard-Boiled Detective Fiction, Working-Class Consumers, and Pulp Magazines." *Colby Quarterly* 36 (2000): 11–28.
Smith, David K. "The Avengers Timeline." *The Avengers Forever*. April 1, 2002. Accessed February 15, 2016. http://theavengers.tv/forever/timeline.htm.
Steinem, Gloria. "Introduction." *Wonder Woman*: New York: Holt, Reinhart and Winston, 1972, 6–12.
Tuchman, Gaye, Arlene K. Daniels, and James Benet. *Hearth and Home: Images of Women in the Mass Media*. New York: Oxford University Press, 1978.
U.S. Department of Labor. Public Service Announcement For Wage Equality Featuring Batman, Robin, & Batgirl (1973). Accessed February 12, 2016. https://www.youtube.com/watch?v=szZsKdJYR-A.
Wertham, Fredric. *Seduction of the Innocent*. New York: Rinehart and Company, 1954.
Wood, Dick (w), and Joe Certa (a). *Jet Dream and Her Stunt Girl Counterspies* [1968] #1 (June 1968). New York: Gold Key Comics.
Wood, Dick (w), and Mike Sekowsky, et al. (a). "Jet Dream and Her Stunt Girl Counterspies." *Man from U.N.C.L.E.* [1965] #7–22 (July 1966–April 1969). New York: Gold Key Comics.
Wright, Bradford. *Comic Book Nation: The Transformation of Youth Culture in America*. Baltimore: Johns Hopkins University Press, 2001.

Social Justice and
Silver Age Superheroes

W.C. BAMBERGER

The relationship between the real world and the narrative universe depicted in superhero comic book stories is malleable. Basic physical laws are generally respected with in-universe reasons provided for their violation, but the line between the possible and the impossible less so; walls between alternate dimensions as well as the almost ungraspable remoteness of other planets to our own are ignored as often as convenience dictates. Even simple geography is subject to the needs of individual adventures: countries and islands come and go, cities are renamed, rendered generic or given see-through aliases. This is done for a number of reasons, one of the simplest being that identifiable nations have real histories, real politics and real conflicts, and introducing connections to such real world facts into a superhero story makes it less realistic—prompting objections along the lines of "So, why hasn't Superman solved that country's resource crisis?" Real world intrusions can easily threaten the integrity of the superhero world.

Still, some comics have dealt directly with particular real world problems—war comics being the prime example. While modern super heroes rarely involve themselves in actual geo-political events, there have been instances where the stories have grappled with real world conflicts that involve the kinds of issues—the fights for honesty, justice and fair-play, for peaceful coexistence, and the insistence on maintaining personal honor—that are the bases on which superhero stories are built. The 1960s were a time of great social and political upheaval, of struggles for freedom and of war. Several *Justice League of America* adventures selected from November 1965 to November 1967—eight months after the first U.S. Marines landed at Da Nang to six months before the assassination of Dr. Martin Luther King—highlight how some of the then current social and political conflicts are addressed (at times rather obliquely) in these pages.

The title of the November 1965 issue of *Justice League of America,* "The Indestructible Creatures of Nightmare Island," suggests a story that will conform to the classic super heroes vs. monsters tradition. However, the first word of the issue, in boldface lettering, is **Conscience**. Conscience as a motivational element, as a story trigger, is certainly not unknown in comics, but here Gardner Fox (who wrote all the stories considered here) uses it to introduce the unusually overt philosophical framework of the story. The introduction reads:

> Conscience is many things, say the philosophers. He who heeds its voice is a virtuous man. Were some man to build a machine which could compel men to heed the "still small voice" of conscience, then he might make earth into a utopia! Or—suffer the same terrible fate that overtook Andrew Helm when he tried to give his native planet a conscience... [59].

Taking in the page as a whole, the juxtaposition of elements, including text referencing Utopian ideals and warnings, the large font title of the story, and the illustration—Flash fighting some kind of whirlwind monster, Green Arrow facing a dinosaur-like creature, and others facing an arboreal menace—form the kind of complex paradox that Fox invested in the best of his tales. Implicit in these seemingly disparate elements is the question "How did an attempt to create a world-wide conscience lead to monsters?" And there is the additional puzzle presented by the box on the cover of the issue that declares, "Solved at last: The age-old puzzler of what happens when an irresistible force meets and immovable object!" So before the action begins we are presented with four large abstractions—conscience, utopia, irresistible force, immoveable objects.

The first page of the story proper reiterates the overriding theme: "The conscience is more wise than science—Whewill" (60). This is a slight misremembering: Fox means to refer to William Whewell. Whewell was a 19th century scientist (in fact it was he who invented the word "scientist"), philosopher and clergyman.[1] The story then opens in the year 1900. An American explorer and his family are approaching "a golden city hidden behind an invisible force-field of kinetic power" (Fox, "The Indestructible..." 60). The expedition is attacked by bandits and everyone is killed except Andrew Helm, the four-year-old son of the explorer. Lamas from the golden city, which is called Ta Ming, find the boy and take him in. As they return to the city—raising the force-field as they do so—the murderous bandit chieftain, Chung Ka, witnesses their passage and tries to follow them, with the intent of looting the city. But he is unable to pierce the force-field. He vows to return one day and steal the riches of the city for himself.

Andrew is raised and educated by the lamas of Ta Ming. At the same time he is learning telepathy and astral projection and more mystical arts,

Chung Ka is serving a long prison sentence. When Chung Ka is finally freed, he and his men return to the golden city. Chung Ka is still unable to break through the force barrier, but he and his men are able to tunnel beneath it: "A tunnel empties out—and then a horde of conscienceless outlaws swarm over [the city]" (Fox, "The Indestructable..." 61). The unusual adjective is, of course, meant to remind us of the theme of the issue.

After the bandits loot the city Andrew Helm is again the sole survivor and he moves to an island somewhere between New Zealand and Australia. There he builds a laboratory surrounded by the same kind of force-field that had protected Ta Ming. He creates a machine "to save mankind from itself." Helms' journeys by astral projection have shown him that conscience "seems to be suppressed in the world," as if it were a psychological problem affecting the brain of the entire population of the Earth. "I shall release it with my invention—the Corti-Conscience machine. Just as the brain can be electrically stimulated to cause a person to feel hate or love, hunger or satisfaction—so my Corti-Conscience, by affecting the cerebral cortex and the brain's amygdala portions—will govern the behavior of a person" (62). In a moment of hubris, Helm reflects that great men throughout history have tried to awaken the conscience in their fellows and failed—he thinks of Moses, Christ, Confucius, Mohammed and Buddha—but where they failed he and his machine will certainly succeed. It seems unlikely that the choice of the name "Helm," the name of the point from which a large ship is steered, was a simple coincidence.

For modern readers Helm's statement, his plan, unavoidably evoke the philosophy behind some of America's post–World War II foreign policy disasters. That is, Helm (who, we must not forget, is an American) is planning clandestinely from a base in another country, acting on his personal vision of how to reshape the rules of conduct for all the people of the world. Helm turns on his machine, and once again employs astral projection to flash around the world. He sees the immediate effects of his Corti-Conscience machine: villains fighting Flash become conscience-stricken and stop; a Caribbean dictator (obviously modeled on Fidel Castro) with an arsenal of nuclear weapons suddenly decides to destroy them all; the Penguin and the equally evil Captain Cold suddenly surrender to Batman.

In contrast to these more extended episodes there is also a quick glimpse—a single panel—of a jungle clearing where guerrilla fighters and uniformed soldiers are laying down their arms and declaring themselves to be neighbors and friends. The country is unnamed, but readers in 1965 would have immediately identified this as a reference to the war in Vietnam. A radio broadcast announces an end to hostilities, war, poverty and oppression around the world. Flash voices what others of the Justice League are clearly feeling as well: "I want to cheer—yet somehow I have a sinking feeling all this news is too good to be true" (67).

In the meantime, Helms realizes he has been out of his body for too long. As he hurriedly returns to his invisible island we are presented with yet another quotation, this one credited to Stanislaw I, an 18th century king of Poland: "Conscience warns us as a friend before it punishes us as a judge." Helms finds he is now unable to reenter his physical body, and will have to spend eternity as an intangible, invisible presence. Without Helm being able to control it, the Corti-Conscience machine is running out of control, and will now begin to have negative effects: "[It's] building up an overdose.... The voice of mankind's conscience will be stilled! The evil nature of men will run riot..." (69). War and gang violence erupt again. The comic book fails to provide a logical explanation for this being the result of an overdose of conscience, but Fox glosses this over in his desire to set up more complex and paradoxical set of philosophical ideas within the limits of his adventure narrative.

Superman urges his fellow Justice League members to help him fight the new outbreaks of trouble. However, instead of the called-for action, a philosophical discussion ensues. Green Lantern—after telling Superman to "cool it!"—says, "What right do *we* have to interfere with the rights of other people?" Flash agrees: "That's telling him, GL! Live and let live—" For his part Batman adds, "If people want to fight and rob and oppress other people, we cannot impose our wills on them! They have rights too, you know!" Aquaman: "Every human should be the master of his own destiny" (70). Similar debates—which were open-ended and widely-ranging enough to encompass questions of the limits of self-determination, of "the rights of man," of anti-colonialism and anti-imperialism, freedoms of many sorts, of cultural relativism, and more—were very much in the air in the mid–1960s. The Cuban Revolution was less than a decade old, and struggles for self-rule were ongoing in many parts of the world. Citizens in the United States were choosing sides on issues such as the Civil Rights movement, anti-war demonstrations, and more. This sequence is surely Fox's nod to the difficulty of arriving at simple answers—answers such as those found within the usually straightforward world of comic book struggle and justice—in a world that was beginning to see (and often to resist) how complex the realities of justice, freedom, etc., actually are. Fox doesn't provide readers with any simple political message, but the way this paralyzing debate is resolved is interesting indeed, in light of the ways in which the political policies of the United States were to proceed over the following 50 years. Superman quickly figures out that the rest of the Justice League members are being affected by some kind of radiation to which he is immune. He then reasons that Green Lantern's ring might be able to dispel it. When he asks Green Lantern for the ring, the response is, "Be my guest—take it! What right do I have to hog it for myself?" a response that makes Superman wince. Superman aims the ring at his co-members and they immediately return to their traditional selves. The Green Lantern: "I feel as if a great weight has been lifted from me!" Flash: "Me too! What kind of gibberish was I spouting anyhow?" Green Lantern again: "Superman, Wonder Woman and I will straighten things out in the world—" (70–71).

It would be unfair to make too much of the resolution of such a complex philosophical debate as worked out through a few panels of an adventure story, particularly as some points are expressed in a form carried to extreme lengths—as with Batman's first statement, about those who rob and oppress having rights, too, so they should not be interfered with. But the conclusion implied by this resolution is clear enough: too much in the way of conscience, a too determined embrace of relativism, too much of a hands-off philosophy are delusions—"gibberish," as Flash says—even a kind of sickness in need of a cure. This is an argument for balance, for finding a middle path.

And after the cure comes action, a straightening out of the world, in line with the Justice League's beliefs. Wonder Woman, for example, seizes a "great dictator" and refuses to unhand him until he agrees to follow the rules she writes on his wall, including "A job for every man! No laws that aid only the rich!" Again, this is particularly interesting—for some even saddening— in light of the next 50 years of American politics. Batman, Flash and Aquaman are attempting to trace the source of the radiation that had so affected them. Their instruments indicate its location but they can, of course, see nothing of the invisible island. The disembodied Helm sees their approach and silently begs them to persevere. They finally locate the island with the help of some porpoises, whose vision is not affected by the force-field. The remaining members now join the others and prepare for the assault on the Corti-Conscience machine.

Part Three begins with yet another historical quote, this one from 17th century churchman and historian Thomas Fuller: "A wounded conscience is able to un–Paradise Paradise itself" (75). They find a way to cross the barrier, but they are "unaware that they have stepped from a normal world into a perilous phantasmagoria!" (77). They encounter a magician, a fiery warrior, a Stegosaurus, and more—the by-now almost forgotten "Indestructible Creatures" of the title. The radiation from the machine that has accumulated inside the force-field "causing"—not, as readers soon discover, actually *creating*—these strange hostile figures. Because passing birds don't see the giant bird attacking Hawkeye he realizes that it is imaginary, and the super heroes realize that these indestructible menaces are "conjured up by our own minds" (79).

After disbelieving the creatures into non-existence, the Justice League members turn off the glowing machine. They find Helms' lifeless body, and this leads into the moral of the tale.

Superman: Too bad he couldn't have lived to realize that conscience cannot be forced on a man.

Wonder Woman: It must come as a result of understanding between men!

Atom: Be they black, red, white or yellow, every man wants happiness for himself, his family and his children! Until that is properly understood, there will always be injustice in the world [82].

This ending, a round-robin statement of the idea of the brotherhood of man, barely addresses the huge, complex questions raised by the story itself. These questions were very much part of the dialogue of ideas in the 1960s, and they were being dealt with, certainly not for the first time, in literature as well. English novelist Anthony Burgess' 1962 novel *A Clockwork Orange*, for example, posed some of these same questions, and came to the same conclusion as Superman.

Echoes of the idea of the forced or violent creation of brotherhood are present, in this instance in a rather frivolous form, in at least one more story following "The Indestructible Menaces" issue. At the end of issue #47, "The Bridge Between Earths," the villains Solomon Grundy and the Blockbuster end a fight by becoming friends with each other and all the Justice League and Earth-Two's Justice Society members. Black Canary says, "They knocked the hate out of each other!" and Doctor Mid-Nite adds, "If only we could get people and nations to knock hate out of each other without going to war!" (256). But this is an unconvincing resolution, little more than a quip.

The December 1966 Justice League adventure is titled "The Lord of Time Attacks the 20th Century." "The Lord of Time" is not a super villain in the sense of those the Justice League usually confronts. He has no super-human powers, no abilities beyond those of an ordinary man. His power lies in his superior technology—specifically, advanced weaponry. "The Lord of Time" is from the future, but the story opens in the present time of the story, in a distant jungle.

After the single panel in "Indestructible Creatures of Nightmare Island" 13 months earlier, America's involvement in the Vietnam War is not referred to until this issue. The first panel is a full-width close-up of an automatic rifle, which "chatters in flaming fury" (286). All that can be seen of the rifleman are his hands on the weapon and his left thigh, leg forward for balance; he is almost nothing more than his weapon. This fierce close-up fills much of the panel. The lower right third, however, shows a half dozen diminutive "V-C," as the shooter's dialogue balloon informs us, flying through the air as bullets strike them. There are no shades of gray in this image—this is a clear depiction of a hero vs. an evil but inferior enemy. The rifleman is Sergeant Eddie Brent, and he is protecting a retreating line of wounded American soldiers. The narration likens Brent to a great warrior of the past: "The Romans had the legendary Horatio—the green berets have Eddie Brent at their bridge" (286).

Two months later, in Gotham City, Brent's younger brother Joey and a large crowd await the arrival of Eddie's train, prepared to give him a hero's welcome. Bruce Wayne and Dick Grayson—who is friends with Joey—are in the crowd. When the train arrives, however, the conductor makes a startling announcement: "Sergeant Brent … suddenly went berserk—knocked out the mail clerk and security guard … grabbed up a sack of money and jumped off the Gotham City Bridge! It was a clean getaway!" (287). This event, seemingly more fit for a Western adventure than for one of the Justice League of America, sets up a subtle set of narrative contrasts: Eddie's violent actions at a bridge in Viet Nam made him a hero, while his actions (not as violent, as no one is killed) at a bridge on American soil bring him disgrace.

Batman and Robin go to the bridge seeking answers. They follow Eddie's footprints to an abandoned, isolated house. Brent aims an unfamiliar-looking weapon at Batman, and when Robin tries to sneak up on Brent from behind the mystery weapon bends itself backward and fires a ray that hurls Robin through the air, straight at Batman. Throwing the weapon over his shoulder, Brent reveals that all his odd weapons only have one charge in them. His next weapon propels all the furniture in the room toward Batman and Robin; Robin is knocked unconscious. Amidst all this mayhem, Eddie's thoughts tell the reader—although not Batman—that he is acting under compulsion: "Behind his harsh laughter, the heart of Sergeant Eddie Brent is breaking! His eyes are glazed with agony, his lips contorted in grotesque mirth … "I don't want to do these terrible things! … I've been ordered to obey—and obey I must!" (289). After Eddie succeeds in knocking out Batman as well, a wraith-like figure appears behind him, telling him he has done a good job. The backstory then begins: As Eddie was riding in the train to Gotham City, the wraith appeared to him and outlined who he was and what he wanted from the sergeant. The Lord of Time of Time had previously appeared in Justice League issue #11. There he had come back in time to loot the 20th century using weapons from the future. He escaped back to his own time but now he can no longer operate his weaponry. He plans to use Brent to "be my warrior and use my array of weapons as I command." In a particularly dark touch he adds, "It amuses me to select you, to turn one of their own heroes against them" (291).

Brent has been under the control of the Lord of Time ever since. The Lord of Time gives him a different uniform and sends him off to steal two seemingly unrelated objects—the gears of a bank vault's time lock and a fossil—which when brought together will allow him to regain the ability to control his own weapons.[2]

Batman soon deduces what is unfolding and Robin joins him as he goes to gather the available Justice League members. When Batman again confronts Brent he punches him, saying, "I'm not hitting you—I'm really lashing out at the Lord of Time" (295). But it is Robin who feels the force of the blow.

The Lord of Time's defensive device for Brent deflects any attack to one or the other of the attackers—this same boomerang effect causes Wonder Woman to be imprisoned by her own golden lasso. Brent then goes on the offensive, wielding the Lord of Time's one-charge weapons against Batman, Robin, and Wonder Woman. In his thoughts, Brent deplores what he is doing and even cheers on his attackers—yet is powerless to resist attacking them.

Stealing the fossil, Brent encounters the remaining members of the Justice League, even as he feels his defensive coating weakening. Brent throws himself into the line of fire from one of the Lord of Time's weapons. The last of the protective coating saves him, and the Justice League are able to recapture the Lord of Time. The issue closes with a full page illustration of Brent, back in his proper uniform, receiving the Congressional Medal of Honor from the U.S. President with the Justice League among others in attendance.

These issues are clear indications of the indelible influence a society has on the stories that are being produced at the time. Even seemingly disposable entertainment targeting adolescents is steeped in issues of morality, prejudice, and war that were permeating American culture in the 1960s. The depiction may be clumsy at times, but the themes that are being explored demonstrate relevancy for both the creators and consumers of popular culture.

NOTES

1. Fox had a jackdaw's eye for the shiniest of interesting facts. He was a lifelong omnivorous reader who gathered in and filed copious amounts of historical and scientific trivia, in the best sense of the word, and he frequently would include such arcane facts in his stories. Sympathetic minds such as Whewell's would have interested him greatly.

2. A strategy unavoidably reminiscent of the famous Lewis Padgett time travel story "Mimsy Were the Borogroves."

WORKS CITED

Fox, Gardner (w), Mike Sekowsy, Sid Greene, and Murphy Anderson (a). "The Lord of Time Attacks the 20th Century!" *Justice League of America* #50 (December 1966). Reprinted in *Showcase Presents Justice League of America* (Volume 3). New York: DC Comics 2007, 284–308.

Fox, Gardner (w), Mike Sekowsy, Sid Greene, Murphy Anderson, and Carmine Infantino (a). "Man, Thy Name Is Brother!" *Justice League of America* #57 (November 1967). Reprinted in *Showcase Presents Justice League of America* (Volume 3). New York: DC Comics 2007, 453–76.

Fox, Gardner (w), Mike Sekowsy, Bernard Sachs, and Murphy Anderson (a). "The Indestructible Creatures of Nightmare Island." *Justice League of America* #40 (November 1965). Reprinted in *Showcase Presents Justice League of America* (Volume 3). New York: DC Comics, 2007, 58–82.

Fox, Gardner (w), Mike Sekowsy, Bernard Sachs, and Joe Giella (a). "The Bridge between Earths." *Justice League of America* #47 (September 1966). Reprinted in *Showcase Presents Justice League of America* (Volume 3). New York: DC Comics, 2007, 233–57.

Relevance in Wonderland
The Mixed Success of Gardner Fox's Message Comic Books

GENE PHILLIPS

Since the inception of the *Justice League of America* feature in 1959, the title's primary focus centered upon spectacle, depicting DC Comics' foremost superheroes having encounters with a dazzling procession of wondrous entities and situations. Beyond the strategy of appealing to a juvenile audience by giving them lots of aliens and monsters, this orientation was also a narrative necessity. Bringing DC Comics' "big guns" together in one feature meant that in most if not all stories, the storytellers had to concoct opponents powerful enough to oppose the likes of Superman, Wonder Woman, and Green Lantern. At the same time, those storytellers also had to find ways to validate heroes who had more limited or specialized talents, like Batman, Hawkman, the Atom, and Green Arrow.

The *Justice League* of the so-called Silver Age was predominantly devoted to evoking the sense of wonder in its juvenile audience. Nevertheless, on some occasions the creators of the feature sought to instruct as much as to delight. Professionals during this period did not maintain precise records as to the genesis of each and every comic-book tale. Nevertheless, in the mid–1960s the dominant process for that genesis was that an assigned writer made a story-pitch to his editor, and when the editor okayed it, the writer wrote a full script that blocked out the story's action and provided captions and dialogue. Penciller, inker, letterer, and colorists then closely followed the writer's script. And though it wasn't impossible for either the penciller or the editor to originate the idea, it seems likely that most Justice League plots originated from the mind of Gardner Fox, who had been writing scripts for comic books since the first superhero boom of the late 1930s and early 1940s. Certain Fox stories from that period reinforce the impression that he engaged in so-called "relevance stories," meant to educate and entertain. Two representative stories from the mid–1960s indicate that Fox was reflecting on the contemporaneous national debates about civil rights and/or the American ideal of equal opportunity. The first story appears in 1965, while the second appears roughly two years later.

"The Case of the Disabled Justice League" appears in *Justice League of America* #36 (June 1965). Of the stories under consideration here, it's the only one that was directly patterned after a similar tale Fox scripted in the 1940s. In the earlier story from *All-Star Comics* #27 (Winter 1947), the Justice Society—a group of DC superheroes, in essence the conceptual template for the 1960s Justice League—reflected upon the societal problems of physical disability. At the end of the tale in *Justice League of America* #36, the characters observe that their own adventure has paralleled that of their Golden Age predecessors. The story also concludes by printing a sort of "resolution of the rights of the disabled" that was originally composed for the Justice Society story.

The story opens on a whimsical note. Six Justice League members—Superman, Batman, Hawkman, the Flash, Green Lantern and Green Arrow—convene in their hidden sanctuary. With no explanation for the reader's benefit, they vote unanimously that Green Lantern should transform Batman into a giant reptilian monster. A little while later, the five un-transformed superheroes make an appearance at a hospital. They've come to raise the spirits of a group of handicapped patients—all boys of middle-school age—who, their doctor claims, "have lost the will to fight their afflictions" (Fox, "The Case..."). The boys all perk up as the heroes begin chatting with them, talking about their super-powers, and so on. Then the heroes contrive to reveal, via Green Lantern's ring, that the JLA sanctuary is being attacked by a giant reptilian monster. The heroes zoom off to defeat their pretend-enemy with the intention of raising the kids' spirits by giving them a rousing show. It is noted that the blind boy in the group has to have all of the events narrated to him.

The well-meaning heroes then get their own object lesson in overcoming adversities. A powerful villain named Brain Storm—introduced a few issues previous—infuses the "Batman monster" with bizarre powers. The Leaguers eventually subdue the monster and the creature transforms back into Batman, who seems no worse for wear. However, the other five heroes have become disabled. Superman goes blind, Hawkman is stricken with asthma, Green Lantern suffers a stuttering disorder that hinders his willpower, the Flash's two legs merge into one, and Green Arrow's arms disappear.

Never daunted, the heroes—all of them aware that the disabled kids are still watching their struggles from afar—track down Brain Storm. The villain unleashes on them various menaces, and the heroes must find ways to use their abilities despite their disadvantages. Given that Green Arrow has no super-powers as such, his feat—that of firing his arrows using his teeth and feet—probably comes closest to the real-world struggles of disabled individuals. Nonetheless, even after the heroes defeat the villains' monsters and revert to their normal capacities, the kids are still motivated to overcome their own difficulties. The story concludes as did the Justice Society story of the 1940s, citing famous individuals who overcame handicaps, like Franklin Roosevelt and Helen Keller. The final page also includes a resolution that "we shall meet those among us who are physically handicapped as fully our equals" (Fox, "The Case...").

Two years later, the struggles for equity in civil rights remained in the forefront of American consciousness. This state of affairs certainly provoked the creators to finally address the matter of racial and tribal divisions in the story "Man, Thy Name Is Brother" from *Justice League of America* #57 (November 1967). During the 1940s a handful of postwar superhero stories had touched on these matters, but the subject had largely disappeared from superhero tales throughout the 1950s. Fox's story on brotherhood was one of a small upsurge of 1960s stories explicitly concerning racism, and though the story is somewhat problematic, it is surely the most ambitious of the three considered here.

Justice League of America #36 focused on disabled middle-schoolers in order to make the story's message more relatable to juvenile readers, and *Justice League of America* #57 begins with a similar strategy. As the story starts, a regular meeting of the Justice League has come to an end and most of the heroes disperse. Snapper Carr, teenaged mascot to the League (as well as an identification-character for young boy readers), mentions to three of the heroes—presumably before they have the chance to get away—that he's doing a term paper on the topic of brotherhood. Snapper wants to investigate unusual events in the lives of ordinary people that relate to this theme, and the heroes—Hawkman, Green Arrow, and the Flash—agree to help their buddy. The three troubled individuals are all in separate geographical places—one in India, two in different parts of America—so the Flash seeks out one locale, Green Arrow another, and Snapper accompanies Hawkman to the third.

Aside from the shared theme, the three episodes of "Brother" are independent of one another. Overall this three-part story is Fox's most ambitious handling of the racial theme, but not every segment is, strictly speaking, "equal." Analyzing the story's segments not in order of occurrence, but in ascending order with regard to the scope of Fox's ambitions, allows us to see the ideas in a format that highlights their consequence, not only their sequence.

The least ambitious segment could easily have been written as a storyline for a 1940s comic strip like *Terry and the Pirates*. Hawkman and Snapper journey to rural India, to investigate the story of an American philanthropist. He and an aide, also American, have brought modern agricultural techniques to a local tribe, the Basas. The tribe has harvested a bumper crop, and have also embraced the Americans' encouragements "to put aside their swords and spears, and to take to the hoe and plow instead" (Fox, "Brother..."). However, the tribe's hereditary enemies, the Uttars, don't agree to disarm, and they rob the Basas of the fruits of their labors. Hawkman and Snapper arrive just as a few of the Basas are about to execute the Americans, apparently for having placed the tribe in this humiliating position—Fox does not provide much motive for the tribe's ire toward the Americans.

After the hero and his teenage mascot save the Americans, the next goal is to prevent the tribal enemies from making war. This is accomplished in a manner that only works because this part of India is so remote: Hawkman poses as a winged messenger of the gods. From the sky he attacks the Uttars, pelting them with their stolen food, until they beg for mercy and pledge to return what's left of the stolen plunder. The hero must then repeat his god-imposture for the Basas, to keep them from counter-attacking, and the tribal leaders agree to make peace. In this segment, Fox's desire to promote an idealistic "quick-fix" leads him to play upon the superstitious fears of natives who are apparently too isolated to have heard of superheroes.

The other two segments are more ambitious purely from the standpoint of meditating on modern racism, rather than on tribal enmities whose causes are conveniently lost in the mists of time. Green Arrow's assignment, occupying the middle position in the comic, is to seek out Jerry Nimo, a high school boy of Apache heritage who mysteriously dropped out of school despite his high scholastic and athletic achievements. However, when the Emerald Archer arrives on the scene—implicitly the American Southwest, though no location is given—the hero meets two white men accusing Nimo of criminal collusion with a gang of train robbers.

The two white men appear only for three panels, but their racism is presented without qualification: one says, "You can't trust these 'Pache kids," while the other agrees, "They come from bad stock" (Fox, "Brother..."). Nimo protests that he never saw the robbers before that day. Green Arrow's solution may seem a bit bizarre by real-world standards, for he invites Nimo to prove his innocence by helping round up the thieves. But in fairness, for the juvenile readers of the magazine, the prospect of a high-schooler of any race getting to team up with a superhero and fight crooks would be a thrill-ride, rather than an imposition.

Fox falls into some stereotypical devices, in that Jerry Nimo is a master tracker just by virtue of being an Apache. Once it's disclosed that the thieves' car had an oil leak, Nimo is able to track them by smelling "the oil under the sand" (Fox, "Brother..."). On the other hand, these skills put him in a position superior to that of the Caucasian Green Arrow, who doesn't seem to have a clue as to how he should track his quarry.

While the superhero and his temporary sidekick drive along the highway, Nimo reveals why he dropped out of school: he asserts that he was ceaselessly tormented for the sin of being an Apache. Fox cuts his own Caucasian kindred a bit of a break when he has Nimo say, "The white boys weren't so bad—it was my fellow redskins who made my life so miserable I couldn't take it!" (Fox, "Brother..."). Still, white racism hasn't been erased by this assertion; Fox simply wishes to make the point that inter-tribal conflicts share racism's tendency to degrade the members of an out-group. Fox is fairly successful at evoking the long-standing animosities between the Apache and their tribal rivals, in contrast to his unsatisfying opposition of made-up Hindu tribes. The artist Sekowsky's best moment appears here as well: the close-up on Nimo's face as he remembers his victimization speaks volumes. Certainly it's more effective than Green Arrow's answering rhetoric, which is nothing more than a standard "tough it out" speech.

Thanks to Nimo's help, Green Arrow overtakes the train robbers. The hero tells the youth to stay out of the actual fighting, so of course, to keep the juvenile fantasy going, the robbers promptly trounce the archer. Nimo gets to strut his stuff by showing that he happens to be a master of judo, which "I've borrowed from the white man—who in turn borrowed it from the yellow skins!" Once Nimo and the archer have beaten the crooks into submission, the young man resolves to return to school and "make something of myself" (Fox, "Brother...").

The lead segment of *Justice League of America* #57 is much in the same mold as the Jerry Nimo segment: a superhero investigates the dilemma of a minority teenager and gives him the inspiration to solve his problems. But the Nimo segment is a little less ambitious, given that American pop culture was replete with many stories of "noble red men." Pop culture was not so generous with stories of noble African Amercians, particularly in the domain of comic books. And though some black heroes and supporting characters had appeared at Marvel Comics in the mid–1960s, Fox and his collaborators were still breaking new ground with the story of Joel Harper. Joel comes to Snapper Carr's attention because Joel saved a person's life but only wanted a steady job as a reward. Snapper wonders, "why—of all the things he could have had—Joel settled for a job" (Fox, "Brother...").

The Flash seeks out Joel in "Metropole City." The name encourages the speculation that either Fox or editor Julie Schwartz may have toyed with depicting Joel as the first black resident of Metropolis—the city in which most adventures in the Superman titles took place, and where persons of color were almost never seen—only to drop the idea as unworkable, since it might have been construed as a criticism of another editor's titles. Such speculation cannot be proven, but the similarity of the cities' names is curious.

Joel is employed in the garment district as a menial "push-boy." But just as he saved a man's life earlier, he can't seem to keep from playing hero. Joel sees armed robbers run out of a bank, and, "acting instinctively," shoves a clothes rack into their path. His instincts almost get him shot, but Flash arrives and saves him. However, one of the thieves blinds the super-speedster with a flare gun. Joel is reluctant to get involved after almost getting killed, but still he helps direct the blinded hero so that he apprehends one of the crooks. The other thieves escape.

Joel then reaps the reward of heroic virtue. His supervisor comes along, sees the apparel on the clothes rack ruined, and promptly fires Joel for being a good citizen. Joel tells the Flash that he wouldn't have been fired if he wasn't black. The Flash makes some rather weak demurrals. Joel replies that "colored boys never get a break" and that though he's been studying men's fashions with an eye to owning his own business, this incident has shown him that his dreams are futile (Fox, "Brother...").

Here, though Fox never explicitly says so, is the answer to the puzzle of why Joel wanted even a drudge job in place of a monetary reward: he wanted to get a foothold in an industry he aspired to join. Sadly. Fox drops the ball at this point. Not only does the Flash offer Joel weak empathy by saying that "everybody has ups and downs in life," he prioritizes the capture of the bank robbers over Joel's unjust firing.

Again, it must be said that a superhero teaming up with a teenager to fight crime was intended to be both exciting and inspiring. When Flash draws upon Joel's knowledge of fashion in order to track the crooks by their garments, the intention is to show Joel as astute enough to be of aid to a superhero. However, it's hard to deny that Joel's "fashion-detective" work is a bit of phony-baloney detective work beside which even Jerry Nimo's miracle nose looks credible.

The real problem, though, is that Fox has raised a question—Joel's imputations of racial intolerance—and that the author then fails to address the question. At least in the Nimo section, Green Arrow's response to the boy's torment may be unimaginative cant. But that response doesn't dismiss the reality of Nimo's complaint.

Joel does help Flash find and apprehend the bank robbers—at which point the segment takes its most problematic turn. Fox certainly could have written an ending in which the Flash used his heroic clout to make sure that Joel got back his menial "push-boy" job. After all, the opening scene states that Joel saved the life of a "wealthy garment manufacturer." One may assume that this is not the supervisor who fires Joel, so it would have been an easy fix for a famed celebrity like the Flash to "go over the head" of the irate manager. But Flash does not do this (Fox, "Brother...").

Instead, he suggests that Joel go to Central City and visit Barry Allen (Flash's civilian identity), because he Flash is sure that Barry can get Joel a job on the Central City Police Force. The segment ends with Joel enthusiastically agreeing with the hero's plan, as he says, "If only more of us differently colored folks would extend helping hands to each other, we'd get along a lot better" (Fox, "Brother...").

To a modern reader, the language has aged badly, but there are other issues to be identified in the story. Some fans have criticized the Joel Harper segment for this "quick fix," given that the happy ending depends on Joel's willingness to give up on his stated dreams. At the same time, one may speculate that Fox wanted to reward his character's heroic actions with something more than a menial job that might or might not fulfill his dreams. One should also remember that in juvenile comic books of this period, the policeman's lot might not have been a happy one, but for the most part the occupation was presented as a noble undertaking.

So the Flash—who can't do anything to advance Joel's fortunes in the garment industry—invites Joel to join his own noble profession. One must take into consideration that to a juvenile reader of the period, "policeman" would sound like a much more exciting and fulfilling profession than that of "garment-store owner." It may also be argued that Fox has imbued Joel with heroic "instincts," and that those instincts might indeed be better served by a job where he used a gun rather than a measuring-tape.

Still, because there has been much justified concern about the ways in which white culture has mitigated or erased the identity of Black Americans, the Joel Harper segment remains problematic. Both Joel and Jerry Nimo are formulaic characters, but Fox puts some real heart into his portrait of Jerry, while Joel is simply a mouthpiece for Fox's "Golden Rule" philosophy. But as I noted before, a commercial writer like Fox—who in 1967 had written comic books for almost 30 years—had many models of noble red men—and sometimes women—on which to draw for inspiration. By comparison, images of noble black men and women were in short supply, and perhaps it might be expecting too much of a white guy in his middle 50s, writing juvenile funnybooks, to conceive a character able to speak to African American concerns about marginalization.

"Problematic," it should be noted, does not mean "bad in every way," though some critics tend to use the word in a condemnatory manner. Fox's reach, his ambition to say something about brotherhood and its complications, may have exceeded his grasp, his ability to relate to make all of his characters equally compelling. Joel is a mouthpiece for a message, but so are the unnamed kids with disabilities in *Justice League of America* #36, while in contrast, Jerry Nimo is a somewhat more rounded characters. Fox's execution is far from perfect, but his overriding intent—his attempt to impart moral messages by associating them with the fantastic adventures of superheroes—cannot be reasonably described as anything but commendable.

WORKS CITED

Fox, Gardner (w), and Mike Sekowsky (a). "The Case of the Disabled Justice League."
    The Justice League of America #36 (June 1965). New York: DC Comics.
_____. "Man, Thy Name Is Brother." *The Justice League of America* #57 (November
    1967). New York: DC Comics.

A Crisis of Infinite Dearth
Winning Vietnam via the Never-Ending War on Earth-X

PETER W. LEE

By 1972 the Justice League of America's silver-aged crown had tarnished badly. A flagship title for National Periodical Publications (DC Comics), the *Justice League of America (JLA)* had showcased the company's bravest and boldest characters battling everything from starry-eyed space crustaceans to inter-dimensional conquerors from apocalyptic dark sides. From its debut in 1960, the team symbolized both the revival of the moribund superhero genre—inspiring fantastical foursomes from rival publishers—and spoke to the optimism of the Kennedy years and the Cold War consensus. Although critics scoffed that a meeting of the JLA often sounded like a one-person conversation and regarded such banal dialogue as a mark of comics' low-brow aesthetics (i.e., disposable kiddy fare), it also affirmed the harmonious nationalism of Earth's greatest heroes. For the superhero crowd, the league's "justice" spoke for anticommunism, patriarchy, and the rhetoric of freedom and democracy (Wright 183–85), or, as DC's ballyhoo put it in one house ad: "to stamp out the forces of evil wherever and whenever they appear!" (Advertisement).

Unfortunately for the JLA, after one decade and one hundred issues, fans had noted the title's slip in the sales ranks. By 1972, the Leaguers skidded from a monthly publishing schedule to bi-monthly status, "an ominous sign" of impending cancellation. "PLEASE CONTINUE TO BUY THE JUSTICE LEAGUE OF AMERICA," reader Joe Arul screamed in the letter pages in issue *#108* (November–December 1973). The fan warned his peers if they did not, the JLA would befall a similar fate to their all-star predecessors in 1951, when the wartime Justice Society of America, a similar all-American band of do-gooders, disappeared from the newsstands in favor of cowboys.[1] The editor remarked upon Arul's perceptiveness, telling readers to "pay attention" to the League's mounting identity crisis lest poor sales put both superhero groups "out of business."

The *Justice League of America*'s uncertain fate during the 1970s paralleled the social discontent plaguing the magazine's titular national namesake. Although President Richard Nixon won a landslide re-election in 1972, in retrospect, his victory played a mean trick on the electoral process and, by extension, American values. The Watergate scandal, then starting to unfold, not only added to the lexicon of political jargon, but became shorthand for a mass civic disillusionment that lasted well into the next millennium.

The fallout from this disenchantment led many Americans to seek escapism in the past. The then-upcoming bicentennial in 1976 encouraged a cultural retreat into history as a sort of spiritual catharsis. The happy days of collective memory had a specific timeframe: World War II. The Second World War was living history for older generations, passed on to baby boomers through stories, movies, and television, and became a popular destination for nostalgic trips down memory lane. The "Golden Age" of various mediums, ranging from comic books to Hollywood movies, anchored the 1940s as the pristine high point of the American century: a decade where the "greatest generation" licked the Depression, stamped out fascism, and brought the United States to international prominence as the defender of the free world. Compared to the troublesome present of the 1970s, the 1940s remained a high point of masculine pride and national fervor. As historian Victor D. Brooks notes, World War II's legacy soldiered on well past V-J Day in the popular consciousness. In the 1950s, white collared men wanted to re-live the "Good War" that recently ended, perhaps as an affirmation of their virility as they dwelled in their grey-flannelled cubicles. In addition, the black-and-white struggle of good and evil provided more moral comfort than the ambiguity of the undefined, but certainly subversive, "un–Americanness" in the Korean "police action," the quagmire of Vietnam, and the Cold War in general. Television programs such as *Combat!* or *The Gallant Men* became standard fare on the boob tube celebrating American heroism, as did the plastic presence of G.I. Joes for maturing citizen-soldiers (Brooks 71, 101).

In the 1970s, boomers in early adulthood appropriated the legacy of World War II to escape from troubled times. The funny books certainly played upon this disillusionment; in the Marvel Universe, unnamed creepy public officials nearly hijacked the Oval Office and built a secret empire, a shadow government which made a mockery of the values Captain America represented (Englehart and Buscema). Looking back from the 1990s, Mark Waid's and Alex Ross's retro-styled *Marvels* positioned the 1970s as a jolting snap-ending to the readers' blind faith in happy endings. As the comic book industry matured in the shadows of Watergate, the motif of good-triumphs-over-evil no longer seemed certain or relevant. In this grim and gritty framework, a timely return to the American victory culture of World War II became a much-needed remedy.

For *Justice League of America*, writer Len Wein played into this sentimentalized nostalgia. Not only would tapping into the popular zeitgeist of World War II make for great entertainment, it would also boost sales. As the historian John Bodnar notes, authors such as Richard Brooks and William Manchester successfully wrote about the "Good War" as a moral beacon to guide the nation from what they received as a loss of patriotism and national prestige (due to Vietnam), emasculinization (blamed on second wave feminism), and the yearning for so-called simpler times (49–50). The world finest heroes, and the comic book industry which had boomed during the Second World War, eagerly turned back the clock to revive the horrors of the Third Reich … if only so they could bash Hitler one more time.

Crisis on Earth-X!

By its one hundredth issue, the Justice League was ready for a change in direction. The fracturing of the Cold War consensus via the counterculture and Civil Rights movements carried the social disenchantment from the front page newsprint to four-colored pulp pages. In *Justice League of America* #98 (May 1972) a three-issue story arc featured the usual pseudo-communist thugs spouting the typical party lines about "imperialist Americanos" meddling with their glorious revolution, which left one long-time reader disappointed. The overt baddies and their tired diatribe "carried a snippet of Cold War puky into the pages that I could've done most easily without," griped Guy H. Lillian III in the letter columns in issue #101 (September 1972). The bland dialogue, stereotyped clichés, and stale villains had left a bad taste for fans who demanded more nuanced fare.

Writer Len Wein succeeded Mike Friedrich for the centennial anniversary issue. Wein avoided contemporary commies; instead, he turned towards the history books. Although DC's comics had regularly featured reprints of Golden Age adventures as back-up features to compensate for the raised prices (from 15¢ to 25¢ per issue), Wein blurred the lines between the past and present. He quickly started reviving heroes whom DC owned, but who had fallen into obscurity during the industry's decline during the postwar years. For his first issue, #100 (August 1972), the Seven Soldiers of Victory, a group of minor characters who had not seen print for decades, returned to DC's leading comic book.[2] Three issues later, in issue #103 (December 1972), the Phantom Stranger, a paranormal figure who ghosted across several titles since the 1950s, graced the pages. The league extended its membership include old-time hero the Elongated Man and in issue #106 (July-August 1973), another defunct hero from editorial limbo, Red Tornado, reappeared and joined the team. Similarly, the JLA's old rogue gallery also started re-menacing mankind. Issue #103 saw the inglorious return of Felix Faux, and #105 (April-May 1975) witnessed the appearance of the Shaggy Man after a seven year absence. Issue #110 (March-April 1974) featured a "new threat from an old villain," namely, The Key from issue #63, who promptly demonstrated his relevancy by murdering another American institution, Santa Claus.

Not only did Wein restore characters from early JLA history, the series began resembling older comic books with revived layouts appealing to older fans. Writer Mike Friedrich had revived a format writer Gardner Fox had used in the 1940s with the Justice Society: segmenting issues into chapters with each segment giving certain characters more panel exposure. Wein continued the trend and expanded on the tradition, using a Leaguer as an opening narrator to recap last issue's events. The retro format struck a chord with readers. In issues #107 (September-October 1973) reader Mike W. Barr commented the "old-style" layouts and logos appealed to nostalgic fans, singing out a "simple little tune that long-time JLA fans are humming; 'Memories, Memories,' for trips down memory lane."[3]

With creators and fans piqued for a past-as-present crossover, Earth's greatest heroes had no choice but to assemble for such a time-traveling tale in *Justice League of America* #107 (September-October 1973) and #108 (November-December 1973). The two-issue tale not only contained arcane 1940s references, but threw the League into a classic "what-if" scenario, namely, a hypothetical world where the Nazi's Iron Cross swayed *über alles*. Although set in the modern year of 1973, the plotline literally brings our heroes back in time. In these two issues, the League, the creators, and readers once again act "to save the soul of a nation [presumably the United States]— and the future of a *world*." Fittingly, the story begins with the JLA's sister team, the Justice Society of America (JSA)—without a comic book title of their own and residing on an Earth in a parallel dimension; the team's appearances are confined to yearly guest-star stints in *Jutice League of America*. The JSA and JLA hatch a plan to bring their worlds closer together. Unfortunately, their experiment backfires and a whirling flash sends several members from each dimension into a third (or, rather, tenth) dimension, named Earth-X. Although stranded in what Flash calls one of "trillions of *elseworlds*" where everything is similar-yet-different, they instinctively know something is wrong. Batman voices the confusion, wondering "what Nazi war tanks are doing in an *American* city." Unfortunately, the world's greatest detective fails to understand the swastikas around them have turned the familiar sights "un–American" by national default. There is no more United States, only the Third Reich. Thankfully, the hated emblem also cues the super friends to the issue's baddies. When a group of startled stromtroopers open fire, the Leaguers immediately rule out diplomacy. Without hesitation, the Earth-II Superman attacks the "Ratzis," grinning, "I cut my *baby teeth* on skunks like you!" (Wein, "Crisis on Earth-X!"). Dr. Fate concurs: "I, too, have battled this madman's *spawn* in years agone!" (Wein, "Crisis on Earth-X!")

The Society and Leaguers recognize their adversaries as far more significant than any mere super-menace they have fought before. If not for the Nazis, many of the heroes would have no reason to exist: many of their origin stories are rooted in America's involvement in World War II. Nevertheless, they express a glee in combating the Third Reich, for "Hitler"—though yet unnamed, but surely lurking behind the scenes in the next page—symbolized an uncomplicated ideology they could rally against: fascism, totalitarianism, and other "isms" anathema to the homespun values of Mom and apple pie.

While the Society waxes nostalgic over the brown-shirted stooges, Wein ups the wistful language with patriotic zeal as more superheroes join the fray. Earth-X's resident super-team, the Freedom Fighters, burst in to help "thwack!" the fascists. The caption notes, "Today is a day of *retribution*—for there may be no *tomorrow!*" (Wein, "Crisis on Earth-X!"). Wein's vengeful text—like Superman's joy in finding someone he can pummel without a second thought—echoed the black-and-white milieu World War II evoked. Of course the Nazis deserved no mercy or hesitation over complex foreign entanglements filtered through social and political dysfunctions. After all, one generation ago, the so-called Master Race almost took over the world.

Thus, enter the Freedom Fighters. Like the Seven Soldiers of Victory, the Freedom Fighters had not seen action for decades, and with good reason. The superhero implosion of the 1950s—when a public panic associated comic books with juvenile delinquency—led one of the leading publishers, Quality Comics, to discontinue all of their titles. DC picked up the copyrights for characters such as Uncle Sam (the group leader and a doppelganger for James Montgomery Flagg's famed World War I recruitment poster), Phantom Lady (whose name primarily refers to her historic minimalist attire and her disregard for prude social guardians), the diminutive Doll Man, the explosive Human Bomb, and the scantily-clad vigilante Black Condor.

Although the Quality superheroes' existence may have eluded younger readers, for longtime comic book fans, such as Guy Lillian III, the "obscure super-heroes from a defunct competitor" signified Wein's continuing excavation of comicdom's rich and largely untapped past. In issue #110 (March-April 1974), Lillian wrote Wein's "masterful feat of verisimilitude" makes the Freedom Fighters "come alive for us kids of the original readers, the original fans." Lillian's comment signified nostalgia as a cross-generational unifier. Readers like Lillian would not have had access to Uncle Sam's original adventures unless they read the decades-old first print run. Lillian represented the next generation who grew up on the Silver Age stuff, but he realized—and enjoyed—the importance of the flashback-esque narrative, one in which Superman and company easily recognize the bad guys and give them no mercy. Lillian notes the Quality heroes are refreshingly one-dimensional in an age of disenchantment: they "spent most of their comix lives battling Nazis" and Wein's tale "still moves down deep in every one of us who loathes despotism." For Lillian and like-minded readers, the Nazis had none of the complexities of communist Vietnam and the recent antiwar movement. Wein's story provided a new basis for a national cultural consensus to coalesce and an affirmation of Superman's motto: the American Way.[4] Paul Emrath summarized many letters in complimenting Wein's tenure as "a Gardner Fox-style with good dialogue."

Reader Scott Gibson expanded on the fanbase's sentimentality, wishing DC would also revive Quality's *Blackhawk*, a series starring an international squadron of aviators battling the Luftwaffe. DC had tried to "update" the Blackhawks in the 1960s as a counterculture group of hipsters—the mod attempt mercifully killed the book. For Earth-X, no such "modernization" was needed since this universe firmly grounded the 1940s as the new 1973. Sitting under a portrait of Franklin Roosevelt, Uncle Sam rehashes how the Good War turned bad: when F.D.R. died in 1944, "the balance of power went the wrong way." Without blaming Harry Truman outright, Uncle Sam simply notes the American government turned corrupt and misguided, leading to an aborted arms race as Germany developed atomic weapons first.

For readers, besides the trans-dimensional borders breached in the story, Earth-X's tragedy crossed narrative borders into their world, creating a partial critique of Earth-I's Cold War. Appropriately, DC's anti-establishment hothead, Green Arrow, questions Uncle Sam's identity and purpose, telling the star-spangled avenger he *"can't possibly* be who you look like." Uncle Sam corrects Green Arrow, informing the archer that, like the Robin Hood mythos he takes up, Uncle Sam also represents an ideal: he "came out of the mists of the past to help his country in her time of greatest need," namely, World War II for Earth-X and the Cold War for Earth-I (Wein, "Crisis on Earth-X!"). For Uncle Sam, both crises are the same: the American nation lost her way, resulting in a usurpation of corrupt power. For readers in Earth-I, the references to a wayward government echoed the quagmire of Vietnam, the antiwar protests, and foreshadowed Watergate and the costs of overconfidence and hubris.

Earth-X had a much more sordid and complex history, even as the implied lessons for a Hitlerian United States rebuked the American follies of the Cold War. According to Uncle Sam, Truman and his successors could not prevent the Allies from fracturing. This breakdown of the "consensus" led to a botched arms race, with Germany entering the atomic age first. The prolonged war killed off the other Quality heroes, namely, the Blackhawk squadron and Plastic Man. Tellingly, Uncle Sam dates their deaths to "five years ago," i.e., 1968, the year Richard Nixon entered the White House. Uncle Sam extends the parallel, stating the Nazis remains in power thanks to a "mind-control ray" which had "the whole world eating out of their [the Nazi] hands within weeks"—perhaps a backhanded explanation of how Nixon hoodwinked the people (Wein, "Crisis on Earth-X!"). The year also resonated among DC readers: as Green Arrow noted in another context, 1968 marked the year Martin Luther King and Robert Kennedy were gunned down—the symptoms of "some hideous moral cancer" which rotted America's very soul and sent many naïve-green heroes on cross-country road-trips to re-find their identities. (O'Neil). Uncle Sam warns the League about the dangers of unchecked power, but at the same time, urges them about the need to maintain a consensual vigilance against foes foreign and domestic.

Our heroes, however, see only one threat: Nazism. The combined JLA/ JSA/Freedom Fighters commit themselves to a Triple-Victory: in defeating Hitler again, they would validate American democracy on three Earths. As Elongated Man quips, "It's not *every* day a fella gets a chance to win *World War II* all over again!" (Wein, "Thirteen Against the Earth!"). Black Condor objects to the outside interference, but Uncle Sam overrides him, explaining liberty is everyone's business. He has "looked into their eyes and seen *sincerity* there and a love of freedom as burning as our own!" (Wein, "Crisis on Earth-X!"). The teams split up to tackle the Nazis' mind-control ray housed in three separate facilities. Their objective takes them from Paris to Mount Fujiyama (where the Japanese regret having joined the axis of evil and now "*pray* for a chance to *regain* lost face!") to Mount Rushmore, where Hitler's visage has joined the American presidents (Wein, "Thirteen Against the Earth!").

In each scenario, the new allies from three worlds fight a robot master mold keeping sentinel watch over the human race. The various teams succeed in destroying the machines with little effort. In Paris, for instance, the mind-control machine renders the Leaguers immobile and plans to put them on exhibition "to strengthen the mythos … to reinforce the dream." But the human subconscious proves more powerful than robotic brainwashing and their human "*reflex action*—more than anything else"—in this case, a combined karate chop—blows up the mechanical monster (Wein, "Crisis on Earth-X!"). Unfortunately, their victories seem to have little effect as the human populace remains in docile passivity to the war around them. Looking for another answer, the heroes encounter a far more sinister menace: each other.

Thirteen Against Themselves!

The happy assemblage of three earths to battle the foe of fascism that no one hero could withstand alone clicked with many readers. However, not every fan applauded the unabashed Nazi-bashing from the American Way. The uncritical patriotism from World War II—the popular faith in the federal government to always do the right thing—had given way to Cold War disenchantment. The failure of American militarism in Southeast Asia, the "-gate" lexicon added to political science jargon, and the counter-culture at large rendered the over-glorification of Cold War orthodox as old-hat hokum. In issue #100 (August 1972), reader Daniel Dasch had faint praise for a retelling of the League's origin story in issue #97, when a downhearted JLA needed a morale boost. Dasch called the re-use of Silver Age artist Mike Sekowsky's pencils as "old." In issue #104 (February 1973), reader James T. McCoy wondered if Len Wein's dialogue deliberately bordered on being corny or, worse, "camp." Significantly, McCoy only singled out lines from the Golden Agers Wonder Woman, Hourman, and Dr. Mid-Nite for their overreliance on bad puns and wisecracks—these "older" heroes reflected a by-gone era no longer appropriate to the current cynicism of the 1970s.

This scrutiny of longstanding institutions slowly infects the virgin populations of Earth-X. Trapped in World War II, the Freedom Fighters prize the memory of the 1940s as their country's heyday. Despite Black Condor's initial suspicion, they followed Uncle Sam's spirited patriotism and accept the League and Society without question. Unfortunately, the JLA and JSA bring with them a pathogen of suspicion and mistrust. When the destruction of the three mind-control robots fail to awaken the people, the world's finest heroes—the League's Batman and the Society's Superman—think they know why. Together, they accuse the Quality characters of conspiring to replace the Nazis and institute a new form of fascism. Ironically, without the Nazis to keep the Freedom Fighters in check, Uncle Sam and his compatriots could easily channel the smashed robots' "dominating energy" and rule the entire planet. Batman reasons, "Who *else* stands to gain from control of such monumental power? With your own super-abilities and the mind-control energy, you *six* planned to gain planetary domination!" The Man of Steel reiterates the Dark Knight: to "turn *traitor* to *America* is the ultimate *sin!*" The crime of "*betraying* America" brings out the fighting spirit from the comic's creators, who had witnessed the fracturing of the Cold War consensus and the counterculture idealism of the 60s, into the comic pages (Wein, "Thirteen Against the Earth!"). Armed with this suspicion, the former super friends proceed to have the usual superhero brawl.

Fortunately, the newest Leaguer, the Red Tornado, resolves the crisis on Earth-X. An android refugee from Earth II, the Red Tornado has continually expressed self-doubt in his ability to function as a full-fledged Leaguer on Earth-I. The Tornado's confused past reflected this fractured identity: a living whirlwind housed in a humanoid shell built by a supervillain, his name originally came from a 1940 funnybook parodying superheroes (originally a hefty, spunky woman who cross-dressed as a "superman" with a pot over her head). From this checkered past, the Tornado's emotional tempest sets him apart from the League, both in mindset as a loser and spatially on the page, as artist Dick Dillion usually draws him moping in the background. For their part, the JLA profess loyalty and encouragement, but, as reader Scott Taylor notes in issue #111 (May-June 1974), the team regards him as little more than a "heap of metal and wires."

As a machine, however, the Red Tornado escapes his biological peers' super-human mistrust and suspicions. He detects his teammates' distrust come from an outside source. While the good guys throttle each other, Red Tornado traces the "dominating energy" to an orbiting satellite (conveniently marked with swastikas) and encounters the true villain: Adolf Hitler. The Third Reich's fuehrer gloats the usual prattle about innate superiority and offers the loner Red Tornado a chance to join the dark side and bring order to the galaxy (Wein, "Thirteen Against the Earth!"). The Tornado declines and strikes back at the space-bound Reich, decapitating Hitler with a single punch.

In this climax, the plot segues into a wordy commentary on the pervasive nature of the Cold War and its corrupting hold on American values. Earth-X's Hitler was actually long dead, even as the *Wehrmacht* triumphed over the United States. Rather, the Hitler doppelganger is, like the Red Tornado, a bucket of bolts: a robot imposter disguised as the German chancellor. The Red Tornado learns the Nazis had lost their hold on the planet years before. Instead, a self-perpetuating war machine, depicted as a large metal box with a mechanical face, had carried on the fight. The android recognizes Earth-X's Third Reich, like the United States on his own Earth, has become subservient to the military industrial complex. "Hitler," unable to change his programming, carried out its function to the most logical end: by brainwashing the Nazis alongside the rest of the civilian population, the computer solidified its control as it maintained the status quo. The mind-control machine dryly explains the robots "were created with superior intelligence … better able to rule the Earth." The computer "took control from the Third Reich … replacing their leaders with android replicas to insure [sic] the governmental shift would go unnoticed" (Wein, "Thirteen Against the Earth!"). Although the Freedom Fighters remain immune to this mind-control—thanks to their super-human drive for liberty—the "dominating energy" has left the rest of Earth-X content to let the world war continue without end. Aside from the repentant Japanese (now allies of Earth-I's U.S. in the struggle against Communist China), civilians do not figure in the deserted battlegrounds of Nazi America.

The permanence of a military industrial complex has turned the once-hot conflict of World War II into a cold war between the guerrilla Freedom Fighters against autocratic automatons programmed to control the humans it supposedly protects. The android leaders masquerading as Nazi leaders espouse the programmed rhetoric of international security and the need for continual vigilance against subversive threats—common language that many readers in the 1970s would recognize as the same stale Cold War ballyhoo.[5] The unnamed robot itself served as an interdimensional counterpart to the Earth-I's war machine that had bogged down in Vietnam. By allegorizing the American armed forces into an unyielding Nazi war machine, Wein posits the folly of the U.S. foreign policy that seemingly built upon a perpetuating military bureaucracy. The mythos—a blind faith in the military to succeed through overwhelming technological might—has become a perpetuating cycle. For the Nazis, the master race could only achieve victory if it subjugates all remaining resistance. For the world of the readers, the fallout from the 1970s disenchantment was the catalyst that led to Len Wein penning this adventure in the first place.

The computer repeats its offer to Red Tornado. Sensing the hero as a *"kindred spirit"* and "a being not unlike yourself," it sees the Leaguer as an outsider among organic beings, a loner in the midst of an identity crisis and needing companionship. Our hero, of course, quickly rejects the computer's offer and generates a windstorm, literally spinning the satellite to its demise. With the "dominating energy" dormant, the rest of the Leaguers awaken from their conspiracy mongering. Somewhat apologetic over the fight, everybody professes unity and make vague promises to meet again. The League and the Society return to their respective homes and allow the Freedom Fighters the first steps to restore their planet to its original prewar splendor.

In this finale, the combined heroes acknowledge the reconstruction and rehabilitation of Earth-X will comprise entirely of Americanism. The League, Society, and readers assume the Freedom Fighters can revert to a pre–1939 era, thereby whitewashing three decades of Nazi "brainwashing." The issue's optimistic conclusion note may have satisfied fans, but it also legitimized the American Cold War rhetoric. Literally left with a "free world" to fashion, the Freedom Fighters will triumph where the Earth-I heroes could not in Vietnam: nation/world-building under American-style tutelage. The story's aftermath, though not depicted, will require Uncle Sam to hunt down the Nazi robot doppelgangers, eliminate them, and then substitute their own sovereignty in place. After all, the "normal" human population, docile for decades thanks to the "dominating energy," will be in no condition to govern themselves. Uncle Sam, as Superman and Batman had suspected, will have Earth-X in his hands.

Writer Len Wein thus partially critiques the military industrial complex for perpetuating the Cold War at home. Even with this criticism, he anchors the story to the idealism of American principles: democracy, liberty, and equality. Just like many critics who have seen Vietnam scandal and the bungled foreign policies as aberrations of the "true" United States, the legion of combined superheroes also rest assured in the sound virtues of the Founding Fathers to prevail on a global scale—even though Earth-X has known only fascism as a form of government for two generations. Since only the Freedom Fighters have the strength to enforce the now-alien values of "America" on the world's people, the story's happy ending suggests they will emerge as the new de facto rulers. DC's creators, their characters, and the readers can take heart this will not lead to totalitarianism, however. The destruction of the mind-control computers, the gruesome demise of "Hitler," and the dispersal of the dominating energy satisfies the comic book expectations. Indeed, good can come even from the most diabolical of Nazi contraptions: Red Tornado manages to salvage a crucial component from the satellite which will allow them to return to their respective earths. In exchange, the League fully accepts him as an equal member, overcoming their suspicions over his dubious origins. In their Christmas issue, #110 (March–April 1974), Black Canary even gives him a new garish costume in issue designed by Len Wein (a costume which the letter column correspondents universally denounced). All parties can take heart in knowing American-style democracy and liberty will reign to the betterment of all.

A Double-V for JLA's USA

In *Justice League of America* #107 (September–October 1973), the Red Tornado plays watchdog as he watches the JLA/JSA take off to win World War II for the second time. He considers the tattered American flag and wonders "if it is worth twelve valiant lives." Readers could also ask the same question as they revisit a history that near-glorified millions of deaths and which had also inaugurated the Atomic Age and Cold War. In issue #110 (March–April 1974), reader Scott Gibson griped, "Why, oh why did Len Wein feel he had to give the Quality heroes an Earth of their own?" After satirizing future crises on infinite earths peopled with characters from Fawcett and other defunct publishers, Gibson lamented the pressure to keep creating new and better stories had taken its toll. "It seems foolish to go to such extremes!" he wrote, concluding "perhaps its time you discontinue the series and allow the JSA to slide back into Limbo." The Justice League might endure as guest stars, but the old-hat of the World War II mythos was, in his view, obsolete.

But readers like Gibson fought against popular nostalgia. The "Good

War," with its clear-cut symbolism of good and evil and a demonstration of American ingenuity and values, had a prominent place in the uncertainty surrounding the 'Nam disaster and the unfolding Watergate scandal and future disillusionment. The grisly aftermath of World War II—the "forgotten" war of Korea, the jungles of Vietnam, and the numerous skirmishes in-between—only reinforced the 1940s as a "simpler" and "purer" time. In a letter from issue #110 (March-April 1974) reader Clint Thomas approved of "the Nazis are downright the group you love to hate." From the 1940s to the 1970s, the Axis of Evil was self-explanatory and deserved no mercy.

In the nostalgic atmosphere of American popular culture, everything old was new again. DC's distinguished competition, led by Captain America, wholeheartedly basked in nostalgia. Even as the star-spangled Avenger tossed aside his costume out of disillusionment with the Nixon Administration's sorry end, his past opened up in new vistas. Writer Roy Thomas revived the "Invaders," a retroactively-applied label for the company's World War II super-heroes. Old faces (Captain America, the Human Torch, the Sub-Mariner) and new (Spitfire) comingled as a timely band made up of an all-winning squad of Axis-bashers, with the villains clearly identified in each issue and their infamous atrocities needing avenging from Earth's mightiest heroes.

For the caped crusaders in Earth-I, II, and X, their rose-tinted historical lens also glorified the Good War which ended the Depression, inaugurated the U.S. as an active superpower, and gave birth to a costumed justice society to enforce this ideology. The JLA's revival of supposedly outmoded concepts perhaps found its greatest manifestation in the return of the original Wonder Woman. Having discarded her classic patriotic garb as un-"mod" in 1968 (the infamous year Earth-X lost Plastic Man and the Blackhawks and Earth-I's Green Lantern/Green Arrow road trip), Diana Prince had channeled counterculture mysticism in an attempt to stay relevant. In 1972, a depowered Prince appeared in the anniversary one hundredth issue (alongside her Golden-Age incarnation from Earth-II); by Justice League of America #110 (March-April 1974), however, the Amazon Princess was already in the stages of returning. DC's letter column scribe, Marty Prasko (a "Junior Bullpen trainee"), explained editor JLA Julius Schwartz had taken over Wonder Woman's series and his vision of a retro-looking DC Universe coincided with writer Robert Kanigher's plans to create new adventures for the original Wonder Woman—based on her 1940s adventures. When Diana Prince returned to the League in Wonder Woman #212, she underwent twelve "labors" to prove herself (Darowski). Her reward: reincarnation of Golden Age heartthrob Steve Trevor and, outside of comics, a television show set in World War II.

As for the Justice League itself, this appeal to the past clicked with readers. Justice League of America #110 (March-April 1974) and #111 (May-June 1974) were one-hundred page tomes, with back-up stories reprinting episodes from the Golden Age—now "new" for 70s readers. Issue #111 also re-introduced the Seven Soldiers of Victory in their original incarnation. By issue #117 (April 1975) after Len Wein's departure, the series returned to a monthly format with an expanded page count. Self-empowered by its continuity, the JLA soldiered onwards; they, like the Freedom Fighters, having transformed their respective Earths into symbolized leagues of justice in American culture.

NOTES

1. In continuity revisionism from 1979, the Justice Society of America disbanded and vanished into self-exile in 1951 to avoid the Red Scare. When the House Committee on Un-American Activities demanded the vigilantes unmask as a form of loyalty oath, the JSA decided to wait out the worst of McCarthyism. See *Adventure Comics* #446 (November-December 1979). Ironically, the hyper-patriotic fervor which gave birth to the Justice League had temporarily killed-off the greatest of superhero communities. In a further twist of comic book history, this issue also marked the end of DC's long-running *Adventure Comics*: the series went into decline with reprints and ended with issue #503 four years later (Thomas 26).

2. Fittingly, the Seven Soldiers of Victory returned on Earth-II, a parallel dimension populated with Golden Age/World War II characters, notably, the revived Justice Society of America. In addition, this issue also saw a price drop (20¢) and the removal of the back-up features.

3. In issue #104 (February 1973), when one reader asked if DC would revive the all-text splash pages rehashing the previous issues, the editors drew the line, calling the old text pages "eyesores" as well as "dizzying condensations of varying storylines." While aesthetic reasons may have prevented full return to older styles, the Justice League's "retro" look continued mostly unimpeded.

4. Fans did not dissect the term "Freedom Fighters," but the label, like "terrorist," was accepted as another name for underground activists seeking to address grievances against an "establishment." In this case, the "man" is the one whose face pasted on the Freedom Fighter's secret headquarters: "The Fuhrer is your friend"—Hitler. By 1983, President Ronald Reagan would dub any group dedicated to resisting communism "freedom fighters," which became the cornerstone of the Reagan Doctrine (Scott 51).

5. Not every reader saw this interpretation. In issue #111 (May-June 1974), reader Bill Henry, Jr., found the story ludicrous. He complained the final robot took over the Nazis "for no particularly convincing reason" and the Freedom Fighters didn't actually do anything noteworthy. Henry's last point is well-taken: as a comic book adventure, the only Freedom Fighter of note was Uncle Sam, whose super power here seemed to be an inexhaustible ability to speak.

WORKS CITED

Advertisement. *Strange Adventures* #129 (June 1961). New York: DC Comics. Print.

Bodnar, John. *The "Good War" in American Memory*. Baltimore: Johns Hopkins University Press, 2010. Print.

Brooks, Victor D. *Boomers: The Cold-War Generation Grows Up*. Chicago: Ivan R. Dee, 2009. Print.

Darowski, Joseph J. "'I no longer deserve to belong': The Justice League, Wonder Woman and The Twelve Labors." In The *Ages of Wonder Woman: Essays on the*

Amazon Princess in Changing Times. Ed. Joseph J. Darowski. Jefferson, NC: McFarland, 2014, 126–135. Print.

Englehart, Steve (w), Sal Buscema (a), and Vince Colletta (a). "…Before the Dawn!" *Captain America* #175 (July 1974). New York: Marvel Comics. Print.

Fox, Gardner (w), Mike Sekowsky (a), and George Roussos (a). "Time Signs a Death-Warrant for the Justice League!" *Justice League of America* #63 (June 1968). New York: DC Comics. Print.

Friedrich, Mike (w), Dick Dillin (a), and Joe Giella (a). "The Day the Earth Screamed!" *Justice League of America* #97 (March 1972). New York: DC Comics. Print.

_____. "No More Tomorrows!" *Justice League of America* #98 (May 1972). New York: DC Comics. Print.

Levitz, Paul (w), and Joe Staton (a). "The Defeat of the Justice Society!" *Adventure Comics* #466 (November-December 1979). New York: DC Comics. Print.

Maggin, Elliot S. (w), Dick Dillion (a), and Frank McLaughlin (a). "I Have No Wings and I Must Fly!" *Justice League of America* #117 (April 1974). New York: DC Comics. Print.

O'Neil, Denny (w), and Neal Adams (a). "No Evil Shall Escape My Sight!" *Green Lantern* #76 (April 1970). New York: DC Comics. Print.

Scott, James A. *Deciding to Intervene: The Reagan Doctrine and American Foreign Policy*. Durham: Duke University Press, 1996. Print.

Wein, Len (w), Dick Dillin (a), and Joe Giella (a). "The Hand that Shook the World!" *Justice League of America* #101 (September 1972). New York: DC Comics. Print.

Wein, Len (w), Dick Dillin (a), and Dick Giordano (a). "Crisis on Earth-X!" *Justice League of America* #107 (September-October 1973). New York: DC Comics. Print.

_____. "Balance of Power!" *Justice League of America* #111 (May-June 1974). New York: DC Comics. Print.

Wein, Len (w), and Dick Dillin (a). "A Stranger Walks Among Us!" *Justice League of America* #103 (December 1972). New York: DC Comics. Print.

_____. "The Shaggy Man Will Get You If You Don't Watch Out!" *Justice League of America* #104 (February 1973). New York: DC Comics. Print.

_____. "Specter in the Shadows!" *Justice League of America* #105 (April-May 1973). New York: DC Comics. Print.

_____. "Wolf in the Fold!" *Justice League of America* #106 (July-August 1973). New York: DC Comics. Print.

_____. "Thirteen Against the Earth!" *Justice League of America* #108 (November-December 1973). New York: DC Comics. Print.

_____. "The Man Who Murdered Santa Claus!" *Justice League of America* #110 (March-April 1974). New York: DC Comics. Print.

Thomas, Roy. "All the Stars are in (Super-Hero) Heaven!" *Alter-Ego* 3.14 (April). Raleigh: TwoMorrows Publishing, 2002. 4–26. Print.

Wright, Bradford. *Comic Book Nation: The Transformation of Youth Culture in America*. Baltimore: Johns Hopkins University Press, 2003. Print.

The Benefits of Doubts
Steve Englehart's Radical Take on Tradition

Jason Sacks

Some of the finest and most insightful art comes from the tension between two opposing and seemingly irreconcilable viewpoints. That creative tension frequently delivers a special relationship between creators, new insights for readers, and an approach that can be read as both revolutionary and evolutionary. That tension is especially powerful in comic book story-telling, as the interaction between smartly designed art and story often results in storytelling that transcends its individual parts.

Steve Englehart's writing represented a different sort of internal tension: it melded the two main conflicting standards of comic art that dominated the mainstream comics industry during the 1970s. It embraced both the tra-ditional approach to character and story that was a hallmark of DC Comics and the radical reinvention of heroism combined with characterization and continuity that Marvel Comics presented. Englehart's short ten-issue run on *Justice League of America* in 1977 was innovative because it demonstrated an appreciation for tradition while delivering new perspectives on that tradition. With just a handful of graceful gestures, Englehart explored those tensions and provided readers with a run that was perfectly in tune with its times while also transcending those times.

The Rule-Breaker Joins the Conservatives

Steve Englehart entered the world of comic books at the perfect time. A conscientious objector from the Vietnam War, Englehart was a prominent member of a new generation of comic book creators who saw in the tumult of the early 1970s the need to reinvent the idea of a super-hero. Starting at

Marvel in 1971 as an artist, Englehart quickly transitioned to working there as a writer. Establishing himself first on romance and horror titles before rapidly rising to some of Marvel's most iconic heroes, Englehart quickly became one of Marvel's most popular writers. He delivered comics stories that both suited their times and reflected a deep respect for tradition. He was a radical traditionalist, a creator who celebrated the history of favorite characters while also delivering his own unique take on their history. Englehart discovered the beating heart inside the characters he wrote while placing them squarely within their existing framework.

Englehart's move to DC was surprising to many longtime fans because his approach seemed different from the writing style that DC's editors emphasized. The strong editorial guidance from highly experienced editors led writers to embrace an adult discipline that contrasted strongly with the sort of unfettered youthful enthusiasm that Englehart and others of his generation brought to their series at Marvel. While Marvel was led by an ever-changing group of baby boomers flush with the radical ideas of the 1960s and '70s, DC was run by men who remembered World War II and had been in the publishing industry for decades.[1] Marvel's rotating door of editors-in-chief[2] were many years younger than their DC counterparts, mostly men in their 20s and early 30s who rose up from the fan community. Reflecting the ethos of the "me generation," there was often only a weak central authority at Marvel. Writers and artists were frequently given a large measure of freedom to deliver the tales they wanted to create.[3] In that open atmosphere, a handful of creators emerged as the radicals of their era and seldom migrated between the two companies. It was thus seen as a major surprise when Steve Englehart crossed over to Marvel's most important rival in 1977.

Englehart is often described as one of the Marvel's "Three Radicals" during the 1970s.[4] He delivered some of the most precedent-breaking comic writing of his era due to his contemporary takes on some of Marvel's most iconic heroes, which placed the characters squarely in the context of their times. Under Englehart's authorship, Captain America witnessed the suicide of President Richard Nixon in the Oval Office[5]; the X-Men's Beast was revived as a pot-smoking slacker scientist who enthusiastically joined the sexual revolution; Doctor Strange and his live-in lover Clea took LSD, died and met God; and the Avengers became involved with (among many other things) a Vietnamese refugee who became a Madonna and an android who became human enough to fall in love and get married.[6] Englehart's rule-shattering approach sparked the attention of critics and fans alike. Most of his comics were acclaimed bestsellers during the time he wrote them.[7] Englehart's approach contrasted strongly with the DC Comics of the era, where even Jack Kirby's bombastic explorations of heroism quickly fell way to a cute Planet of the Apes pastiche.

Englehart's rise to prominence happened strikingly quickly, with him ascending to the peak of his profession within four years of entering the industry. That ascendance came to an abrupt end in 1976. After a dispute with Marvel's editor-in-chief of the time, Englehart bolted from the comfortable halls of Marvel and took on a surprising set of new assignments. After his meteoric rise to stardom at Marvel, one of comics' most radical writers came to work at conservative DC in late 1976. Few observers of the time could have expected that Englehart would combine his rule-shattering approach with a deep reverence for DC's long traditions, but that is what he delivered. In his DC stories of 1977, Englehart displayed a deep respect for the history of those characters along with a rethinking of the implications of that history, finding the space to transcend. Steve Englehart embraced a radically traditional approach to his DC Comics work. Some of the finest writing of Englehart's career came on a short ten-issue run he produced for *Justice League of America*.

A Radical Traditionalist

Englehart's radically traditional writing at DC combined his approach towards bold storytelling and thoughtful characterization with a devotion to the characters' traditions. In each of the comics he delivered during his year-long tenure at DC, Englehart displayed keen insights into the most compelling aspects of the characters he wrote. These insights were based on close readings of the texts that preceded him but also on his new conclusions from those texts. Englehart's writing explored fresh areas in its depiction of the past, a feeling that beneath the placid surface portrayed in these comics was a more interesting and slightly weirder world that wasn't always obvious, succesfully melding DC's traditionalism and Marvel's radicalism in a slick, crowd-pleasing approach.

In 1977, Englehart wrote three comics that were the apex of his career: an intriguing revival of Jack Kirby's Mister Miracle, an eight-issue run on Batman in *Detective Comics* that some would call the definitive Batman; and a much-loved ten-issue run on *Justice League of America*. During his year on *Detective Comics*, Englehart revived the classic villain Hugo Strange, who had previously appeared in *Batman* #1 some 37 years earlier. His takes on iconic Batman villains the Penguin, the Riddler and the Joker brought to the surface attributes of those characters that had long been forgotten. Englehart showed those same virtues on *Justice League of America*; as letter writer Peter Sanderson noted, "Among Steve Englehart's greatest talents is his ability to take already existing characters and concepts and fill them with new life and vitality."

On *Detective* and *Justice League*, Englehart was assigned the great Julius

(Julie) Schwartz as editor. Schwartz was 32 years his elder, but Englehart found their collaboration fruitful. As Englehart relayed in a 2003 email:

> I mentioned [to DC Publisher Jenette Kahn] that Julie had a rep for controlling his books, whereas I wanted to control my books. I assume she spoke to Julie about that, because on both titles he left me pretty much alone. He did make some changes around the edges but was not involved in plotting or execution. And he was always, then and later, fine with that. I believe Julie just wanted the best books he could get. I also believe, but do not know for sure, that in the earlier days of comics, he generally dealt with writers who were less able than he was of crafting a good book. That is to say, he took the lead to make sure he got what he wanted. The problem with that theory is that I think John Broome, for one, was a very good writer. So maybe Julie just took the lead because that was his way. And maybe, by the time I showed up, he was tired of taking the lead—or maybe he was spoken to strongly by Jenette and told, truthfully, that DC had nothing going for it at that point except for this *wunderkind* who'd come over from Marvel. However it happened, the bottom line is that he let me do my thing and never showed any resentment about it. In fact, he was a strong proponent of my stories. He treated me as an equal. There may have been various reasons for it, but I do think the main one was that I was giving him good stories and that was all he really wanted for his books.

Schwartz had one more thing in common with Englehart: the editor's reputation was built in large part on his own radically conservative reinterpretations of many of DC's best-known heroes. Schwartz edited the revivals of Flash, Green Lantern, Hawkman and the Atom (among others) in the 1950s and 1960s, delivering new versions of some of the most iconic 1940s comic characters. That approach paid off and the new heroes helped to usher in the Silver Age of Comics. It's likely that Schwartz felt a kinship with the approach of the young writer. Schwartz was well known to be one of the most deeply involved editors in comics, often sitting with writers to help them plot and deliver their stories. It's thus a great sign of his respect for Englehart that Schwartz mainly left him alone.

Englehart's run on *Justice League* encompassed a 17-page prologue in issue 139, and 33-page stories in issues 140 through 146, and 149 and 150. *JLA* 147 and 148 presented the then-annual Justice League/Justice Society of America team-up, which Englehart opted not to write. All ten issues are illustrated by Dick Dillin, the very definition of a solid but unspectacular comic artist, and inked by veteran Frank McLaughlin. Dillin does a fine job on the book— Englehart noted in his email to me that "Dick Dillin [was] a long-time DC stalwart I was very proud to work with. I love being part of comics tradition"—but the real star is Englehart.

The Early Stuff Mattered

The first thing that jumps out in reading the ten issues of *Justice League* is Englehart's respect for the work of those who came before him. Each issue has an aura of deep respect for history. As he noted in his email:

I tend to believe in the reality of my characters (not psychotically; I know they're fictional; but I say to myself "Now, if these guys really existed, who would they really be?"). Therefore, I try to accept everything they've ever done as real history for them, unless it just absolutely can't be. And that leads to wanting to make use of that history to delineate their characters. I was trying to make the 2-D JLA characters 3-D, so I had to put them in their contexts. So the actual idea and execution was all mine, but the flip side to Julie's treating me with respect was my treating him with respect, and certainly a part of what I did was to pay homage to the DC that he had been a major force in creating. I wanted to say that that early DC superhero stuff mattered.

Englehart's love of the characters' history was made immediately clear with his first issue. In his initial 17-page story in *Justice League of America* #139 (February 1977), for instance, there were six footnotes,[8] a large amount for a DC book of the era. DC generally ignored continuity, with each issue of each comic running as its own world unto itself. This level of footnoting made the comic feel like it was part of a larger world, a shared history that all the characters had lived through. Marvel grabbed their readers in part because they were made to feel part of a shared universe; Englehart's take on the JLA placed them in a larger context in which threats seemed more real, with a more extensive history.

Englehart's Justice League delivered a panoramic view of DC history. His first extended sequence built on several classic DC storylines, providing context for the Guardians of the Universe (the blue aliens who created the Green Lantern Corps) by connecting the Guardians to a classic Golden Age character and a modern character from just a few years previously. Englehart had the Guardians create the Manhunters, as a precursor of the Green Lantern Corps that Englehart ingeniously connected to both a much loved Joe Simon/Jack Kirby creation from the 1940s and a much less loved Kirby creation of the 1970s. Englehart took pains to make those connections completely clear even for readers who weren't familiar with that tangled history. When a rogue Manhunter crashes into *Justice League* #140 (March 1977) it holds the promise of a grand, galaxy-spanning adventure that connects to the past and the future.

In fact, Englehart even drew connections that readers might never have expected: he added continuity that referred to his long *Avengers* run. One of the protagonists of *Justice League of America* #142 (May 1977) is a beautiful green-skinned woman named Willow. The alien escapee from an interstellar robot called the Construct speaks in unique speech patterns that are similar to former Avenger Mantis. Mantis always referred to herself as "this one," which Willow also does. The alien woman is pregnant, and Mantis became pregnant as she left *Avengers*. There are even some sly allusions to other *Avengers* plotlines in Willow's story. After the events of that two-part story, Willow/Mantis disappeared forever from DC continuity, to reappear next when Englehart and his *Detective Comics* partner Marshall Rogers took on Marvel's Silver Surfer.

Englehart's love of comics history was also reflected in an area that DC traditionally neglected: characterization. From *Justice League of America* #139 (February 1977), characters call each by their first names and make reference to previous adventures. His love for history is especially evident with his portrayal of Hawkgirl. The heroine had a long and happy marriage to Hawkman and she would often battle alongside her husband. She was a brave and forthright heroine who held her own in battle. Yet for the most arbitrary of reasons, Hawkgirl was denied formal membership in the League. The JLA had a long-running rule preventing members who duplicated powers from joining them (a fact that didn't leave out Superman, who had virtually the same powers as founding League member the Martian Manhunter). There was certainly no real reason for the rule in the fictional world of the Justice League; instead, it was probably a writer's conceit that it would be difficult to write characters who had duplicate powers. Indeed, the rule really made no sense in its fictional context: why wouldn't the Justice League want to have both Superman and Supergirl, or both Hawkman and Hawkgirl as members? Englehart faced that rule head-on, and through wonderful storytelling, insightful characterization, and respect for the characters' histories, showed how arbitrary it was. In a delightful scene, Hawkgirl argues for her admission with her peers and succeeds in her argument. Englehart's writing presented a radical take on the events, showing that tradition would logically lead to change. That approach flowed through all of Englehart's work on the series.

Justice League of America #145 (August 1977) showed the inner struggle that led to Hawkgirl joining the team and demonstrated the power of Englehart's approach. That issue featured the team's battle with a supernatural sorcerer named Count Crystal who used magic to kill Superman (Superman got better). In the midst of an all-out battle, Crystal manages to kidnap Hawkgirl and made a half-hearted attempt to win her love. Though it ran counter to the way she lived her life as a police officer on the planet Thanagar, Hawkgirl pretended to fall for the villain's ploy until she overpowered Count Crystal and turned the battle in the League's favor. This scheme caused the heroine real emotional pain; as the narrator says in a caption, "To some, the solution to Hawkgirl's dilemma would seem self-evident ... but not to her! The easy pleasures of our modern world are not the norm on her native Thanagar. There, marriage is a sacrament! Since voicing vows to Katar Hol, she has never once looked at another man." Even as a ruse, Shayera Hol is sacrificing a bit of her soul to defeat the evil sorcerer. In light of her sacrifice, how could the JLA deny her membership? In the next issue she fought valiantly to battle the plans of the evil Construct, once again showing she was at least as brave as her husband. By the end of issue 146, the choice for the League was obvious, and Shayera was inducted to join her husband Katar.

A second character joined the JLA in issue 146 (September 1977), although to be more accurate, the character rejoined the Justice League. Eternal second-rate hero the Red Tornado had been killed and revived twice by previous writers, who apparently felt he was both too dull and too complicated to include in their stories. Englehart saw complexity in a character other writers saw as simple. The robotic Tornado gave the writer a chance to explore the idea of an eternal outsider with a profound inferiority complex who still was allowed to sit at the big kids' table. In doing so Englehart extrapolated from the character's history to rediscover complexity in a character that lesser writers found uninspiring. By *Justice League of America* #150 (January 1978), the Tornado was in the front line of his team, singlehandedly defeating the villain and even laughing at his own foolishness earlier in the story. The Tornado grew a great deal during Englehart's run, but his progression was so smartly presented that it feels completely natural.

Then there's the case of the JLA member who was ignored by nearly all the other writers on *Justice League*: the Phantom Stranger. The Stranger was a supernatural character who didn't fit in with most of the JLA's pseudo-science fiction adventures. However, he was inducted as a full member after he helped the League defeat the nefarious plans of Felix Faust in 1972's *Justice League* #103 (December 1972). The Phantom Stranger had only appeared with the League one more time in 36 subsequent issues before Englehart used him four times within ten issues. He had the Phantom Stranger defeat the main villain in issue 139 (February 1977) and save the whole team in issue 145 (August 1977). Between 1977 and the cancellation of *Justice League of America* in 1985, the Phantom Stranger only appeared five more times. Englehart's knowledge of the mystical hero helped him seem a logical part of the Justice League, something that escaped all previous and subsequent writers of the series.

Englehart's reverence for the Justice League's history even extended to their mascot. He revived Snapper Carr, the League's young buddy for the team's first ten years of the team's existence. Englehart casts Carr as half of the evil Star-Tsar in issues 149 (December 1977) and 150 (January 1978), revealing that Carr had long been nursing resentments towards the League due to his feeling that the heroes didn't pay him any respect. As Carr ponders in *Justice League of America* #150 (January 1978), "Maybe I am just a mascot and not a grown man, like I said. I never seem to know what to do when I'm on my own. I haven't seen these guys in months! How much of my anger is justified—and how much is sour grapes?" This isn't the same boy who was friends with the League when it first started; Carr was a man who had grown and changed, and not necessarily in the most positive ways. Carr could be seen as representing the anxieties of baby boomers being trusted by the older generation. Englehart gives the ending of Carr's storyline an ambiguous grace note that shows his complex emotions, taking a character that had been more-or-less forgotten, and breathed new life into him.

Secret Origins

Englehart's finest and most respectful exploration of DC history lay in his radical take on the team's origin. *Justice League of America* #144 (July 1977) revealed the true "secret origin" of the Justice League, Englehart examined the timing around the JLA's first appearance and concluded that the dates generally accepted for the story didn't quite seem correct. The generally accepted origin for the team included Green Lantern, but that hero hadn't debuted until several months after the Justice League was formed. Englehart took that time discrepancy and created a thoughtful and compelling tale that melded DC history, post-war paranoia, and a Martian invasion into a grand adventure yarn.

Justice League of America #144 (July 1977) centered another revived Leaguer, albeit revived only in flashback. Long before he became the Oreo-loving hero in Keith Giffen and Kevin Maguire's '80s *Justice League* series and a leader in Grant Morrison's *JLA* run, the Martian Manhunter was written out of the League. This story revealed that the Martian Manhunter was the reason the Justice League was formed. J'onn J'onzz was accidentally transported from Mars to Earth in 1955 and was living a happy life as a New York police detective. J'onzz was happy, that is, until the evil Martian Commander Blanx and several of his lieutenants were accidentally transported to Earth by Martian Manhunter four years after he arrived on Earth. The Martians' arrival triggered widespread panic—this was at the height of the Red Scare era, and paranoia was rampant—and also brought together nearly every action hero in the DC Universe at that time. Not only did *Justice League of America* #144 (July 1977) feature Superman, Batman and Robin, Wonder Woman, Aquaman and the Flash, but it also featured such moribund characters as the Challengers of the Unknown, Plastic Man, the Blackhawks, Congorilla, and even Rex the Wonder Dog. All were gathered together by Roy Raymond, TV Detective, to fight the Martian invasion. Along the way, Adam Strange, Jimmy Olsen and Rip Hunter make cameo appearances as the combined heroes defeat the menace of Blanx and the evil Martians.

It's a moving story that celebrates DC's long history while giving that history a modern sheen. Englehart finds the heart of J'onn J'onzz in the Martian Manhunter's self-sacrifice and intelligence. As well, Englehart gives each of the guest-stars a perfect unique moment in the story. Showcasing Englehart's considerable skills gained in the previous five years, *Justice League of America* #144 (July 1977) never feels like an issue in which too much is going on; it's a tribute to Englehart's abilities that this issue flows amiably instead of being busy and overcrowded. "The Secret Origin of the Justice League" fully embraces super-hero tradition and classic team-up tropes. It's a grand joining of characters of the type that fans love; it splits the super-heroes into sub-teams who all fight one part of a large battle[9]; it also takes pains to present characterization of characters in ways that stay true to their character. In that way the story can be read as a radically conservative work because it takes existing storytelling techniques and tropes, giving those traditions new power while still staying true to their foundational integrity.[10] Englehart loves the story as well; as he said in an interview: "I tried very much to be true to those characters as they had been in the fifties and write them in that style—it was supposed to have taken place in the Brave and Bold era, so it definitely was an homage to DC in the fifties—not so much Gardner Fox, but DC in the fifties" ("JLA Satellite..."). Since its publication, this origin has taken its place as the definitive origin of the Justice League of America.

Characterization was an important part of Englehart's stories. In the main, though, his characterization was most interesting when used in the context of the stories themselves. For instance, his portrayal of J'onn J'onzz in issue 144 (July 1977) and of Hawkman and Hawkgirl in the issues she appears in, are wonderful ways of using character to illuminate story. However, his characterization seems more awkward in other places. For example, he has the Atom express feelings of uselessness in issue 142 (May 1977), but that complaining rings somewhat untrue. It's clear from Englehart's portrayal that the Atom is a veteran crime fighter and a trusted member of the JLA for many years, so it seems confusing that the hero suddenly doubt his abilities and usefulness. Similarly, Englehart portrays the Flash as a tongue-tied country boy from the Midwest when talking to Wonder Woman, which seems to go against so many of the adventures he had had previously with the League.

However, other characterizations ring true. For instance, Wonder Woman had recently been forced to spend two years going through a series of trials to regain her status in the League after a period where she had lost her superpowers. It made sense for the character to be resentful about being treated so poorly, especially since she was quite literally an Amazon princess. Another character handled well by Englehart was Superman. He was portrayed as a true hero, who felt the weight of the world on his shoulders and handled it gallantly. The relationship between Green Arrow, the eternal rebel, and Hawkman, the interstellar policeman, was seldom handled better than by Englehart, adroitly moving beyond cliché to find the heart of both characters. In doing so, Englehart definitely fulfilled his assignment of adding life and character to DC's sedate pantheon of heroes be restoring than to their core values.

Lo! There Shall Come an Ending

Ironically, Englehart was succeeded on *Justice League of America* by Gerry Conway, who had replaced him on *Avengers* one year earlier. Conway went on to write the JLA's adventures for nearly 100 issues, but he never came close to matching the quality of Englehart's short run. His radical retake on the Justice League as "Justice League Detroit" in the early 1980s was condemned by many readers as moving too far away from the League's traditions.

Perhaps the best summary of Englehart's ten issues on *Justice League of America* comes from Englehart himself. He notes on his website that the JLA was the reason DC hired him to come to their company. As Englehart states,

It was the JLA that I was recruited to DC for. They wanted to give the characters personalities—like The Avengers—after decades of being simply "costumes." I knew that would require a lot of work on each individual, and that would be tough in a traditional format, so I asked to make the book double-sized—and keep it monthly. Nothing like this had ever been done before, but they went for it—the result was a nice run where there was room for characterization and superheroics ["Justice…"].

He added in his email, "That run did reestablish the JLA, and I was very pleased that the first story in the current *Justice League* animated series was taken directly from my first story way back then, the Green Lantern/Manhunter thing—which Julie, of course, lived long enough to see.[11] I'd say he and I both got what we wanted out of our time together."

Steve Englehart's ten issues of *Justice League* are among the most interesting comics of the 1970s, and his origin story in issue 144 is a textbook example of how to juggle two dozen characters in a story without the story suffering. His run on *Detective Comics* is justifiably called a classic, but Englehart's work on *Justice League of America* also demonstrates his radically traditional approach to DC's characters. When one of comics' most rule-shattering Baby Boomer writers joined with one of its most senior editors, they produced a run on *Justice League of America* unlike any that came before.

Notes

1. In fact, Julius Schwartz, who edited Englehart on *Justice League of America*, was a fan-turned-pro as well. He co-published the very early fanzine *Time Traveler* before working as a literary agent for many writers of classic science fiction. Among Schwartz's clients were H.P. Lovecraft, Ray Bradbury and Robert Bloch.

2. Between 1971 and 1977, Marvel had five different editors-in-chief leading the line. Up until Jim Shooter's ascent to the role in the first week of January 1978, writers were generally given the freedom to deliver the sorts of comics that they wanted to write, with little or no editorial guidance. This meant that writers like Englehart, with good sales, had almost complete freedom.

3. Roy Thomas, who served as editor-in-chief at Marvel from 1972 to 1974, was born in 1940. He specifically embraced an ethos that left writers alone unless they required intervention.

4. The other two radicals are generally considered to be Steve Gerber, who brought a brooding level of existential doubt to his work on *Howard the Duck*, *The Defenders*, "The Guardians of the Galaxy" in *Marvel Presents* and *Man-Thing*, and Don McGregor, who brought a deep emotional resonance to his stories of Luke Cage Power Man, the Black Panther and Killraven, Warrior of the Worlds.

5. Making matters worse, Nixon was the head of a criminal conspiracy dedicated to the overthrow of the United States. In the climactic battle, Captain America and the members of S.H.I.E.L.D. fight on the White House lawn to defeat the evil Sons of the Serpent, with the entire event broadcast on network television. Clearly, hatred of Richard Nixon ran strong in 1976.

6. The Vietnamese woman (Mantis) and the artificial man (the Vision) participate in a double wedding to Swordsman and Scarlet Witch, respectively, in a memorable 1975 issue.

7. Indeed, *Captain America* was moribund and slated for cancellation when Englehart took over the series. Within two years, the series was at the top of Marvel's sales charts.

8. In *Justice League of America* #140, Englehart footnoted comics such as *Detective Comics* #443, from 1974; *First Issue Special* #5, from 1975; and *Flash* #168, from 1967.

9. This tradition goes back to the 1940s, when stories of the Justice Society of America in *All-Star Comics* often had a framing story at the beginning and end of a story, with stories featuring individual characters in the middle chapters.

10. This approach was deliberately also taken by Grant Morrison during his run on *JLA* that began in 1997. As Morrison reports in his autobiography *Supergods*, "I wanted to do intelligent superhero comics that didn't rely on sexualizing cartoons, excessive violence, or nihilistic gloom. It felt like time to plunge the desiccated, over-analyzed superheroes back into the molten four-color pit where they could stew for a while in their own incandescent juices and reclaim their collective mojo."

11. Englehart is referring to Season 1, Episode 1 of *Justice League*, titled (appropriately) "Secret Origins."

WORKS CITED

Englehart, Steve. "Justice League of America." http://steveenglehart.com/Comics/ JLA%20139-150.html. Retrieved November 28, 2015. Web.

Englehart, Steve (w), Dick Dillin (a), and Frank McLaughlin (i). "The Ice Age Cometh." *Justice League of America* #139 (February 1977). New York: DC Comics.

_____. "No Man Escapes the Manhunter." *Justice League of America* #140 (March 1977). New York: DC Comics.

_____. "The Origin of the Justice League—Minus One!" *Justice League of America* #144 (July 1977). New York: DC Comics.

_____. "The Carnival of Souls!" *Justice League of America* #145 (August 1977). New York: DC Comics.

_____. "The Key—or Not the Key." *Justice League of America* #150 (January 1978). New York: DC Comics.

Kelly, Rob. "JLA Satellite Interview with Steve Englehart." http://jlasatellite.blogspot. com/2008/04/jla-satellite-interview-with-steve.html. Retrieved January 23, 2016. Web.

Morrison, Grant. *Supergods*. New York: Spiegel & Grau, 2011.

Sanderson, Peter. "JLA Mail Room." *Justice League of America* #144 (July 1977). New York: DC Comics.

The Not-So-Golden Age
Gender, Race and Nostalgia
in All-Star Squadron *1981–1987*

RUTH MCCLELLAND-NUGENT

Nineteen eighty-one was a promising year for Americans nostalgic for World War II. Indiana Jones was a hit at the box office, wartime veteran Ronald Reagan was inaugurated into presidential office, and superheroes from its comic books re-entered the battle against Nazism in the pages of DC's *All-Star Squadron.* Debuting in September 1981, the comic presented a new version of the 1940s Justice Society, re-imagined by Roy Thomas, former Marvel writer and editor. In its pages, Thomas brought together old heroes, new heroes, and heroes that had been the property of other publishing houses in the 1940s, but that now belonged to DC, all into one new Earth-2 history. He invented the phrase "retroactive continuity" in the letter page of *All-Star Squadron* #18 (February 1983) to explain this process, which made it possible for Phantom Lady (formerly a Quality Comics character) to fight side-by-side with Hawkman, and for the wartime Captain Marvel (originally a Fawcett Comics property) to come face-to-face with Golden Age Superman.

But although Thomas's carefully researched storylines made his affection for the 1940s clear, he was not content to make the comic a mere nostalgia piece. *All-Star Squadron,* richly informed by social and political history, presented tales that were both action-packed and driven by serious moral criticism of World War II-era cultural prejudices. For Thomas, the Golden Age of comics was not a golden age for American social justice to some extent in terms of gender bu more particularly in terms of race. And while the letter pages were full of glowing reviews praising his approach, a minority of angry missives demonstrated that, for some conservative-leaning readers, Thomas' complex view of World War II was unwelcome. In a 1988 article, "The 'Good War' Myth," historian Michael C. C. Adams identified this uncritical nostalgic

91

view of history as a myth, one that some American clung to after the social upheavals of the 1960s and 1970s and the moral ambiguities of Vietnam. In this view, the "issues appeared simpler, the larger world was more understandable, [and] everything seemed to work out better for a 'can do' generation" (60). Adams expanded his thesis in a 1993 book, *The Best War Ever*, in which he argued that this mythmaking actively suppressed historical analysis in favor of simple nostalgia, shutting down criticism of wartime social unrest and political disagreement, and preventing later generations from learning any real lessons from the war (1–18). Clearly, Roy Thomas was one who did not accept the "Good War" myth as factual history. In the pages of *All-Star Squadron*, he used his considerable authorial freedom to offer in his stories implicit criticisms of that era's gender inequality as well as frequent critiques of 1940s racial and ethnic prejudices.

From the comic's earliest days, Thomas charted a clear difference in gender balance between the historic 1940s era Justice Society and his new umbrella team, the "All-Star Squadron." In December 1981's *All-Star Squadron* #4, eighteen heroes flew on the splash page, with an overall ratio of women to men was 1:6, slightly better than the Golden Age JSA's 1:8. These included Wonder Woman, Liberty Belle—a revived DC property from 1943's *Boy Commandos*—and a new, gender-swapped version of the Golden Age hero Firebrand. The latter was Thomas' first brand new character, a retconned sister of Rod O'Reilly, the original Quality Comics' Firebrand.

In Thomas' version, Rod had given up his crimefighting disguise for a Navy uniform and was badly injured at Pearl Harbor. His sister, Danette, while investigating his apartment in January 1982's *All-Star Squadron* #5, discovered his uniform and adapted it to her own use. A volcanologist in her civilian identity, she had developed mystical powers via an encounter with magical lava which allowed her to control fire and plasma blasts; this rendered her one of the team's most physically powerful members. Although her budding love interest Sir Justin, the "Shining Knight" of the Seven Soldiers of Victory, objected to her going into danger, she shrugged him off, and no more was said of preventing her from taking part in the team's exploits.

For the most part, reader reactions to the new female lineup as published on the letters page, were positive. In *All-Star Squadron* #14 (October 1982), Gary L. McCullock, of Charlotte, North Carolina, called the "unusually large number of women characters" a "refreshing" development. August 1982's *All-Star Squadron* #12 saw readers pleading for even more revived female characters, such as Red Tornado and Black Cat (the latter, Thomas explained, was not a DC property). But Thomas was not only changing the quantity of female characters. He was changing the quality of their stories as well, placing them in positions of leadership and plot focus. Perhaps the most dramatic example of this came with the leadership role Thomas devised for Liberty Belle.

In her civilian identity as Libby Lawrence, the hero was a star athlete and famous journalist; as Liberty Belle, she sported a mask and a belt buckle carved from the American Liberty Bell in Philadelphia. When the bell was rung, the belt produced a mysterious "adrenal rush," enhancing her powers further and giving her some control over shockwaves. In this identity, she joined the Justice Society in the comic's inaugural issue as they accepted FDR's command that they "mobilize every one of this nation's costumed heroes—men and women—into a single, super-powerful unit—a sort of All Star Squadron, so to speak!" (Thomas, "The World..."). While less formidable than Firebrand in terms of her powers, Liberty Belle became the key leader of the team. In December 1981's *All-Star Squadron* #4, as the heroes discovered the devastation at Pearl Harbor, Liberty Belle called for action as the team debated a waiting for an official declaration of war: "You stay here and wait for the legal niceties, if that's your style. I'm for finding the Nip fleet that launched this sneak attack, and sending it to the bottom of the Pacific!" (23). In *All-Star Squadron* #13's story from September 1982, "One Day During the War," her leadership role was formalized. Hawkman joined the Army, leaving a leadership gap. As the All-Stars debated whether the rest should follow his lead, Liberty Belle argued that there were many roles to play in support of the war effort: "Every group is doing what it can: businessmen are working as dollar-a-year men ... labor has pledged no strikes for the duration ... can we do any less? If eight JSA-ers decided to do their bit in uniform instead of costume—that's their right. But we on the home front can play an important role too" (4).

In response to her rousing speech, the team unanimously elected Liberty Belle to serve as their leader. Some readers loved this development. In January 1983's *All-Star Squadron* #17 letters page, Dennis Perado of Ft. Lee, New Jersey, expressed strong approval: "Belle is the only one of the five recently appointed woman leader of a super team (Zatanna, Dream Girl, Storm, and the Wasp being the others) that I thought was a wise choice." Kevin E. Patterson (no address given), however, disagreed: "You seem to be moving the All Stars toward what in the 1940s would be a radically liberal bent.... I shouldn't wonder that the American military brass or even FDR himself might press for a male hero to replace Liberty Belle as leader of the Squadron. What kind of image would the sexist public see in a super-hero group led by a woman?" Thomas gave no direct response to Kevin, but in response to another reader he called Belle's leadership "natural," and continued to present Belle's leadership as unquestioned by male or female team members. He also continued to add other major supporting female heroes to the lineup, often granting them intelligence and physical prowess their Golden Age counterparts may have lacked. Hawkgirl, for example was presented as an enthusiastic and competent warrior, eager to prove that she is "more than just a debutante with feathers," in August 1982's *All-Star Squadron* #12. In January 1985's *All-Star Squadron* #41, he revealed that Sandra Knight (Phantom Lady) was a scientific genius in her own right, often tinkering with new improvements to her super-powered weapons. Clearly, Thomas had no interest in simply replicating the stereotyped, sexist roles for female characters as they had existed in the 1940s. Yet he avoided explicit criticisms of gender prejudices, preferring oblique commentary such as the mockery of Wonder Woman's position as secretary to the Justice Society.

Thomas established early on that Wonder Woman was the most physically powerful member of the Justice Society proper, and, other than Superman, of the extended All-Stars. In December 1982's *All-Star Squadron* #16, she easily outmaneuvered her fellow team members when they attempted to physically overwhelm her while she was under a villain's hypnotic influence. In November 1983's *All Star Squadron* #27, a visiting general was astonished as she easily lifted a huge piece of equipment over her shoulder. "And she's only their secretary?" he exclaimed (8). The most elaborate discussion of her serving as "only" the secretary came in February 1984's *All-Star Squadron* #30. As Wonder Woman moved a heavy robot in the All-Star headquarters, Liberty Belle laughingly exclaimed: "Just thinking of the humor inherent in the idea of you—one of their strongest members—merely acting as the Justice Society's Secretary!' Wonder Woman responded, "Oh, the boys mean well ... and besides, I write faster than any of them can even type" (2). True to her word, Wonder Woman finished writing an entire notebook for a report before Liberty Belle has finished a page. "I'd have written faster, but the pen started to melt," she tells the wondering Belle (21).

Readers were aware of the absurdity. Jason Carr, of Chesterfield, Indiana, wrote on the letters page of July 1984's *All-Star Squadron* #35, "Thank heaven you guys finally let Liberty Belle tell the truth about Wonder Woman's being one of the most powerful All-Stars.... I have loved Wonder Woman since I was a little kid ... and it's about *time* someone told the truth about her." Delmo Waters of the Bronx s questioned why Thomas continued to replicate the sexist Golden Age dynamic: "[E]vidently all that Wonder Woman did was sit around the Justice Society headquarters, doing nothing.... That's like letting Superman stay and clean the sphere while the All-Stars do their thing." Thomas agreed that the Golden Age dynamic was ridiculous: "That's the whole point, in fact, of Liberty Belle's laughter on p. 2 of issue #30—that guys like Dr. Mid-Nite, the Atom, and Sandman, would have been fighting spies, while Wonder Woman sat on her bracelets! Times have changed, have they not?" Yet while Thomas acknowledged that times had changed, he was content to leave Wonder Woman as the group's secretary, perhaps to preserve the continuity he was so carefully re-fashioning. In contrast to these implicit criticisms of 1940s sexism, from very early on he made explicit criticism of racial bias a major dramatic focus of his story-lines.

One of the earliest of these featured the new female Firebrand. In September 1982's *All-Star Squadron* #13, set a month after Pearl Harbor, Firebrand, Liberty Belle, and speedster Johnny Quick boarded a plane for a military hospital. When speaking of the attack on Pearl Harbor, Firebrand's emotions got the better of her: "It's the Japs! I—I can't help it! Every time I think of them, I'm filled with such hatred—for what they did to Rod—and so many others—I … I do hate all Japs—and nothing can change that! Nothing!" (7). She is gently countermanded by Liberty Belle, acting as the voice of conscience, but was unmoved. At the hospital, visiting with her brother, she vowed to "get even with those dirty yellow scum." Rod then revealed that he was saved at Pearl Harbor by an American Army soldier named Ken Hosokawa, who lost his own life dragging Rod to shelter. Rod explained that his savior was the American-born son of Japanese immigrants: "And he died, giving his life for a country that denied those parents citizenship. Well? Still think they're all dirty yellow scum?" (21). In tears, Firebrand begged forgiveness for her anger and prejudice. Liberty Belle answered: "There's nothing for me to forgive. But the next time you meet one of the Nisei—the second generation Americans born of Japanese parentage—you might ask him for forgiveness—for the prejudices many other Americans are heaping on him, just because of his skin color" (23).

It was a timely topic. In the 1970s, popular culture and activism had drawn increasing attention to the historical injustice of Japanese-American internment. 1971's *If Tommorow Comes*, a made-for-TV movie, had examined the romance between a Nisei man and a white woman at the start of the war, emphasizing white prejudice and racial hatred. In 1973, Jeanne Wakatsuki Houston published *Farewell to Manzanar*, an autobiographical novel of her family's internment; it was adapted as a television film in 1976. Real-life activism followed closely in the wake of these popular fictional portrayals. In 1978, the Japanese-American Citizen's League spearheaded an effort to draw attention to Japanese-American internment during World War II. In July 1980, the Commission on Wartime Relocation and Internment of Civilians began what would be a multi-year investigation into wartime internment (Oyama). Monetary redress was one goal of the JACL's leaders, public education and work to prevent another similar incident was even more important (Middleton 1439–41).

Intentionally or not, Roy Thomas was certainly aiding with the public education effort, right down to correcting his own missteps in regards to racial insensitivity. As he responded to a reader in the letters page of June 1982's *All-Star Squadron* #10:

We wanted especially to thank ALL-STAR Squadron reader Tom Kumamoto of San Jose, California, regarding an exchange of letters with the writer of this book on our use of the term "Nip" (short for "Nipponese," from the Japanese name for their homeland.) As we explained to him, a Japanese- American co-worker told said writer some years ago that the term was far less offensive than certain others, so it was used issues #1–5. However, after thinking the matter over, we prefer not to use *any* term that can be reasonably construed as a racial slur.... We're interested in chronicling the wartime adventures of Earth-Two's greatest heroes—but not in keeping old prejudices and epithets undeservedly alive.

Thomas would also explore prejudice through the experiences of Japanese-American characters. He was not the first DC writer to address anti–Japanese racism this way. In the pages of December 1977's *Wonder Woman* #238, writer Gerry Conway had broached the topic of internment camps and anti–Japanese prejudice, introducing Thomas Morita as an embittered son of Japanese emigrants. Although technically a villain in his guise as the shapeshifter Kung, Conway had told the story sympathetically, thought he eyes of Thomas's sister Nancy, who remained loyal to the United States despite its racism. Thomas would re-introduce Kung in April 1982's *All-Star Squadron* #8, retconning him into the new continuity, and joining Thomas's own new characters of Japanese descent.

He began this multi-issue exploration of prejudice again Japanese-Americans in February 1984's *All-Star Squadron* #30. As members of the Justice Society set out to investigate the sabotage of eight American inventors by agents of Japan's Black Dragon society, Wonder Woman reminded her team-mates: "Don't forget—not everybody with slanted eyes and sallow skin is an enemy of America!" (13). It was a needed admonition. When Morrie Fushido, an American of Japanese descent, tried to help the Atom, he was nearly beaten for his trouble. "I'm as American as you are!" Morrie protested. (In a helpful sidebar on page 14, Thomas reminded his readers that "Issei" is "one born in Japan, but living in the U.S." and defined "Nisei" as "children of the Issei, born in the U.S. and thus automatically citizens.") With Morrie's help, the JSA determined that the Black Dragons were indeed recruiting, but that neither Issei nor Nisei show much interest in joining (15). Regardless, Wonder Woman voiced concern in the closing pages about the future of Japanese-Americans: "The Nisei problem ... brings out other passions ... hidden ones ... often ugly ones" (21). On the very next page, a cut scene takes the reader to the White House, showing Roosevelt talking about a document he is about to sign, finally concluding that "there's a war going on—a war that's got to be won—no matter who gets hurt—so I suppose I've got no choice!" Thomas ended the story with an editorial text box:

Thus is Executive Order 9066 issued on this day—February 19, 1942—by the hand of the president of the United States. As an eventual result of this order, more than 100,000 persons of Japanese ancestry living in the U.S.—most of them natural-born citizens—will be interned in hastily-erected relocation centers ... stripped of their property for the duration, denied their civil rights. There are those who will say, years later if not at once, that this date should live in infamy as surely as that of the Imperial Japanese Attack on Pearl Harbor on December 7, 1941.

And maybe, just maybe … they are right! [22].

Thomas' emphasis on Roosevelt's personal responsibility echoed the findings of the 1981 Congressional commission, which had been widely reported in the news, the *New York Times*, for example, wrote of their findings in a 25 February 1983 article:

[Relocation] was motivated by "racial prejudice, war hysteria and failure of political leadership," and not by military considerations. [The report] placed particular blame on President Roosevelt.… "All of this was done despite the fact that not a single documented act of espionage, sabotage or fifth column activity was committed by an American citizen of Japanese ancestry or by a resident Japanese alien on the West Coast," the report said [Miller].

Some readers appreciated Thomas tackling the topic. As Melissa Zitovysky of Chicago wrote in the letters page of July 1984's *All-Star Squadron* #35: "After all, if you'd wanted to, you could have simply said 'the Americans of the 1940s had no hatred for the American Japanese.' But your story this month showed many different opinions about the Nisei and Issei, and made me think about how we often let our hatred overpower our reasoning. Cheers—and thanks!"

In May 1984's *All-Star Squadron* #33, Thomas introduced his first original super-powered character of Japanese descent, who would soon join Kung as a complicated and sympathetic anti–American agent. Under the name "Tsunami," she controlled ocean waves and caused earthquakes, but as Miya Shimada, a Kibei (Nisei who had returned to Japan) she first appeared trying to persuade a group of Nisei and Isei to join her in fighting for Japan. When her listeners insisted upon their loyalty as "good Americans," Miya rebuked them: "I was a 'good American' once too—until I was called 'Jap!' one time too many!" (15). Tsunami also faced prejudice on the basis of her gender, portrayed as emanating from those who share her race and ethnicity. When she revealed her skimpy Tusnami costume to the Issei and Nisei in the same issue, they chided her that this was "no way for a girl to dress." In June 1984's *All-Star Squadron* #34 Captain Nishino of the Imperial Navy blamed her gender for failing to recruit the Japanese-Americans—"I told Admiral Yamamoto no good would come of bringing a woman into war—not even one such as you" (16). This sexist treatment did not spur her to question her loyalties; the betrayal of Japanese values by a Japanese agent, however, would.

In *All-Star Squadron* #42, the February 1985 issue, Prince Daka (a villain Thomas revived from the 1943 *Batman* serial films) recruited Tsunami, Kung, and a third super-powered agent, Samurai, in a plan to steal Starman's rod from the All-Stars (15). In the next issue, *All-Star Squadron* #43 of March

1985, Daka commanded the trio to kill the All-Stars while they were helpless; both Tsunami and Samurai refused, arguing it would be a dishonorable act counter to Japanese bushido values (3). When Tsunami was then taken prisoner by the All-Stars, she was surprised that the team did not torture her, and slowly became impressed with their sense of honor. When Daka attempted to kill Liberty Belle after agreeing to a prisoner exchange, Tsunami saved the American and rejected Daka entirely for his lack of honor.

But Tsunami could not side with the Americans either: "While your government persecutes my own people.... I am Kibei—dweller in two worlds, at home in none." As Miya fled into the darkness, the American heroes decide to let her go, although they knew Washington would prefer her in captivity. Liberty Belle, often the voice of racial equality in the group, mused that they had a higher obligation: "Warriors, of any stripe, must act—in the end—by their own code. First Sumo, then Tsunami acted by there, tonight—and we all know it cost them dear. Can we do less—and still say we fight for justice?" (21).

Readers had a mixed reaction to the storyline. In July 1985's *All-Star Squadron* #47 letters page, T.E. Pouncey suggested that Thomas' focus on the Japanese villains was itself racist: "They are drawn and written as very stupid people." Other readers praised Thomas for his racial sensitivity and for avoiding the "Good War" trap. Larry Schulz, of Springville, New York, wrote: "I was worried that ALL-STAR SQUADRON would just be syrupy nostalgia and racism. Well, the Japanese therein don't look like toothy monkeys, and the Germans don't display the camp villain of a silent film nasty." Robert T. Joschonek, of Jonestown, Pennsylvania, specifically thanked Thomas for showing the white heroes struggling with their own racist thoughts: "heroes are human, no matter how great the man, pettiness and prejudice may still exist within him."

Thomas was interested in portraying the complexities of racism in the United States, but he did not ignore Nazi racism. His most overt comment on the matter came in May 1982's *All-Star Comics* #9, in which he reintroduced two characters who, like Kung, were creations of Gerry Conway: Nazi villain Baron Blitzkrieg and American hero Steel, the "indestructible man." Thomas "retconned" their stories so that they now connected, reshaping Blitzkrieg's origin as the product of Nazi experimentation to bring Steel into the picture. Shot down on a secret mission over occupied Poland, the hero was hunted down by Hitler's favorite concentration camp commandant "Ein Schlachter," The Butcher. Captured, beaten unconscious, Steel awoke to a nightmarish scene, as emaciated prisoners in striped uniforms surrounded him.

A woman explained, "[t]he Nazis call it a Konzentrationslager ... but we know its true name. This is hell.... They brought us here in freight cars

... they told us it was a camp ... a place of 'protective custody.' They took us from the ghettoes ... they brought us here to experiment upon us—to kill us! And the horror of it is... we did not fight back!" (8–9). The point about fighting back became clear when Steel attempted to escape against desperate odds, fleeing a Nazi medical facility with a vial of acid. Grazed by a bullet, he was stunned dropping the bottle. A prisoner saw this, and, as Steel explained later:

> It was the young Jew I had talked to before—staring downward with eyes like sullen fire raging in the ravaged, shadowed sockets. With an emaciated hand, he grasped the bottle— as if, instinctively, he knew what he was going to do with it. And, as the Butcher led his trigger happy goons into the yard ... he did it! A splatter of breaking glass—a hiss—then a scream of mortal anguish— a scream which burbled into an incoherent moan, even as Nazi bullets cut down the madly grinning prisoner [13–14].

The camp commandant would be reconstructed into the super-powered Blitzkrieg, but in Thomas' telling, the focus was put on the young Jewish man's desperate act of resistance in the face of overwhelming despair. Adrian Gonzales and Jerry Ordway's art underlined the horror of the camp scenes, with prisoners gone bald from hunger, eyes portrayed as dark holes, under an ominous sky filled with black smoke from chimneys. In another panel, eyes and mouths contort grotesquely from a green fog, suggesting the scenes of mass gassing. In the space of only a few pages, Thomas, Gonzales, and Ordway imbued the series with a deep moral seriousness, underlined by the nightmarish imagery of the unimaginable death camp. While not accepting the facile "Good War" construction of unquestioned American virtue, Thomas also made it clear to his audience that, as far as the Holocaust was concerned, there was no moral grey zone.

Not all of his readers were appreciative. The October 1982 letters page of *All-Star Squadron* #14 included a lengthy diatribe from Heino Mueller of Coat Mesa, California, that accused Thomas of being anti–German:

> Portraying Germans as Nazis has been a growing trend for many years now in motion pictures, television magazines, and, of late, in your stories as well. The high point, in terms of sheer popularity, was probably the "Holocaust" series on NBC-TV, which I consider to have been extremely one-sided in its account. No one denies the atrocities that were committed by all sides during the war, but the persistent focus on the tragic fate of the Jewish people in Europe shows a blatant lack of historical balance.... This type of publicity only provokes a cycle of antagonism and intolerance among ethnic and racial groups.

Thomas did not agree that "all sides" had created morally equivalent atrocities. He replied:

> We must admit that we feel that the "persistent focus" on the fate of six million mostly civilian Jews in Europe—a goodly percentage of the war's casualties by any reckoning— does not in any way show, as you claim, "a blatant lack of historical balance." In our minds, and despite such murderous acts as those committed by Russia against the Poles in such

places as the Katyn Forest, the aptly-named "Holocaust" so dwarfs most other atrocities of World War II that we can never apologize for considering, not Germans, but Nazism and those who espoused it, to have been among the greatest curses of humankind.

And lest you wonder about Roy's own ethnic origins: it's never been anything he's been either especially proud of or ashamed of, but his own great-grandparents, on both sides, came to this country from…. Germany. —R.T.

As the letter mentions, the 1978 miniseries *Holocaust* had indeed launched a new awareness of the tragedy into American popular culture. Rebroadcast in 1979, it reached an estimated 220 million viewers in the United States and Europe. It had an incredible impact on American media discussion of the murder of Jews in Nazi Germany; in the last two weeks of April 1978, after the broadcast, over 20 items referencing the series appeared in the *New York Times* alone (Shandler). Its emphasis on Jews not believing the truth until too late, on launching hopeless resistance in the Warsaw ghetto foreshadowed Thomas' themes, if it did not inspire them directly. The public interest was matched by government action. In 1978, Jimmy Carter launched a commission on the Holocaust, with the stated purpose "to make recommendations on establishing and funding an appropriate memorial to victims of the Holocaust, and to recommend ways for the Nation to commemorate April 28 and 29, 1979, the 'Days of Remembrance of Victims of the Holocaust'" (Peters and Woolley). In 1980, the Commission's findings helped launch the National Holocaust Museum, educational programs to help educators better teach about the tragedy, and a renewed commitment to prosecuting Nazi war criminals inside the United States (Report to the President).

But as Mueller's letter suggests, the 1970s and 1980s also saw pushback against those who sought to memorialize the Holocaust. There was a visibly resurgent racist movement within the United States in this period. In 1977, the American neo–Nazi party sought a permit to march in the predominantly Jewish community of Skokie, Illinois, prompting a highly publicized court struggle over freedom of speech and assembly in the United States (Horowitz 535–45). The Institute for Historical Review, founded in 1979, lent a pseudo-academic legitimacy to Holocaust denialism, publishing a non-peer-reviewed journal that pumped out articles arguing that evidence of the Holocaust was faked or exaggerated (Rosenfeld 376). And Holocaust denialism in the United States intertwined with other racial hatreds; the Ku Klux Klan, for example, embraced Holocaust denialism and anti–Semitic conspiracy theories in the 1970s, which helped drive its growth in the 1980s (Kielsgard 152–53). In light of this racism, it is not surprising that Thomas received pushback from readers when he turned to the theme of anti-black prejudice in wartime American, told through the story of the only prominent African American character in the series: Will Everett, the hero called "Amazing Man."

In his fictional backstory, Everett had been an Olympic athlete who experienced Nazi racism at the Berlin Olympics of 1936, and racism at home in the United States. Stuck with a low-paying custodial job in a lab, he experienced an accident that rendered him able to absorb the properties of any substance he touched. By touching steel, for example, he could become nearly indestructible, as explained in July 1983's *All-Star Squadron* #23. Recruited by Superman foe Ultra-Humanite to steal Dr. Fate's magic helm, he first appeared as an antagonist to the All-Stars. They foiled his attempted through the combined efforts of Green Lantern, Steel, Liberty Belle, the Atom, Tarantula, Batman and Robin, prompting Everett to quip: "The story of my life! A bunch'a white guys—ganging up on me!" (23). When, in October 1983's *All-Star Squadron* #24, Everett discovered that the Ultra-Humanite planned to attack his hometown of Detroit, he reluctantly sided with the All-Stars, whom he does not trust because of their affiliation with the racist United States government.

Readers' reactions, as presented on the letters page of November 1983's *All-Star Squadron* #27, were mixed, but largely positive, particularly among those readers who identified themselves as African American. Willie Holmes of Chicago wrote: "This may sound strange, but I'm glad to see one of "us" as a really powerful villain during World War II. Come to think of it, a black wasn't even shown as a petty thief, let alone someone like Amazing-Man." While DC Hampton (no address given) thanked Thomas for the portrayal but critiqued his use of stereotyped speech patterns:

> Throughout the comics world all Afro-Americans and Afro-American males in particular possess identical speech patterns; they all speak "street classy." This means that slang terms are used in excess, that most parts of speech are used improperly, and that the final letter of any word in the present participle is omitted. If ever a printer's error results in fault [sic] skin coloring in a comics magazine, fear not, for one may always identify any Afro-Americans present in the story by the way they talk!

Thomas agreed that Amazing Man had been "a bit too slangy," and noticeably changed Everett's speech patterns for his next appearance in October 1984's *All-Star Squadron* #38.

In this issue, as team members were catching up on an explosion of housing-related racial unrest Detroit, they were shocked to see their old friend Amazing Man, Will Everett, on the newsreel, being attacked by a white mob in robes of the "Klan-Like Phantom Empire" (16–17). To the horror of the watching All-Stars, the robed men chained Everett to a cross, doused him with gasoline, and lit the flames. Using his abilities to mimic the properties of the iron chains holding him down, Everett barely escaped with his life. A mysterious figure wearing red white and blue and a Klan-like hood, calling himself the "Real American," led the crowd in a chant of racial hatred (19).

The story continued in November 1984's *All-Star Squadron* #39, as Thomas told his version of the real-life Detroit housing protests of 1942.

Several of the All-Stars sped to Detroit, where they found a white supremacist rally advertised by a flyer in a diner window: "Help the White People to keep the district White. MEN NEEDED to keep our lines solid.... DON'T BE YEL-LOW COME OUT" (4). Firebrand's dialogue explained why housing segregation is such a problem: "Most negroes are forced to live in a hellhole of an area nicknamed 'Paradise Valley' ... and there are a lot of people who don't want to see them move out it!" (5). Investigating further, Johnny Quick and Liberty Belle located Everett's mother, and fiancée Rachel, and offered to alert President Roosevelt to the problem. Rachel, initially friendly, responded angrily. She condemned Roosevelt for suppressing A. Phillip Randolph's planned civil rights protest march, rejecting pleas of wartime necessity: "Our people have been fighting their own damn war for near a century—why should we worry about Hitler—when we've got gangs like the Klan and the Phantom Empire right here at home?" (10).

Shaken by Rachel's skepticism, the heroes nevertheless confronted the white supremacist crowd in their civilian identities as journalists Libby Lawrence and Johnny Chambers. An angry white woman confronted them as "East Coast Liberals" come to spread "Communist poison!" (11). Thomas' audience might well have recognized these epithets as coming, not from the 1940s, but from far-right organizations of the 1960s and 1970s to criticize a media they believed were controlled by racial and ethnic minorities, trying to brainwash Americans with totalitarian propaganda (Gillis 213–17). But in Thomas' story, it was the "Real American" who was the real brainwasher. Using the mysterious power of his voice, he was not only able to whip the white crowd into a frenzy, he hypnotized Amazing-Man into believing he was weak and powerless, unable to overcome the white supremacist villain. Meanwhile, the All-Stars have succeeded in standing between the white mob and the black crowd, but are stunned to find that their "neutral" peacekeeping results in arrests only for black protestors, not for the whites who had begunt he violence (19). Thomas emphasized in this case that resistance to biased authority could be virtuous, via Everett's resistance, as well as that of the black crowd who were prepared to die for their rights. Unlike the Nisei and Issei, who proved their loyalty via non-resistance, Thomas paints the black protestors more like the Jews who resisted in the face of overwhelming odds.

As Everett and his father were being arrested, in Washington, D.C., Green Lantern and Hawkman begged FDR to intervene. As Rachel had pre-dicted, the president refused, calling the situation "regrettable" but a "local matter." Stunned, Green Lantern and Hawkman decided they had a moral imperative to address the riots themselves. Hawkman observed that if they cannot resolve the race riots, "we may just be working to win one war—while setting the stage for another one—in America itself!" (20).

In December 1984's *All-Star Squadron* #40, Thomas cited Alan Clive's

State of War: Michigan in World War II for a real-life narration of how the historic riots had played out on "our" world, before returning his narration to his fictional world, where the All-Stars had fallen under the Real American's hypnotic influence (2). Robotman deduced out that his mechanical ears gave him immunity to "Real American's" hypnosis. Lending them to Amazing-Man, he assisted the black hero in battling Real American to a standstill. Everett discovered that his foe was not human, but an android, hooked into special-mind influencing technology. Amazing-Man got to save the day, rather than the white heroes; if he could not triumph over all racism, at least he could defeat one racist villain. To the surprise of the other All-Stars, Amazing Man also announced that he would join their ranks, despite his suspicions of American wartime society:

> I figure I can do more good as Amazing-Man, battling alongside the All-Stars, than I can as one more "colored man" in Detroit or anywhere else. Maybe that'll show we negroes should be allowed to fight in this white man's war—not just deliver toilet paper.... I'm signing on for the duration—long as the All-Stars' goals and mine look like the same ones.

"And any time they're not," Green Lantern responded, "we're counting on you to tell us *why* not." Hawkman adds, "Then—we'll talk, okay?" (21). The willingness of the white All-Stars to operate in good faith and listen to black criticism has persuaded Amazing Man to join them, and his father to take the battle to the courts. Even if the government was unmoved by racial injustice, Thomas' story suggested, individuals might still make progress.

On the letters page in April 1985's *All-Star Squadron #44*, reader responses were mixed. T. M. Maple of Toronto, Canada, wrote:

> Though comparisons between Nazi Germany and wartime America are, of course, ludicrous, it is still clear that many evils were tolerated in the name of fighting what was perceived to be a far greater evil. Maybe FDR was right, that America could not both fight Hitler and suffer the upheaval that would surely have accompanied attempts to achieve true racial justice. Still, this does little to justify injustice from those who suffered from it.

Not every reader agreed. Steve Smith, of Tipp City, Ohio, accused Thomas of promoting Communism with his positive view of A. Philip Randolph and the civil rights struggles of the 1940s. In support of his argument, he cited the John Birch Society publication *It's Very Simple: The True Story of Civil Rights*, by Alan Stang, to argue that Soviet agitation had been behind civil rights movements since 1918, and that the National Negro Congress (of which Randolph became president in 1947) was a "communist operation ... associated with twenty organizations identified as hard-core communist fronts by the House Committee on un–American Activities as early as 1958!" The smear that the civil rights movement was a communist plot had been founded mainly in the fantasies of J. Edgar Hoover, and promoted with enthusiasm by Southern segregationist governors such as Lester B. Maddox and

George Wallace. But by the 1980s, the idea existed mainly on the fringes of right-wing discourse; mainstream conservatives like Ronald Reagan voiced more muted discomfort with the breadth of desegregation, and equal opportunity legislation, arguing that government intrusion into citizen's lives had become a greater problem than racial prejudice (Berlett and Lyons 183–85). Thomas's response left little doubt that he did not share these concerns about the civil rights movement, even if he thought there was room for criticism:

> Even if the Civil Rights movement were found to be in regular communication with the Kremlin, it wouldn't invalidate most black claims of injustice done to them over the years.... But I'm certainly not going to condemn the cause, or even the name of A. Philip Randolph, on the basis of HUAC findings, either, since the "guilt-by-association" tactics of the so-called McCarthy years was as distasteful to me as anything the real "Reds" ever did.... (And no, I've never been a total supporter of everything CORE, SNCC, the Black Panthers, the NAACP, or anybody else ever did either.) I'm just a writer—an American writer of German descent, using at present the medium of the super-hero comic books— which I happen to love—trying something a bit different from a run-of-the-mill action take.

Thomas certainly succeeded in producing something "a bit different," if for no other reason than his success in stitching together a new history for DC's fractured Earth-2 continuity. Ironically, it was a concern for continuity that proved the popular comic's downfall. DC's *Crisis on Infinite Earths* erased all of DC's 'alternate earths" from existence, including Earth 2. Although Thomas was allowed to finish certain key storylines by removing them to hyperspace, editorial disorganization hampered his carefully plotted story arcs. According to Thomas' editorial on the letters page of May 1986's *All-Star Squadron* #57, he had been promised he would still be able to use the "Big Three" in his stories—Wonder Woman, Batman, and Superman—as well as Robin and Aquaman. But editorial opinion shifted, leaving Thomas without these "Forbidden Five," and story arcs that could not be easily resolved without them. Despite his best efforts to introduce replacements, years of continuity were lost, and the comic folded in 1987. Before its demise, however, *All-Star Squadron* had established a unique place in DC's lineup as a work of historical fiction and social criticism. Roy Thomas' heroes fought Nazi racism and Japanese aggression, but some of their most poignant battles were against prejudices within American society and themselves. Even if World War II was not a "good war," the All-Star Squadron was presented as a good team— a golden example of egalitarianism illuminating a not-so Golden Age.

Works Cited

Adams, Michael C. C. *The Best War Ever: America and World War II*. Baltimore: Johns Hopkins University Press, 1993. Print.

_____. "The 'Good War' Myth and the Cult of Nostalgia." *Midwest Quarterly* 40.1 (1988): 59–74. Print.

Berlet, Chip, and Matthew Nemiroff Lyons. *Right-Wing Populism in America: Too Close for Comfort*. New York: The Guilford Press, 2000. Print.

Commission on Wartime Relocation and Internment of Civilians. "Personal Justice Denied: Report of the Commission." Washington, D.C., 1982. National Archives. Web 12 November 2015.

Conway, Gerry (w), Jose Delbo, and Vince Colletta (a). "Assassin of a Thousand Claws!" *Wonder Woman* #238 (December 1977). New York: DC Comics. Print.

Gillis, William. "Say No to the Liberal Media: Conservatives and Criticism of the News Media in the 1970s." Diss., Indiana University, 2011. Web. 29 February 2016.

Holocaust. Dir. Martin Chomsky. Perf. Joseph Bottoms, Tovah Feldshuh, Michael Moriarty, James Woods, Meryl Streep. NBC Productions, 1978. DVD.

Horowitz, Irving Louis. "The ACLU and Politics; the Politics of the ACLU First Amendment Blues: On Downs, *Nazis in Skokie.*" *Law and Social Inquiry* 11.3 (1986). Web. 13 November 2015.

Huston, Jeanne Wakatsuki. *Farewell to Manzanar.* Boston: Houghton Mifflin, 1973. Print.

If Tomorrow Comes. Dir. George McGowan. Perf. Patty Duke, Frank Michael Liu. Aaron Spelling Productions, 1971. *Amazon Prime Streaming.* Web. 18 December 2015.

Kielsgard, Mark. *At The Confluence of Law and Politics: Responding to Modern Genocide.* New York: Routledge, 2015. Print.

Letters Page. *All-Star Squadron* #10 (June 1982). New York: DC Comics. Print.

Letters Page. *All-Star Squadron* #14 (October 1982). New York: DC Comics. Print.

Letters Page. *All-Star Squadron* #1 (January 1983). New York: DC Comics. Print.

Letters Page. *All-Star Squadron* #27 (November 1982). New York: DC Comics. Print.

Letters Page. *All-Star Squadron* #35 (July 1984). New York: DC Comics. Print.

Letters Page. *All-Star Squadron* #44 (April 1985). New York: DC Comics. Print.

Letters Page. *All-Star Squadron* #47 (July 1985). New York: DC Comics. Print.

Miller, Judith. "Wartime Internment of Japanese Was 'Grave Injustice,' Panel Says." *New York Times* 25 February 1983. Web. 15 November 2015.

Middleton, Martha. "Commission Hearing Probes Reparations for Japanese-Americans." *American Bar Association Journal* 67.11 (November 1981): 1439–41. Web. 16 November 2015.

Oyama, David. "In 1942, Internment. In 1981, an Inquiry." *New York Times* 9 July 1981. Web. 15 November 2015.

Peters, Gerhard, and John T. Woolley, *The American Presidency Project.* Web. 10 November 2015.

President's Commission on the Holocaust. Report to the President. Washington, D.C., 1979. United States Holocaust Museum. Web. 15 November 2015.

Rosenfeld, Gavriel D. "The Politics of Uniqueness: Reflections on the Recent Polemical Turn in Holocaust and Genocide Scholarship." In *Holocaust: Critical Concepts in Historical Studies Volume 3.* Ed. David Cesarani and Sarah Kavanaugh. New York: Routledge, 2004. Print.

Shandler, Jeffrey. *While America Watches: Televising the Holocaust.* 1999. Oxford: Oxford University Press, 1999. Kindle AWZ File.

Thomas, Roy (w), Rich Buckler, and Jerry Ordway (a). "The World on Fire." *All Star Squadron* #1 (September 1981). New York: DC Comics. Print.

_____. "Never Step on a Feathered Serpent." *All Star Squadron* #5 (January 1982). New York: DC Comics. Print.

_____. "Day of the Dragon King!" *All-Star Squadron* #4 (December 1981). New York: DC Comics. Print.

Thomas, Roy (w), Adrian Gonzales, and Mike DeCarlo (a). "One Day During the War." *All-Star Squadron* #13 (September 1982). New York: DC Comics. Print.

Thomas, Roy (w), Adrian Gonzales, and Rick Hober (a). "The Magnetic Marauders." *All-Star Squadron* #16 (December 1982). New York: DC Comics. Print.

Thomas, Roy (w), Adrian Gonzales, and Jerry Ordway (a). "Mayhem in the Mile-high City," *All-Star Squadron* #6 (February 1982). New York: DC Comics. Print.

_____. "Afternoon of the Assassins." *All-Star Squadron* #8 (April 1982). New York: DC Comics. Print.

_____. "Should Auld Acquaintance Be Destroyed..." *All-Star Squadron* #9 (May 1982). New York: DC Comics. Print.

_____. "Doomsday Begins at Dawn!" *All-Star Squadron* #12 (August 1982). New York: DC Comics. Print.

Thomas, Roy (w), Rick Hoberg and Bill Collins (a). "The Battle of Santa Barbara—Times Two." *All-Star Squadron* #33 (May 1984). New York: DC Comics. Print.

_____. "The Wrath of Tsunami." *All-Star Squadron* #34 (June 1984). New York: DC Comics. Print.

_____. "Nobody Gets Out of Paradise Valley Alive!" *All-Star Squadron* #39 (November 1984). New York: DC Comics. Print.

Thomas, Roy (w), Rick Hoberg, Bill Collins, and Mike DeCarlo (a). "Detroit is Dynamite!" *All-Star Squadron* #38 (October 1984). New York: DC Comics. Print.

Thomas, Roy (w), Richard Howell, and Bill Collins (a). "The Rise and Fall of the Phantom Empire." *All-Star Squadron* #40 (December 1984). New York: DC Comics. Print.

Thomas, Roy (w), Arvel Jones, and Bill Collins (a). "Oh Say, Can't You See?" *All-Star Squadron* #42 (February 1985). New York: DC Comics. Print.

Thomas, Roy (w), Mike Machlan, Richard Howell, and Sam de LaRosa (a). "Day of the Black Dragon," *All-Star Squadron* #30 (February 1984). New York: DC Comics. Print.

Thomas, Roy (w), Jerry Ordway, and Mike Machlan (a). "When Fate Thy Measure Takes...!" *All-Star Squadron* #23 (July 1983). New York: DC Comics. Print.

Gritty Levity
The Giffen/DeMatteis Era
of the Justice League

CHARLES HENEBRY

When *Justice League* dropped "of America" for a 1987 relaunch after a decade-long decline in sales, no one expected the group to become one of DC's top sellers. Keith Giffen claims in the introduction to the 2008 trade paperback that he and his co-writer, J.M. DeMatteis, both worried that the book would tank and they would quickly lose the assignment (6). Instead, the series became one of DC's mainstays, generating two spin-off titles, *Justice League Europe* and *Justice League Quarterly*. Responsible for plots and layouts and working with a mixed roster of dialogue writers and artists, Giffen dominated a peculiar corner of the DC universe for the next five years, a space that bustled with ironic antiheroes, snappy dialogue, and comic misadventures.

Today Giffen and DeMatteis' *Justice League* is remembered chiefly for bucking the "grim 'n' gritty" trend inaugurated a year earlier by the runaway success of Frank Miller's *The Dark Knight Returns,* followed almost immediately by Alan Moore's bestselling *Watchmen.* Yet, for all its reputation as antidote to those authors' dark meditations on superpowers and society, the series' vision was often gritty, and sometimes even grim. Like both Miller and Moore, Giffen crafted stories that questioned whether superpowers could solve the world's profound sociopolitical problems. The key difference was that Giffen did so to comic effect. This tonal shift owed a lot to DeMatteis' snappy dialogue, filling panels with banter and sarcastic commentary. It also owed something to Kevin Maguire's mastery of facial expression, broadening the comic's range from heroic standards like rage and fierce determination to include jealousy, boredom, even embarrassment. Together, Maguire and DeMatteis allowed Giffen to move much of the action indoors, foregrounding interpersonal squabbles and painting a picture of superheroes living (or, rather, enduring) ordinary life. Thus, the lighthearted tone of the Giffen-DeMatteis *Justice League* was not a rejection of the emerging trend in superhero comics so much as an idiosyncratic implementation. Giffen and his collaborators joined with Miller and Moore, critiquing the tradition of comic-book heroism and satirizing contemporary society. But their delivery leavened dread with laughter.

The cover of the first issue promised "a return to greatness for the all-new *Justice League*." Three years earlier, in *Justice League of America* Annual #2, the old series had shifted the team's headquarters from a gleaming space satellite to the gritty streets of Detroit, and had replaced the team's most famous regulars (Superman, Wonder Woman, Green Lantern, Batman, and Flash) with unknowns Steel, Vibe, Vixen and Gypsy. These newly minted heroes had greatly enhanced the League's gender and racial diversity. But, as series editor Andy Helfer told the story in the letters column of *Justice League* #2 (June 1987), that bold attempt at reinvention had failed miserably with readers: "We looked out onto the great sea of faces that is comic book fandom, and saw red, fevered eyes, yellowed fang-like teeth, and up raised fists. We heard the cries for blood." Helfer declined to mention race or gender explicitly as a factor in fans' rejection of the "Detroit League," though a cynic might be tempted to note that the "all-new *Justice League*" assembled on the front cover of Giffen and DeMatteis's first issue hearkened back to the nearly all-white and nearly all-male Silver Age team of 1960's *Justice League of America* #1. Helfer instead dwelt on the series' tradition of superheroic teamwork:

> The *Justice League of America* defines the greatest of DC's heroes in a way which "solo" superhero books can not—that is, it defines the individual heroes in the context of their peers—it deals with the *fraternity of heroes,* and allows readers, for a few brief moments, to enter into that private world, and see how heroes interact with *each other,* rather than the "ordinary" people the heroes are sworn to protect, or the villains they are duty-bound to battle [emphasis in the original].

Yet, Helfer noted, the demand for continuity with past tradition competed with an equally powerful demand for reinvention:

> This was, after all, 1986—the year that brought readers the most sweeping, comprehensive series of positive changes ever to hit the DC Universe. Beginning in January with the *Green Lantern Corps,* then in mid-year, with *Dark Knight [Returns], Batman Year One, Man of Steel,* all three new *Superman* titles, and last, but not least, the new *Wonder Woman.*

In short, in rejecting the Detroit League's failed experiment in gritty urban diversity in order to embrace the epic scope and Arthurian idealism of the Silver Age League, the new League would nonetheless need to update that tradition to make it relevant for a new era.

Perhaps the most obvious such move was the decision to cut "of America" from the series' title. The original series had debuted at the height of the

Cold War, when presidential candidate John F. Kennedy was warning darkly of a "Missile Gap" with the Soviet Union. In that era of national paranoia, many Americans regarded their nation as preeminently committed to justice on a world scale. The book's title thus hearkened to an America that looked back with pride on the great deeds of World War II and saw racial injustice as a regional issue peculiar to the Deep South. Later developments would call that confidence into question: the village massacres and carpet-bombing campaigns of Vietnam, the racial divide exposed by riots in Los Angeles, Detroit and other urban centers outside the South, the criminal activity that led to a sitting president's near-impeachment and resignation. Through all those years of mounting disillusion with the myth of a Just America, the comic's title stood unchanged. Of course, by the time Giffen and DeMatteis took over in 1987, President Reagan had taken steps to reinvigorate that myth, celebrating "Morning in America" while fulminating about the "Evil Empire" (Rossinow 170, 107). But just six months before the new title's launch, the Reykjavik summit with Gorbachev signaled a shift in Reagan's international policy, foreshadowing an end to the Cold War (Rossinow 230). That seems to have provided DC with the opening it needed to finally ditch the old name, with all its jingoistic, parochial connotations. As Helfer explained,

> We'd immediately decided that the "*of America*" part of the logo had to go. Despite what Ronald Reagan might tell you, these times are somewhat different than the "good old days" when the JLA first hit the scene. Sure, we're still proud of our country, and yes, we still sometimes fear the same foreign influences we did way back then. But this planet is a lot smaller than it used to be. In a world where trans-global communication is an everyday fact of life, where the term "Global Village" is as commonplace as "Chicken McNuggets," the old rules don't apply. So we were no longer dealing with a group of card-carrying Americans here—instead these heroes are citizens of the *world* [emphasis in the original].

Helfer's characterization of the 1960s team as "card-carrying Americans" may strike us as odd, given the mythic or extraterrestrial origins of four of its seven members. His phrasing, though, comments on the breezy confidence with which the original title conflated its heroes' dedication to "Justice" with the ideology "of America."

Giffen's plots and layouts quickly made good on Helfer's promise of a newly international League. Issue #1 (May 1987) saw its heroes defeat a group of terrorists who had taken the UN General Assembly hostage. In the two issues following, the team confronted the problem of weapon stockpiles, tangling with three superpowered antinuclear activists as well as Russia's state-sponsored Red Rocket brigade. Admittedly, issues 4–6 shifted focus away from geopolitics, adding a new hero, Booster Gold, and then helping Dr. Fate deal with the Gray Man, a supernatural menace. But international affairs returned in issue #7 (November 1987): the team defeated a killer satellite and thereby won official recognition from the United Nations. This new status, achieved on the final page, was forecast on the front cover with a new series title, *Justice League International.* A worldwide system of embassies swiftly followed, completing the group's transformation from a nominally American to a genuinely international organization.

Yet, as suggested by Helfer's passing reference to McNuggets, the creative team realized that the "Global Village" of the 1980s was as much a creation of multinational business conglomerates as international treaty organizations. Within the story, the impetus behind the Justice League's change in status came not from its members, but from a shadowy businessman, Maxwell Lord, who managed over the course of the same seven issues to worm his way into a position of authority in the League. Always dressed in a thee-piece suit, and frequently pictured in front of a bank of televisions showing news from around the world, Lord behaved in those early issues like a puppet-master, one of the standard types of comic-book villain. Yet Lord seemed to have the League's interests at heart, working to mend its tattered public image and eventually winning it UN status. Indeed, it's tempting to think that Giffen and Maguire modeled Lord's character on Adrian Veidt, Ozymandias in *Watchmen,* another master-manipulator of global media who sought to save the world by uniting it. In a key visual parallel, Veidt was repeatedly depicted in the last three issues of *Watchmen* standing in front of a bank of televisions. But those issues hit the stands several months after Maxwell Lord's first appearance in *Justice League* #1 (May 1987). Giffen, a longstanding DC regular, may have gotten hold of Alan Moore's notoriously detailed scripts. But it seems at least as likely that Veidt and Lord represent independent developments of a shared anxiety over the growing power of international corporate media to shape global events—an anxiety mixed, oddly, with optimism. For while business interests were coming to dominate world affairs, they promised an end to the militarized nationalism of 19- and 20th-century geopolitics. Just three years after Giffen introduced Maxwell Lord, McDonald's opened its first restaurants in the Soviet Union and mainland China (Times Wire Services, United Press International). Six years after that, Thomas Friedman, noting that no two countries with a McDonald's had ever gone to war, advanced his "Golden Arches Theory of Conflict Prevention." Friedman attributed this phenomenon to the influence of prosperous middle class consumers, not that of McDonald's CEO, but the basic idea is the same: business multinationals spreading international concord.

While Maxwell Lord succeeded handsomely in reversing the League's fortunes in issues 1–7, the performance of the team's heroes was far more mixed. They triumphed over terrorists in issue #1 (May 1987), but the final page revealed that the crisis was all a set-up created by Lord to generate positive publicity for the team. Confronted with an actual challenge in next two issues, the League was first stymied by international law and then daunted by nuclear radiation, and so wound up standing un-heroically on the sidelines. In issue #4 (August 1987) they beat a longtime adversary, the Royal Flush Gang, but once again their victory had Lord's fingerprints all over it, a diversion pushing the League to accept his role in recruiting two new members, Dr. Light and Booster Gold. In issues #5 (September 1987) and #6 (October 1987) the League seemed to be offering crucial support to Dr. Fate in his struggle against the Gray Man. But that conflict was resolved at the start of issue #7 (November 1987) in a manner that suggested the mystic hero had never really needed their aid. And the rest of the issue was taken up with a third trumped-up menace, a deadly satellite deployed by Lord as the *pièce de résistance* in his campaign to win UN recognition. The pointed contrast between the League's fumblings and the successful scheming of its shadowy patron offers a second striking parallel to *Watchmen*: as Veidt said in that series' final issue, "Your schoolboy heroics.... What have they achieved? Failing to prevent Earth's salvation is your only triumph" (Moore 17). Though *Justice League* lacked *Watchmen's* somber tone, anticlimax was a dominant trope in both books.

Giffen thus joined Moore in doubting whether costumed heroes could really address world problems, a lesson hammered home by the fate of the Silver Sorceress, Wandjina, and Blue Jay in issues #2 (June 1987) and #3 (July 1987). A trio of heroes from an alternate timeline ruined by nuclear Armageddon, they arrive on Earth with the laudable aim of destroying the world's nuclear arsenals, one silo at a time. Their quest was a timely one: driven by American defense spending, 1983 had seen superpower tensions rise to nearly unprecedented levels (Rossinow 101). Nuclear war became a cultural touchstone, as witnessed by popular music from a range of genres, from the metal apocalypse of Iron Maiden's "2 Minutes to Midnight" (1984) to the mournful post-apocalypse of Alphaville's "Forever Young" (1984) to Sting's "Russians" (1985), with its ticking clock and half-despairing refrain, "I hope the Russians love their children too." Superman took up the cause of nuclear disarmament in *Superman IV: The Quest for Peace,* a movie which opened in July 1987, about a month after the second issue of *Justice League* hit the stands. Given the size of the movie's publicity campaign, it's hard not to imagine that Giffen's comic wasn't plotted at least in part as a response to Superman's pledge before the UN in the movie's trailer: "Effective immediately, I'm going to rid our planet of all nuclear weapons." Silver Sorceress and her compatriots act even more decisively, showing up at a military base in the fictional third-world nation of "Bialya," and taking unilateral action to destroy its nuclear-tipped missiles. "We've leveled your silo—we're about to destroy your missiles—and if you try to *interfere* ... well, let's just say it won't be pleasant," they proclaim to the astonished soldiers. "We mean you no harm. We are, in fact, here to *help* you, to *save* you—from yourselves" (Giffen et al., "Make War No More," 8–9, emphasis in the original).

Their powers prove equal to the immediate goal of destroying the missiles, but not to the larger aim of saving these soldiers from themselves. For Bialya's crafty dictator, Colonel Rumaan Harjavti greets the trio as heroes and offers his help in selecting their next targets. They know he can't be trusted, but they need an ally in this strange world. Before long, he's sent them off to strip Israel of its nuclear weapons. By the time the Justice League springs into action, the trio is moving on Russia, with predictably disastrous results. The scenario thus expresses a darkly comic insight: that supers are all-too-readily coopted by the powers that be. Frank Miller suggested something similar in his portrait of Superman in *The Dark Knight Returns:* trapped within the ironclad binary of Cold War ideology, the well-meaning idealist became a tool in service to the near-maniacal, war-hungry President Reagan. But Giffen's version offers more than a commentary about comic-book superpowers; it's also a parable about America *as* a superpower. Like any number of U.S. presidents in the second half of the 20th century, his antinuclear heroes blunder into an ill-advised partnership with a glad-handing third-world dictator. And the canny villain employs their might to serve his ends, not theirs. Notably, Giffen plotted this story three years before Saddam Hussein became America's enemy in the first Gulf War. Before that, Hussein was our ally, an ally we armed, an ally who in the 1980s was using those weapons to fight a savage war of his choosing against Iran.

Thus, when heroes' powers prove effective, the heroes are often being used, manipulated in a way that subverts their noble aim. But *Justice League* also liked to focus attention on the physical limits of superpowers, as in issue #3 (July 1987) when news of a nuclear meltdown broke the three-way standoff between the League, the Soviet Rocket Reds, and the Silver Sorceress's antinuclear group. The looming catastrophe, reminiscent of the Chernobyl disaster of April 1986, united the three opposing teams by giving them a shared cause, but to no avail. Turning away from longstanding *Justice League of America* tradition, the heroes didn't find an easy fix, didn't come up with a clever application of someone's little-used power. Instead, for a full page readers watched the assembled heroes give vent to despair: the Silver Sorceress laments "We were supposed to come and save the world, not watch it happen all over again." The Rocket Reds know their armor is useless: "Dimitri—our armor won't protect us, will it?" "Nothing will protect us, Alexei, nothing at all." Mr. Miracle wants to act, but Batman holds him back: "They're like the Firepits on Apokolips! I've got to go in there and—" "Scott—No! Not even *you* could make it out of there alive" (Giffen et al., "Meltdown," 18). There's nothing to be done. And then Silver Sorceress' ally Wandjina, equal parts rage and idealism, hurls the others out of the way and breaks into the containment vessel, presumably in a bid to quell the reactor's excessive heat with his weather powers. Tellingly, Giffen and Maguire don't focus on what Wandjina does to cool the reactor, but instead on the price he pays for taking action: a page later, the hero stumbles back outside, terribly poisoned.

Issue #7 (November 1987) offers a second, less somber instance of the series' effort to impose realistic limits on super-powers. Confronted with the peril of a killer satellite, the Leaguers are forced to hitch a ride into orbit aboard a Star Labs ship that looks suspiciously like a real-life space shuttle—and then pile out of the cargo bay wearing blue Star Labs spacesuits. Attacked by a swarm of miniature missiles, they face great peril, as Beetle notes: "One rip in these suits and we're dead" (Giffen et al. 26). Yet the encounter is more comical than dramatic, a bunch of blue figures flailing their arms about in a desperate effort to maneuver in the vacuum. The episode reads as a rebuke to the cosmic melodrama of *Crisis on Infinite Earths,* the 1985–86 series in which a panoply of DC's greatest heroes fought and conversed on small, presumably airless planetoids. Less than a year later, working with penciller Steve Leialoha, Giffen and DeMatteis repeated the joke in *Justice League International* #15 (July 1988), when Martian Manhunter, Captain Atom and Rocket Red flew up in a different Star Labs ship to face the space fleet of Manga Khan. This time they piled out of the airlock wearing orange suits, only for Atom to realize, "Uh.... J'onn? I just remembered something. If I use my powers, I rupture my suit. and if I rupture my suit—" "You die. Wonderful" (8). Yet the title wasn't entirely consistent in its treatment of the rigors of space. Issue #10 (February 1988), the League's obligatory tie-in with DC's 1988 Millennium crossover series, sent a mixed group of old and new team members into deep space to take on the home base of the evil robotic Manhunters. The assembled group—Martian Manhunter and Captain Atom among them—all fly through space unaided, surviving the vacuum without any special equipment. The episode both begins and ends with the heroes standing about on a tiny, presumably airless planetoid, conversing. Given DC's recurrent penchant for cosmic melodrama, Giffen and Maguire's joke here was a subtle one, enacting one of its silliest tropes with a straight face.

This analysis poses three interrelated questions: Why did Giffen and his fellow creators expose and mock the silly contrivances of comic book tradition? If their aim was to eliminate contrivance, didn't they worry that their embrace of realism wound up undercutting heroism—and even tipping the story over into bathos and bickering? In short, how could they quietly encourage readers to deplore the cosmic melodrama of *Crisis on Infinite Earths* while at the same time peddling a far more explicit brand of silliness, one where heroes banter while flailing around in borrowed space-suits?

It all comes down to "the blue big blue schoolboy"—not Superman, but the savage critique of that character in the fourth issue of *The Dark Knight Returns* (34). Miller's scorn for the pieties of superhero comics can be seen as tapping into the cynical mood of the mid–80s. After all, even though Reagan and his allies trumpeted national pride and traditional morality, to many observers "Morning in America" was a highly produced TV commercial, not a lived reality. In this reading, Miller was criticizing the "schoolboy" for being gullible, for pledging faith in "Truth, Justice and the American Way." By questioning both Superman's patriotic idealism and Batman's old program of incarceration and rehabilitation, Miller tore down and reinvented the superhero for an America riven by culture war, its cities blighted by crime, yes, but also by the endless debate of talking heads on television. The medium had become the message.

Giffen responded to Miller's critique of heroism in the media age by making news coverage a running theme in *Justice League,* a debt he signaled by appropriating Miller's distinctive way of rendering television in the medium of a comic book.[1] The first and fourth issues found the heroes besieged within their headquarters, a cordon of journalists lined up around the compound. In the second issue, Blue Beetle turned from the League's monitor station to give an alarming update: not an earthquake or an alien invasion, but news that a particularly aggressive journalist, Jack Ryder, was targeting the League. Likely modeled on Geraldo Rivera, Giffen's characterization of Ryder presented the League's heroes with a challenge that, like the nuclear meltdown of issue #3 (July 1987), could not simply be punched into submission. Of these two threats to the possibility of heroism, the journalist was by far the more fundamental: for whereas the meltdown offered an opportunity for genuine self-sacrifice, media coverage occasioned merely the appearance thereof—as in issue #7 (November 1987) when Mr. Miracle appeared to brave death when he entered the beam of a "killer satellite" that (he realized) was actually a device used to train warriors on New Genesis and would not harm him. What's worse, most of the new League's members were motivated at least in part by the desire for fame. Mr. Miracle came from a background in show business, and he turned up at headquarters in issue #1 (May 1987) with Oberon, his manager, standing beside him. Something of a huckster, Oberon gleefully assured Miracle that League membership would be a great career move: "Ah, Scott, m'boy—never fear! When word of this gets out, your box office receipts will skyrocket!" (Giffen et al. 3). Blue Beetle showed a similar outlook: "What's wrong with a turn in the spotlight? A little Blue-Beetle-Mania?" (3). Only the Martian Manhunter had the wisdom to know that good press cannot create genuine heroes—and the painful experience to report that bad press can destroy them: the journalists waiting outside "are wolves, waiting to consume us. To them, we're novelties—sideshow freaks—viewed with amusement one moment, reviled the next" (4). Manhunter's cynicism stood in marked contrast with the idealism of the team's youngest member, Captain Marvel. Described in issue #5 (September 1987) as "a fifteen-year-old kid in a super-human body" (Giffen et al. 17), Giffen and DeMatteis' reinvention of Captain Marvel brilliantly literalized Miller's satirical critique of Superman: Marvel didn't just believe in the "schoolboy" morality of classic comic books, he really *was* a schoolboy.

But the energy of Miller's rejection of superheroic idealism drew from something much closer to the vital heart of the genre than the cynical zeitgeist of the 1980s. Superman and Captain Marvel weren't despised just because their morality was out of date, but more fundamentally because these Golden Age characters tied the genre to a past that both fans and creators were eager to outgrow. By the 1980s, comics had become a niche market, with an increasing fraction of readers purchasing their books from specialty stores. Aware of the higher status of comics in Japan and Europe, these dedicated fans longed to escape the opprobrium of reading children's fare. They perceived the Comics Code not merely as an outdated restriction on artistic freedom, but as the principal obstacle preventing the emergence of an adult comics market in America. In point of fact, as detailed by historian David Hajdu, comics of all stripes—Superman and Wonder Woman included—faced attack in the decades leading up to the 1954 Senate hearings that resulted in the comics code (80–81). However, the narrative circulating in the 80s and 90s gave particular prominence to those hearings, to their assumption that comics were a medium for children, and to the pointed questioning endured by EC's Bill Gaines. This led Frank Miller to suggest, in the letters column of *A Dame to Kill For*, that the publishers of superhero comics had crafted the Code not only out of "utter cowardice" but in a "cynical effort to put William Gaines, the best publisher in comics history, out of business." According to the logic of this Cain-and-Abel story, not only were "adult" comics necessarily violent, noir-themed affairs, but superhero comics—with their saccharine morality— had murdered their adult kin.

Of course, not everyone agreed with Miller's recipe for producing adult comics by stirring in equal parts cynicism and violence. But even Scott McCloud, creator of the sweetly sentimental teenage love story *Zot!*, chose to characterize the superhero tradition as a trap to be escaped, whether through outright defiance or parodic subversion: "I'm not one of these 'stamp out super-heroes and only read *American Splendor*' types. After all, I got started on super-heroes myself. It's true! I'm a fanboy! Put on the cuffs! There's no denying it now. But, at least I'm smart enough to see how the super-hero *formula* has us artists by the short hairs." In the hope of exorcising this demon, McCloud created *Destroy!!*, a 31-page, jumbo-size comic marketed as "The Loudest Comic Book in the Universe!!," featuring 29 pages of non-stop, pulse-pounding action as two beefy heroes duked it out over a girl, laying waste to New York City in the process. Thus, strikingly, although McCloud's work shared almost nothing in common with the grim tone of Miller and Moore, his *Destroy!!* is in one key sense identical to both *The Dark Knight Returns* and *Watchmen:* it wrestles with the tropes of the superhero tradition in an effort to (yes) *destroy* them. As McCloud himself put it in the Author's Note to the book, "By blowing the works in *Destroy!!* I hope to do just that: get it out of my system, and maybe encourage others to do the same. Now that it's done, I plan to get back out there as soon as possible and do some *real* comics (y'know, with *real* people, *real* stories…)" (emphasis in original).

McCloud's phrasing suggests the challenge that DC faced in capitalizing on the positive fan response to Miller's and Moore's books in 1986–87. On the one hand, their success suggested not only a taste for adult-themed comics, but a willingness on the part of readers to pay premium prices ($2.95 an issue for *DKR* and $1.50 for *Watchmen,* at a time when ordinary comics were just 75¢) for advertisement-free comics printed with premium inks on high-quality paper. On the other hand, while "Blowing the works" was undoubtedly an attractive solution for independent creators like Miller and McCloud, it was hardly workable for DC, with its wealth of legacy properties.

Seen in this context, Giffen and DeMatteis's gritty, humorous, and sometimes grim *Justice League* offered an ingenious solution: embracing the silliness of the superhero tradition while at the same time mocking and subverting it. Whereas Moore and Miller both used "schoolboy" to label what they were working to eliminate, *Justice League* wore the schoolboy label proudly. Captain Marvel was only the most obvious of the team's juveniles. Guy Gardner sauntered around like a schoolyard bully. Blue Beetle and Booster Gold played the role of class clowns, leaving the long-suffering Martian Manhunter in the role of the put-upon, overworked teacher. This dynamic is perhaps best captured in issues 5–6. The cover of issue #5 (September 1987) promised readers the "showdown" between Batman and Guy Gardner that everyone had been eagerly anticipating since issue #1 (May 1987). But the fight lasted only from the bottom panel of one page to the top panel of the next—a brilliant and hilarious anticlimax: "One punch! One punch!!" laughed Beetle (Giffen et al. 14). The episode drew on and subverted one of the sillier comic book traditions, when two heroes fight. Such combats are often motivated far more poorly than Batman's decision to put an end to Guy's preening arrogance. For fights like these generally have less to do with character development than fan service. Whether justified by reference to interpersonal conflict, a misunderstanding between new acquaintances, or a villain's psychic possession, the fight allows readers to answer the burning question, "Who would win if…?" Notably, Giffen refused not only to gratify readers' desire to witness a knock-down, drag-out fight, but even to answer that crucial (but silly) question. For Guy, goaded by Batman and filled with braggadocio, took off his power ring in the interest of making it a "fair fight," thus making the fight *unfair* by the standards of the superhero showdown.

But the following issue featured another superpowered fight, this one carried out precisely in accordance with tradition. The cover forecast the exciting conflict, depicting Captain Marvel, eyes glowing eerily red, about to crush the Martian Manhunter beneath a great rock: "Possessed by the Power of the Gray Man!" And the book did not disappoint: the fight began on page 7 with a villainous speech by the possessed hero, and ran for four pages, with the Manhunter taking the lead role against Marvel while his teammates scrambled to find the elusive Gray Man. As for the crucial question, the final page of the fight suggested Marvel would have won if the Gray Man's psychic grasp hadn't slipped, allowing the Manhunter to deliver a devastating upper-cut.

Yet even as the issue acceded to the demand for a knock-down drag-out combat between two of the team's heroes, it also offered a subtle commentary on that tradition. For not only did the fight between Captain Marvel and the Manhunter enact that trope on the heels of an issue that subverted it, but, what's more, the fight was an extended homage to Scott McCloud's *Destroy!!*

page 9, panels 1–4: Manhunter flies up swiftly from behind the rampaging Captain Marvel, but Marvel knocks him back a long ways.	pages 5–9: Captain Maximum runs up swiftly behind the rampaging Red Basher, but Basher knocks him back 60 city blocks (Cap's flight backward runs three pages).
page 9, panels 5–6: Captain Marvel flies over to the Martian Manhunter, but Manhunter picks up a giant pointed rock and bats him away like a baseball player swatting an easy pitch	page 12: Captain Maximum flies over to where the Red Basher is standing, holding the pointed tip of the Chrysler Building, but Basher bats him into New York Harbor like a baseball player swatting an easy pitch.
page 12, panels 1–4: Captain Marvel, having beaten Manhunter into submission, suddenly recovers his sanity, only for Manhunter to level him with a final devastating punch.	pages 26–27: Red Basher, having punched Captain Maximum all the way to the moon, recovers his sanity and gives himself up to the police, saying "I'll come quietly now," only for Cap to leap all the way back to earth, pounding from above Red with meteoric force.

In this side-by-side comparison, *Destroy!!* comes off as by far the funnier and more extreme combat, filling up more pages with far more destructive action. Even as Giffen and Maguire worked to recapitulate McCloud's epic battle, they set it in a sleepy Vermont town and, in keeping with that reduced scale, substituted a blow knocking Manhunter perhaps 60 feet for a blow knocking Captain Maximum some 60 blocks—and a 15-foot pointed boulder for a 15-story fragment from the top of the Chrysler Building. This reduction in scale and the loss of specificity can be read as a sly reference to the editorial limitations imposed on Giffen and Maguire. By contrast to McCloud, who published through the independent press Eclipse, they could not afford to destroy New York City. But it also suggests the fun to be had with smaller acts of destruction: why blow the works and bid farewell to the comics of your youth when you can keep coming back, month after month, having fun? Rather than asserting their maturity by denying the pleasures of childhood, Giffen and his compatriots proposed that readers revel in childish pleasures even as they knowingly laugh at their folly in doing so.

Or, perhaps more accurately, Giffen and company offered the possibility of knowing self-laughter but didn't insist upon it. Reading through the letters page of the first ten issues, it's hard not to be struck by the range of responses from readers. In a letter published in issue #6 (October 1987), Tim Downey looked forward to the "big brawl" he could see coming between Batman and Guy Gardner. Perhaps half-worried that Downey had been disappointed by the results, which had by that time run in issue #5 (September 1987), editor Helfer responded teasingly,

> Gee, Tim—you were right about that brawl between Guy and Batman—bud did ya think it'd turn out the way it did? We originally planned for a big, multi-page, slam-bang, knock-down, drag-out fight between the two—but once Keith sat down to plot it out, he realized that there could have been only *one* way to handle the fight. After all, Bats is one of the few heroes without any super power, so, on a purely *human* level he is without equal. But we bet we had you goin' there, right?

Perhaps Helfer needn't have worried; in issue 9 he was able to print three letters praising the creative team's handling of the showdown between Batman and Guy. Of these, Stephen Kinsey's is particularly striking, in that he anticipates my analysis of the fight as upending a comic-book cliché:

> Every time you turn around, it's this hero against that one, or this team versus that group.... With that said, let me say that I thoroughly enjoyed *Justice League* #5, where Batman had it out with Guy Gardner. This fight was not what one would normally expect to see in a comic book. It was not one of those fights that took up the bulk of the story. It was over before it really got started.... One punch was all that was needed to remedy the impending confrontation. Loved it.

But while no one appears to have complained about that fight, in a letter published in issue 10 Chris Garcia wrote in praise of the more traditional dust-up between Captain Marvel and the Martian Manhunter. This is to suggest that as one of DC's headline titles *Justice League* drew a broad readership and had to cater to a wide range of tastes. Some, like Frank Milos (issue #6 [October 1987]), were dyed-in-the-wool Marvel Comics fans converted to DC by *Crisis on Infinite Earths*. Others, like Mike Christiansen (issue #5 [September 1987]), wanted a return to "the simple and pure camaraderie of the early League." Some, like Doug Stanley (issue #7 [November 1987]), complained that Guy Gardner's personality made him unfit for League membership, while Mike Downey (cited above, issue #6 [October 1987]) singled out

Guy as his favorite: "he is consistently amusing and just plain cool"—an assessment that toes the line between appreciating Guy as a source of comedy and admiring him as a tough guy. Overall, most readers appreciated the title's humorous treatment of superheroes, but that didn't mean there weren't hold-outs, like John Andrew Lay (issue 10), who complained that "every hero (with the exceptions of the Batman and the Martian Manhunter) seem to act like petulant nine-year-olds." Only a few readers seemed to perceive how humor functioned in the title to lighten grim realism: "Too many comics nowadays ... are beginning more and more depressing each month. *Justice League* has shown itself able to deal w serious topics such as terrorism and nuclear disaster and yet provide enough comic relief so that it doesn't become bogged down." In short, some readers were there for the tradition, others for the knowing subversion of tradition.

The Giffen-DeMatteis *Justice League* was more than a parody; it offered a gentle satire *of the practice of reading comics.* Rather than insisting on "adult-only" themes, *Justice League* invited adult and juvenile readers alike to enjoy superheroes in all their goofy folly. Writing in the *Boston Globe* in 1989, in the wake of Tim Burton's *Batman,* Jay Carr commented on the cultural impact of Miller's and Moore's work:

> There's something picturesquely despairing about them all. These graphic novels are the late-20th-century equivalent of the 19th century's gothic novels, expressions of existential dread. Like *The Dark Knight Returns, Watchmen* no longer can quite believe in its heroes, or even in the cities in which they operate. Neither is in a class with the Holocaust-themed graphic novel that rendered the genre respectable, Art Spiegelman's *Maus,* but *Batman* will move this new noir form from specialty stores to mainstream acceptance. It may not be a great time for costumed heroes, but it is for comic books about their discomforts.

It seemed comics had finally grown up, and in so doing they had at last found a national audience of serious readers. Giffen's *Justice League,* by contrast, was only a success in specialty stores, failing to achieve anything like the national prominence of those other titles. Yet it offers a compelling alternative vision as to what a "grown up" comic might look like: one that engages with contemporary social and political issues, comments ironically on the capacity of superpowers, and yet responds not in bitterness but in laughter.

NOTE

1. I credit Giffen rather than penciller Maguire because Giffen was responsible for page layouts; issue 1, pp. 18 and 25; issue 2, pp. 2 and 13; issue 7, p. 28.

WORKS CITED

Carr, Jay. "Holy Batgeist, Readers!" *Boston Globe* (pre–1997 Fulltext): 33. 23 June 1989. ProQuest. Web. 29 April 2016.
Friedman, Thomas L. "Big Mac I." *New York Times* 8 December 1996, E15. Print.
Giffen, Keith. "Introduction." *Justice League International Vol. 1.* New York: DC Comics, 2008, 5–6. Print.

Giffen, Keith (w), J.M. DeMatteis (w), Steve Leialoha (p), and Al Gordon (i). "Gnort and South!" *Justice League International* 15 (July 1988). New York: DC Comics, 1–22. Print.
Giffen, Keith (w), J.M. DeMatteis (w), Kevin Maguire (p), and Terry Austin (i). "Born Again." *Justice League* 1 (May 1987). New York: DC Comics, 1–25. Print.
Giffen, Keith (w), J.M. DeMatteis (w), Kevin Maguire (p), and Al Gordon (i). "Make War No More." *Justice League* 2 (June 1987). New York: DC Comics, 1–22. Print.
_____. "Meltdown." *Justice League* 3 (July 1987). New York: DC Comics, 1–22. Print.
_____. "Gray Life Gray Dreams." *Justice League* 5 (September 1987). New York: DC Comics, 1–22. Print.
_____. "Justice League.... International." *Justice League International* 7 (November 1987). New York: DC Comics, 1–38. Print.
_____. "Soul of the Machine." *Justice League International* 10 (February 1988). New York: DC Comics, 1–17. Print.
Hajdu, David. *The Ten-Cent Plague: The Great Comic-Book Scare and How It Changed America.* New York: Farrar, Straus and Giroux, 2008.
Helfer, Andy. "Justice League [Letters Column]." *Justice League* 2 (June 1987): n. pag. Print.
McCloud, Scott. *Destroy!!* New York: Eclipse Comics, 1986.
Miller, Frank. "Batman: The Dark Knight Falls." *[The Dark Knight Returns 4]* (1986). Print.
_____. "Blam! [Letters Column]." *A Dame to Kill For* 3 (February 1994). Print.
Moore, Alan. *Watchmen* 12 (October 1987). Print.
Rossinow, Douglas. *The Reagan Era: A History of the 1980s.* New York: Columbia University Press, 2015. Print.
Times Wire Services. "'Beeg Maks' Win Big 'Da' in Moscow Debut." *Los Angeles Times* 31 January 1990, P1. Print.
United Press International. "China's 1st Big Mac Attack—Diners Crave 'Pork Buns.'" *Los Angeles Times* 8 October 1990, P3. Print.

"I'm Batman! Bwah ha ha!"

Comedy in the Grim 'n' Gritty Eighties

BRIAN COGAN

While the Justice League of America has had numerous versions of the classic team (with new ones to follow after the recent *Convergence* and upcoming *Rebirth* reboot), one thing has usually stayed the same and that is a sense that the Justice League as a team was the best hope of both America and the world. No matter what threats lay ahead, the combined powers of (usually) Superman, Batman, the Flash, Wonder Woman and Green Lantern (and other heavy hitters) would be there to save us all from cosmic menaces and homegrown super-villains.

But what if sometimes the world needed was not to be saved, but just a little levity? In the 1980s, J.M. DeMatteis and Keith Giffen, along with artist Kevin McGuire, reinvented the Justice League not only as an international organization (the JLI)[1] but also brought to the franchise a sense of usually subtle but sometimes verging on slapstick comedy that was a cross between the Three Stooges and Abbot and Costello, with Booster Gold and Ted Kord, the Blue Beetle serving up the majority of the chunks of silliness. However, while the JLI *was* silly, the real changes that DeMatteis and Giffen made was to bring back a sense of the everyday and the mundane that had been lost over the years. In treating the Justice League members not as cosmic gods (even if that was an apt description for a few of them), but as ordinary human brings, reminiscent of the early days of the Fantastic Four or Spider-man, DeMatteis and Giffen created the perfect antidote to the new "serious" and dark characters that dominated comics in the 80s and 90s. DeMatteis and Giffen did not simply make the League comic; they made them human again, with equal proportions of light and dark in an increasingly dark industry.

From Justice League America to Justice League International: A New Direction

Lets face it, the late 80s and early 90s, while being one of the most innovative patches in comic book history, also took well known comic book characters in increasingly dark directions. Frank Miller's *Dark Knight* and the new wave of British authors that flocked to DC's Vertigo imprint (Alan Moore, Neil Gaiman, Grant Morrison and Jamie Delano, to name a few) brought a new sense of maturity as well as horror and fantasy infused stories that were darker than anything most fans had seen before. Many mainstream books followed suit, but there was one prominent exception, the Justice League of America. As Mathew Pustz wrote,

> in the mid eighties, DC transformed its long-running Justice League of America into a lighthearted super team comic. Fans were divided about whether the comic was an appropriate place for humor, but the series provided readers with an alternative to the always serious, constantly universe shaking adventures of teams such as Avengers, X-Men and Teen Titans [218].

This was largely because in 1987, the new creative director, Keith Giffen, decided to shake up the status quo and change the direction of the JLA. Because Giffen "felt uncertain about his dialogue, he brought in J. M. DeMatteis on Dialogue" (Darius). Giffen and DeMatteis were in some ways doing exactly what Frank Miller and the British wave were doing, upsetting the status quo and changing the direction of a moribund industry. But, while the others writers were going darker, Giffen and DeMatteis decided to keep some darker elements, but also add a lighter, often comic touch. As Julian Darius wrote:

> Giffen decided to make the series different by infusing it with comedy. In 1987, this was a fairly radical step: revisionism was going mainstream and super-heroes were becoming darker and more realistic. This was especially true of the rebooted versions of Superman, Batman and Flash. Marvel was no exception, among it most popular characters were Wolverine and the Punisher, both arguably psychotic and certainly murderous. Comedy titles didn't succeed anymore in American super-hero comics. Yet Giffen was allowed to succeed and the resulting series would make the justice league one of DC's most popular titles.

As the new status quo was "darker" and "more realistic" there were already fans, and many within DC, that did not approve of the new direction. To many, the idea of comic books not being "gritty" in the post-mid–80s grit boom (Miller, Moore, etc.) doomed comics to be just a source of comic relief or escapism.

But, while the Justice League was meant to be funny, it was not meant to *just* be funny. There were still cosmic adventures and deadly threats to the team. As Chris Sims noted, "While JLI was a book with a lot of very funny, very memorable parts, comedy was not really the main focus of the series. Or at least it wasn't the focus at the expense of anything else." Despite the comic touches, there was a lot more going on at JLI then simply changing the book's tone.

As Sims goes on to explain, JLI was "balanced" in that it had

> all the super heroic action, drama and melodrama that marked every other great superhero comic of that era, it just also wasn't afraid to be funny while it was at it. And in the mid–80s, when comics were increasingly being defined by darker storylines, when DC had just redefined their universe with a series where Superman was crying in anguish on the cover while holding the dead body of his cousin made JLI stick out even more.

Just by virtue of not having a major tragedy every issues, JLI stood apart from its contemporaries.

The JLI (along with Justice League Europe, its sister book; for the sake of brevity I will refer to both as JLI from now on) was defined by the balance of sometimes slapstick comedy, along with genuine world shaping events. Characters were not designed to be comic relief, but to be analogous to real life, where both comedy and tragedy were potential in any give week. As Chris Sims wrote, "the groundwork is laid through comedy and character work, so that when the action starts, it hits harder."

As compared to other bickering superhero teams such as the classic Fantastic Four and the X-Men, Sims notes,

> Giffen and DeMatteis' scripts were different. If only because they had an ear for dialogue that made their characters seem slightly more real than most comic book heroes at the time. Extremely quippy and caught up in bizarre situations, sure, but in the real way that characters in sitcoms and movies (you know, people who *aren't* superheroes) sound real. They were vain, petty, grumpy, and most of all, they were extremely sarcastic. It gave them a level of relatable authenticity that nobody had ever really had in a superhero comics before that.

The writing was surprisingly mature, despite the light hand and this help to counter-balance the sometimes-darker elements of the new storylines. A particularly telling aspect of this came in the second reboot of the JLI in 2005's *I Can't Believe It's Not the Justice League.* After a reconstituted league frees Ice from (a version of) Hell, they are forced to walk back out without looking back to see if Ice is still following behind them in a nod to the myth of Orpheus. After a wrenching five-panel sequence where Guy Gardener and Fire walk in front of Ice looking anxious, the next page reveals in the first panel Fire's eye darting to look backwards. Ice smiles sadly, saying, "Beatriz, you always *did* care too much." As Ice smiles she fades away, leading to a dramatic final full page of Fire and Guy Gardener hugging while crying inconsolably (Giffen and DeMatteis, 2005). In an interview years later, DeMatteis argued that this was part of the appeal of the JLI that "we would set up gag, after gag, but then hit the readers with something very powerful and very emotionally real. I thought that was a wonderful sequence and that Kevin Maguire drew it so beautifully too." Chiming in, Keith Giffen added that "we used to call it 'being punched in the stomach while you're laughing" (Santori-Griffith). This was the tone that set the JLI team apart from its contemporaries, that the tone, like real life, could change at a moment's notice. As an online comic book collective pointed out,

> So much has been written about the JLI era, with numerous retrospectives focusing on the "bwah ha ha" aspect of the book, that its essay to forget that humour was only one of the components in the book's success rather than the driving force. It's true that many of the characters in the book laughed, joked and played pranks, but this didn't mean that times of sadness and darkness did not enter their lives. Indeed, the gravity of such situations is even more profound because the reader sees the effect ion characters they have come to know and love [The BGCP Team, "JLI Retrospective: Death and Remembrance"].

Overall, and somewhat surprisingly, JLI could be compared not as much to Avengers or X-Men at the time, but instead could be seen as a super-heroic version of *Cheers* or even yet-to-be-born-sitcoms such as *Seinfeld*. "In many ways the book read like a sitcom, particularly as the personality traits of the characters became more established and Giffen and DeMatteis settled into a seemingly effortless rhythm" (The BGCP Team, "JLI Retrospective, J.M. DeMatteis Interview"). This rhythm was aided by the fact that before they had even started, Giffen and DeMatteis were prevented from using most the characters that fans regarded as the heart and soul of the Justice League. Instead, like all good comic writers, they would be forced to improvise.

Bring on the Second Tier Characters! Blue Beetle, Booster Gold, Fire and Ice and Guy Gardner

However, even though Giffen and DeMatteis were charged with creating a "back to basics" book, they found that other editors and authors were not as keen on having big names such as Hal Jordan and other major superheroes be involved and Andy Hefer, editor of JLI as well as Green Lantern, "suggested using Guy Gardener because he was a newer character" (Darius). While the original team initially had familiar characters such as Batman, Doctor Fate and even Captain Marvel for a few issues, for the most part, the team was anchored by the buddy duo of Blue Beetle and Booster Gold. The Blue Beetle (Ted Kord), who was actually yet another iteration of the original Blue Beetle concept this version created in 1957 (Goulart 56), was one of the Charlton Comics' characters that DC comics acquired in the mid–80s. After rebuffing attempts for acclaimed author Alan Moore to include them in his seminal

Watchmen series (Moore instead created thinly veiled characters analogous to the original Charlton comics characters, in Blue Beetle's case, Nite Owl), DC had several new characters but no place to put them. Giffen took Beetle and within a few issues paired him with Booster Gold for a long lasting comedy team that continues to this very day (despite Beetle being killed and brought back after several changes in continuity) in the new series *Justice League 3001*. As J.M. DeMatteis noted, "we could have put these two characters together and it would have become evident really quickly that they had no chemistry. We would have had to spin them off with different characters. But something happened with the two of them" (Santori-Griffith).

Booster's avarice, Beetle's quick witted rejoinders and Guy Gardeners relentless sarcasm and short fuse defined the book, especially in the early days and in some issues, it appear that the team would never actually getting around to doing anything "super." As Chris Sims wrote, "For every battle with a powerhouse like Despero or The Grey Man, there were get rich quick schemes from Beetle and Booster, or stories that focusing on the trials and tribulations of super heroics on the heroes personal lives." Along with turning Booster and Beetle into comic relief, Giffen and DeMatteis also tweaked other characters. Guy Gardner became an arrogant jerk, analogous to a Sylvester Stallone movie character, and also memorably introducing Maxwell Lord as a potentially egomaniacal global tycoon Giffen's Justice League was in some ways a more comedic version of the original Fantastic Four, with internal squabbles played for laughs instead of the realism of living in close quarters with fellow team mates.

While Beetle and Booster were a team, it was a daring choice to even bring in Booster Gold in the first place. Booster was not a contemporary comics hero, but came from the future due to a desire to "participate in what was remembered as the classic age of super-heroes, exploiting his knowledge to become rich and famous" (Darius). While previously other wealthy characters, Batman for example, were shown to selflessly use their wealth to fight crime, Booster Gold was instead "a character" whose very conception is based around materialism and opportunism" (Darius). Booster and Beetle when not providing comic relief, were busy creating plot twists and complications, even memorably starting their own resort casino on Kooey Kooey Kooey in *Justice League International* #33 (December 1989).

In many ways, the JLI could be looked upon as a way of rewarding long term fans, by elevating some of the best fan-favorite second tier characters, and giving them witty and realistic dialogue. Giffen and DeMatteis were telling fans that they respected the fan's dedication to the second tier characters and in a sense, the fans' own quirks and idiosyncrasies. In *Justice League International* #46 (January 1991), Guy Gardner is seen attending a comic book convention to buy a thinly disguised (General Glory) issue of *Captain*

America #1. As Mathew Pustz noted, his dialogue indicated at first contempt for the hardcore fans, but he later softens and says to himself, "Y'know, now that I think of it, maybe they ain't geeks. Maybe their as good a bunch of eggs as yer ever gonna find! In fact, I'd rather be hanging around with this bunch than those jerks in the League any day!" (153).

But even as the team was starting, many fans remained skeptical, not just because of the new creative team, but because the supposed rigidity of genre in comic books. It's not as though comic books had never been light or even silly, most of DC's 50s and 60s output leaned towards light-hearted camp, but that once the innovations of the late 60s and early 70s had been codified, humor was not expected as a primary part of the plot. Many works that continued in a comic vein when comic books had become "serious" were labeled as simply "escapist." As Versaci wrote, "Unsurprisingly, creative works that fall under the banner of escapism are regarded with great suspicion by those that like to consider themselves 'well-read' and that "because from this perspective, escapist entertainment is all about 'hiding' from what really matters—namely the real world" (Versaci 3). Because of this, the new humorous direction "caused the opinion of the team to be lessened in the eyes of both the public and former members" (Serchay 1105). While the were some jokes about the team being looked at askance by their fellow superheroes, overall sales were robust and within a few issues, the new JLI was setting itself not just apart from previous incarnations of the Justice League, but also from contemporary mainstream comics in general.

A Ray of Light in a Dark World

Among the many things that set the League apart from other costumed heroes was that the League, and on several occasions the League's villains, realized that sometimes, their adventures were, to put it bluntly, decidedly silly. This is epitomized the famous (infamous to some) repetition of the "bwa ha ha!" laugh, which quickly became a catch phrase of both the comic, and symbolic of the era. The laugh first appear in *Justice League International* #8 (December 1987), and is uttered by Blue Beetle as he is increasingly amused at Booster's lack of success with the beautiful new Paris bureau chief, Catherine Cobert. As the sequence goes, Beetle's laugh gets louder and louder, even appearing a caption on the last panel of a two page spread when Beetle is off panel laughing so loudly Booster can hear him from rooms away. If any phrase to either fans or detractors epitomized the humor of the JLI, it was the parody of a super-villain laugh that became an enduring staple of the Justice League's villains as well as heroes.

As Bradford Wright noted, in the mid–80s after the success of *Watchmen* and *The Dark Knight,* superheroes were becoming more complex and the plots increasingly dark.

> In this cynical era, however, it was the superhero who was the aberration. Superheroes became a force for relentless morality in a corrupt society that hated and despised them. Theirs was a seemingly impossible task that no sane individual would undertake, and indeed, the sanity of superheroes did come into question. Once confidant symbols of hope, superheroes now spoke to the paranoia and psychosis lurking beneath the rosy veneer or Reagan's America [266].

While initially sales had been good and the comic had gained critical acclaim as well as fan support, DC could not help but second-guess the JLI/JLE and Giffen and DeMatties were out as writers after issue #60.

After the League: The Darkness Returns

When major comic book companies decide to change directions, there are techniques both in terms of story telling and in comic book visual that help to indicate to new readers, or returning old ones, that the comic has been rebooted in such a way that it is now less intimidating for people just jumping on. The use of a "swipe" is a common visual method in terms of the front cover design. This is a visual reference where a traditional cover is recreated by the cover artist via a "swipe" which is "copying the basics of an image, changing some details to make it fit new characters to make it fit new characters and situations" (Pustz 144).

Although there had been initial support for changing the Justice League to "light hearted superhero adventures" in the long run not all fans were pleased with the new direction and five years later DC decided to change formats yet again. As Pustz noted, "in response to fans mixed reactions, the editors decided in 1992 to return to the original's more serious traditions. To signal this change, the covers of the April 1992 issues of both *Justice League America* and *Justice League Europe* featured swipes imitating classic covers from the comic's early days" (146). The message was clear that the "fun" JLI had been an experiment, but now the show was over and it was back to dark and gritty. Fun comics had had their turn, now it was time for the tortured near-psychopaths to resume their ascendency, often at the literal expense of the JLI.

It seemed almost two decade later that DC was somewhat embarrassed by the JLI's hijinks. Surely, comics couldn't be taken seriously if people joked and talked to each other as if they were actual people? Soon, in retcon after retcon, DC almost systematically either changed, or killed off many of the major characters that had made JLI so memorable. Blue Beetle was killed by a megalomaniacal Maxwell Lord (who was later killed by Wonder Woman), followed into oblivion by Scott Free, Big Barda and of course, Ralph and Sue

Dibny (who in the acclaimed *Identity Crisis* is shown in a flashback to have been raped before she was eventually killed), which made many fans wonder, as the BGCP authors asked, "Why was DC seemingly intent on erasing them from existence?" (The BGCP Team, "Justice League International").

While the JLI ex-members may have been put on a virtual hit list, the Justice League itself has remained a constant in one iteration or another since the demise of the JLI. After the retcons of Justice League International and Justice League Europe, the Justice League did not always exert quality control (when did it ever?) leading some to believe that since the early 90s departure of Giffen and DeMatties, "JLA has waxed and waned in years since then" (Goulart 214). While there were several best selling runs, including an interesting take by Grant Morrison, in some ways the league seemed to flounder, unsure of what tone to take or even what the core membership should be (thanks to retcons, in the past, present or future). Blue Beetle and many other characters were killed in particularly vindictive ways and despite some other characters designed to be lighter the trend towards darker characters continued. But, as in any reboot, old characters sometimes return (albeit in new formats) and in 2003, the JLI rode again.

The Return(s) of the Justice League International

In 2003, DC announced plans for a mini-series featuring may of the characters from the original JLI case. The first mini-series, *Formerly Known as the Justice League*, reunited key members Booster Gold, Blue Beetle, Guy Gardener, Fire and Ice, along with newcomer Mary Marvel and stalwarts Captain Atom and Fire. The issues, drawn by long time JLI artist Kevin McGuire lacked only Guy Gardener's sharp edge to truly make it the classic Justice League International.

In 2005, most the same team returned again in JLA Classified as *I Can't Believe It's Not the Justice League,* including a heart rending story where the characters journeyed to hell (or, at else a possible version of Hell, one reminiscent of a fast food restaurant) in order to rescue the missing Ice, Guy Gardeners love/hate interest. After the 52 relaunched, members of the classic lineup were again tried out, this time written by Dan Jurgens, but the comic was cancelled after issue number 12 and an annual in August 2012. Since then, Giffen and DeMatteis have collaborated in *Justice League 3000*, which ended in 2015 and was relaunched as *Justice League 3001*, where Booster, Blue Beetle, Fire and Ice (primarily the latter two at this point) have returned as the "Supper Buddies 3000," a variation on the team that Maxwell Lord was trying to restart in *Formerly Known as the Justice League*. While it's unclear (while waiting even more reboots and universe changing events to come) how the new iterations of some of the most beloved icons of the classics JLI will fare, the original books, now released as collections, can still evoke a time period that is not dead (there are numerous great solo and team books that use a bit of the JLI template, most notably Matt Fraction's run on *Hawkeye* over the last few years) but still stands out as a contrast to the mainstream orthodoxy about team books both now and in the present. During the reoccurring ages of the Dark Knight and "women in refrigerators," the comedic, but ultimately more realistic version of the Justice League International demonstrates how in the end, "the JLI brought back some sunshine to the often dark world of super hero comics, just one of the many reasons to cherish it" (The BGCP Team, "Justice League International").

NOTE

1. The book was called *Justice League* for the first six issues of Giffen and DeMatteis' run, the *Justice League International* through issue 25, and re-titled *Justice League America* for issues 26–60.

WORKS CITED

The BGCP Team. "JLI Retrospective: Death and Remembrance." http://bigglasgow comic.com/jli-retrospective-death-and-remembrance/. Accessed February 1, 2016.

The BGCP Team. "JLI Retrospective, J.M. DeMatteis Interview." http://bigglasgow comic.com/jli-retrospective-j-m-dematteis-interview/. Accessed February 1, 2016.

The BGCP Team. "Justice League International: A Retrospective." http://bigglasgow comic.com/justice-league-international-retrospective/. AccessedFebruary 1, 2016.

Darius, Julian. "On the First Year of Keith Giffen and J.M. DeMatteis' Justice League International." Sequential Art. http: Sequart.org/magazine/16465/om-the-first-year. Accessed July 17, 2015/

Giffen, Keith, and J.M. DeMatteis, et al. *I Can't Believe It's Not the Justice League* New York: DC Comics, 2005.

_____. *Justice League International Volume I.* New York: DC Comics, 2008.

_____. *Justice League International Volume II.* New York: DC Comics, 2008.

Goulart, Ron. *Comic Book Encyclopedia* New York: HarperCollins 2004.

Pustz, Mathew. *Comic Book Culture: Fanboys and True Believers* Jackson: University Press of Mississippi, 1999.

Santori-Griffith, Mathew. "Super Buddies: Giffen and DeMatteis on Blue Beetle and Booster Gold." http://www.comicosity.com/super-buddies-giffendematteis-on-blue-beetle-and-booster-gold/. Accessed February 19, 2016.

_____. "Super Buddies: Giffen and DeMatteis on Fire & Ice." http://www.comicosity.com/super-buddies-giffendematteis-on-fire-ice/. Accessed February 29, 2016.

Serchay, David. "Justice League International." In *Comics through Time: A History of Icons, Idols and Ideas, Vol. 3.* Ed. M. Keith Booker. Santa Barbara, CA: Greenwood, 2014.

Sims, Chris. "Ask Chris 227: Does Justice League International Have a Legacy?"

http://comicsalliance.com/ask-chris-227-does-justice-league-international-have-a-legacy/. Accessed December 2, 2015.

Versaci, Rocco *This Book contains Graphic Language: Comics as Literature* New York: Continuum, 2007.

Wright, Bradford C. *Comic Book Nation: The Transformation of Youth Culture in America* Baltimore: John Hopkins Press, 2001.

Lacking Leadership

The Justice League Europe's Place in the DC Universe

Fernando Gabriel Pagnoni Berns *and* Leonardo Acosta Lando

The fall of the 103-mile wall between East and West Germany in November 1989 came with some of the largest geopolitical consequences of any event of the 20th century. The Berlin Wall was a physical icon of the Cold War and its fall redefined the significance of Europe on the global stage and also allowed for the redefinition of a multi-nation union on the continent. But, as hope for a unified Europe encountered difficult political circumstances, it was isolated regional events, such as the crisis on the Balkans, that became the driving force for the integration process of European Union and the period in which the Europeans started talking seriously about defense. The results were quite weak agreements such as the European Security and Defense Policy (Milzow 166) rather than a strong policy. In addition, the European Union's lack of leadership in international affairs raised con-cerns about the EU's ability to consolidate Europe as an "identity project" through economic integration and cohesion. In fact, "during the 1990s the EU seems to have stepped aside almost everywhere in the world, leaving the leadership to the United States" (Menéndez-Alarcón 46).

In this scenario, DC launched its new comic-book series, *Justice League Europe*, a spin-off comic book series that would chronicle the adventures of a "brother" organization to the Justice League of America. The quotation marks around "brother" signal the fact that, more than equal sibling, the European branch was always considered "inferior" to its American counterpart. This situation of inferiority and the scenario of general disorganization that underlined the Justice League Europe replicated in many ways the geopolitical scenario of Europe after 1989.

U.S.-EU Relations

Andrew Moravcsik argues there are a series of commonly accepted historical claims about the relationship between the U.S. and Europe that do not hold up to close examination. First, the author explains, there is the popular idea that in the "good old days" of the Cold War transatlantic relations were good because Europe and America had a common purpose, and they showed great unity because there was a common threat. After the end of the Cold War in 1989, Europe and the United States did not have the same common purpose (203). However, it must be remembered that the Cold War was far from a period of Western agreement with, for example, significant disagreements between the United States and Europe over various programs targeting Russia (204). Another exaggerated claim is that the United States asserted itself unilaterally because Europe lacked unity and common purpose. "The best evidence, according to the conventional view, is the lack of a serious Euro-pean security and defense identity. If it existed, according to this view, then there would be stronger opposition to the United States or at least some coherent alternative" (204). As Philip Gordon and Jeremy Shapiro explain, "the image of a militaristic and unilateralist America and a pacifistic and inward-focused Europe certainly has a measure of truth to it, but it is also a caricature" (5).

However, Moravcsik acknowledges the fact that these unwarranted claims are part of popular wisdom. And what permeates popular culture and constructs cultural artifacts is popular imagination rather than factual truth. Even if the relationships between U.S. and Europe were in fact far more complex than historical narrative acknowledges, it is not that rare that cultural artifacts were constructed around popular wisdom. Products of popular culture such as films, television, music, and comic books illustrate, in part, the cultural climate of an era. Popular culture not only reflects its social context, but shapes it as well. Cultural artifacts, such as comic books, legitimatize popular wisdom.

In terms of European/U.S. relationships, the 1980s saw a number of paradigmatic changes including the Intermediate Nuclear Force crisis of the early 1980s, the rise of Gorbachev, the end of the Cold War and of the Soviet Union, the Gulf War, and the powerful rise of Al-Qaeda. In this decade of fundamental changes, the year of 1989—the same year as the fall of the Berlin Wall—sees the coming of the Justice League Europe featured in a comic book of the same name which ran for 68 issues,[1] the last issue coming out in 1994. Those were not easy years in global relationships: as Federiga Bindi states,

> the first half of the 1990s witnessed a relaunch of the foreign ambitions of the European Community. With the United States, the relationship continued on its ambiguous path. On the one hand, both sides claimed to attach great importance to closer cooperation and to stronger relations; on the other hand, they have been involved in petty disputes, threats, retaliation measures, and counterretaliations [33].

The general climate was that "as the dust settled on the post–Cold War world, the balance swung back again towards convergence between U.S and Europe. But, as the popular wisdom espouses, this trend was reversed as the Clinton era came to an end" (Howorth 13) and a new administration seemed prepared to execute unilateral policies while Europe remained fragmented and timid.

The Justice League Europe

Justice League Europe was a DC Comics book series that was a spin-off of the more comedic *Justice League* series written by Keith Giffen and J.M. DeMatteis. Like Justice League America, *Justice League Europe* featured whimsical humor but was a much more action-centric series. The initial group was composed by some ex-members of the Justice League of America such as Captain Atom, who serves as the leader of the team, and Soviet Rocket Red, together with new members such as Flash, Metamorpho, Animal Man, Power Girl and Elongated Man. The team was originally headquartered in Paris but later moved to a castle in Great Britain.

Like many superhero team titles, stories revolve around superheroic exploits and the group's daily life. The novelty of the Justice League Europe was the incorporation of diplomacy and global politics. The team was led by Captain Atom who, even if American, was the perfect embodiment of Europe's perceived lack of leadership on the world stage at the time. He sees himself as a poor leader to this new incarnation of the Justice League. His main source of anxiety is the fact that he doubts his capacity to face and resolve all the potential problems which will come out from the different personalities of the team members. Captain Atom doubts his capacity to gives the team unity and common purpose during situations of assault and stress. Of course, he was right and by the end of the first issue he is the butt of the joke of almost every member.

This situation resembles the serious problems that Europe had to face through the 1980s and 1990s. Among these problems was the lack of a concrete leadership once the world's geopolitical status evolved past the stalemate of the Cold War. The 1980s presented a scenario in which the Europeans sought to take advantage of the relative freedom from restraint offered by the end of the Cold War to maximize their global role and impact. The main problem was the fact that Europe is a continent, not a country. As such, it involves many wills and subjectivities, languages, cultures, contexts, idiosyncrasies, governments, interests, policies, territories, and borders. There were a lot of identities, but there was no "natural" leader. As a result, Europe had problems defining itself as an economic and political entity but also in reformulating its role within the world.

In the first meeting of the Justice League Europe, a self-doubting, timid Captain Atom is the official chairman. His weak presence as leader is interrupted by Maxwell Lord, the businessman in charge of the Justice League International. Via television screen, he interrupts Captain Atom's disorganized and wandering inaugural speech to give his own welcome to the new JLE. Unlike Captain Atom's, Lord's speech is smooth and concise, right to the point. Even Captain Atom is grateful for the interruption. The scene provides a sharp contrast between the lack of leadership in the JLE and Maxwell Lord, embodying American economic corporatism. The very idea of forming a European branch of the Justice League was Lord's. Thus, the idea of Europe as a geopolitical space existing under the United States' shadow is enhanced.

Both Captain Atom and Europe shared the goal of achieving union from diversity, of defining a common purpose beyond the individual preferences and values of the members. Without a dominant leader or coalition, Europe was at risk of falling apart as just an incoherent amalgam of nations without a common purpose. In *Justice League Europe* #3 (June 1989), some members of the League choose to act without Captain Atom's acknowledgment. Tired of the leader's attitude of sitting and waiting, Power Girl, Flash and Elongated Man go out to investigate a murder. After their furtive mission goes horribly wrong, Power Girl defends her decision against Captain Atom: "If anyone's is to blame, I'd say it's you! Without strong leadership, we have to make our own decisions!" (Giffen, "Another..." 20).

Even in an American comic book, these words are indicative of Europe's complex situation: each country wanted to keep its self-determination but, also, keep Europe growing as a strong-willed continent with clear direction and common purpose, as a model for building and integration. Europe was making its best efforts to overcome the discrepancy between autonomy and coherence. The immediate danger that Europe confronted was some countries doing what Power Girl, Flash and Elongated Man did and acting unilaterally putting whole group in danger.

Dealing with Middle Eastern Countries

Justice League Europe #5 (August 1989) deals with the consequences of an unauthorized mission to Bialya, a fictional country modeled after Lybia. The country is governed by the evil femme fatale Queen Bee, who, together with the criminal Jack O'Lantern,[2] started a campaign to discredit the European branch of the Justice League. Her ultimate goal was twofold: first, carrying out an act of vengeance against the Justice League for past interventions, and second, halting the installation of a Justice League branch in Europe, a fact that would place rogue country Bialya more prominently into the view of global justice.

The story explicitly mirrors the delicate situation of U.S. and Europe in regard Middle Eastern countries. Through the 1980s, the United States disagreed with Europe on a number of foreign policy issues, including the Middle East. The election of President Ronald Reagan, who was decisively against any European initiative regarding Middle Eastern countries, and the Israeli invasion of Lebanon on June 6, 1982, put an end to European activism in the area. Previously, during Jimmy Carter's presidency, when Americans at the U.S. embassy in Tehran were held hostage, the United States immediately responded with an economic boycott and froze Iranian assets in the United States. The EEC (European Economic Community), however, did not support the call for sanctions.

After terrorist attacks at the airports in Vienna and Rome in December 1985, the EEC foreign ministers agreed to intensify their cooperation in several areas linked to security. The United States, however, insisted that Libya should be singled out as responsible for terrorism in Europe. While the divided Europeans were discussing the issue, the United States took action and, informing only the United Kingdom (and using their bases), launched a punitive raid on Libya, an act that was strongly criticized by the rest of the Europeans. Despite the turmoil of the 1970s and 1980s, the early 1990s "witnessed the convening of the Madrid Conference for Peace in the Middle East, in which the United States played a key role. Despite Europe's active political and economic participation in the Madrid process, its role was clearly secondary to that of the United States" (Emara 197).

Furthermore, Operation Desert Storm in the Middle East in 1991 clearly established the supremacy of the U.S on the international arena. In years dominated by the Operation Sand Storm, tensions and disagreements between America and Europe over Middle East issues proliferated (Hadar 112).

In *Justice League Europe* #5 (August 1989), Captain Atom is questioned about his unauthorized excursion into Bialya by Maxwell Lord (and, by extension, the U.S). Captain Atom explicitly acknowledges the division about

America and Europe regarding foreign interventions when he mentions Batman not having to respond for his actions with his team (Giffen and DeMatteis, "Stagg..." 5). Two issues intermingle here: first, the problem of Captain Atom as a weak leader commanding a disorganized group and, second, the proclivity to unilateralism that the United States demonstrated during the Cold War. Captain Atom, now an integral part of European policies, must answer for his team's actions within Middle East. This division is explicitly marked by Captain Atom when speaking to Lord: "The JLE deserves the same operational status as the JLA. We're not some cut-rate copy!" (Giffen and DeMatteis, "Stagg..." 12). But it is clear that the European branch did not have the "exceptionalism" that the established Justice League had.

JLE as a Cut-Rate Copy

The business with Bialya is just an example of how the JLE, in representation of Europe, has to deal with the fact of its inferior condition in respect to established Justice League. For starters, the center of operations is named "Justice League International: European Division Headquarters" so the "international" tag comes first and the European identity is second billed. Second, the group has not vehicles of transit of its own, so them must be taken borrowed from the Justice League (Giffen and Jones, "Conquest"). Furthermore, the image that the individual members of the group are frequently made inferior while serving on the Justice League Europe. The powers of Power Girl are reduced by half while on the team, Wonder Woman has no lasso of truth in her brief tenure as a member, Metamorpho has amnesia, Animal Man has problems controlling his powers and Flash, in this case Wally West, is constantly compared to his uncle, the older and more experienced Barry Allen, a comparison in which the young Wally always loses. Thus, the idea of the Justice League Europe as a copy of inferior quality is sustained.

Perhaps more importantly, the group sorely lacks European members. With exception of Russian Dmitri Pushkin, every other member is American. This issue is not subtly managed, but, rather, it is made central focus of issue #3 (June 1989). Captain Atom meets Charles Villard, a representative from the French government and the meeting ends in a sour note when it is revealed that the chairman of the JLE does not speaks French. This lack of interest in learning native European languages and the lack of European members is taken as a form of offense towards Europe. In a condescending note, Captain Atom points to the fact that "it's not my fault that there are no European super-heroes worth their salt" (Giffen and DeMatteis, "Another...").

The pejorative gaze framing the Justice League Europe is shared also by the perfect American Boy Scout: Superman is called into action by Sue Dibny in *Justice League Europe* #9 (December 1979) to help with some problems involving Power Girl. In the issue Superman thinks, "That group [the JLE] seems to have so many members they need a newsletter just to keep us up to date on their rooster" (Giffen and DeMatteis, "Under…"), an idea that mirrors the real-world political fact that "the EU member states were further shackled by increasing membership, making it difficult to achieve a unified position from within" (Milton-Edwards 179). Superman seems to think that too much many members make things harder at the moment of taking decisions. This derogatory remark is, in fact, unsupported: there are no more members in the JLE than in the Justice League and, leaving aside Wonder Woman (who leaves the team after only one issue), there had not been any substantial changes. It looks as if Superman shares some common beliefs of superiority with America.

Lastly, the Justice League Europe, unlike its American counterpart, was more female-centered. This is not a minor detail. National identity and gender studies intersect reciprocally in many ways. As Yuval-Davis articulates it, "constructed notions of nationhood usually involve specific notions of 'manhood' and 'womanhood'" (1). For example, women are culturally charged with reproducing nation through the education and socializing of children. Even so, there is another way in which countries can be gendered: through the framing of whole countries within the binary category of "masculine" or "feminine." In popular imagery and within an ideological framing, whole countries are gendered as masculine or feminine depending of their values and culture (Russell 66). A country is called masculine or feminine based in supposedly clearly distinct gender roles and the existing stereotypes that sustain them: men are supposed to be assertive, tough, and focused on material success through competition, whereas women are supposed to be more gentile, tender, and concerned with the nurturing of children and caring values. Not surprisingly, and following the gender stereotypes, the feminine countries were considered modest while the masculine countries were assertive. This is not to say that men from feminine countries are effeminate, nor are women from masculine countries masculine. Instead, this dimension deals with how conflict is handled.

Masculine countries tend to dominate and exercise power in traditional terms through military action upon other countries (Soeters 56). In feminine countries, emphasis is placed on cooperation. Still, these categories are mobile and constantly shifting. For example, the U.S. is gendered male because its aggressiveness in regard to internal protectionism and foreign policies, which make it tough and driven. When the terrorist attack of September 11 occurred, the United States was framed as feminine: some journalistic accounts talked about the nation as if it were a raped woman (Lemelle, Jr., 13). Even if nations within Europe, such as the U.K. are "pro-active," Europe, as a continent, can be gendered (especially through the 1980s) as feminine. A "mighty" America versus a "faltering" Europe (Redwood 1).

In which ways are the JLE gendered feminine? First, there is the strong presence of active non-superpowered women within the group. Sue Dibny takes charge of monitoring for the team and also Catherine Cobert is declared leader of the team in issue #21 (December 1990), to the total relief of Captain Atom. Second, the group is gendered thanks to its emphasis in diplomatic relationships. Unlike the Justice League, diplomatic interactions are major plot points in this series. Forms of diplomacy can be gendered as "feminine" (Petersen 23) when compared with more action-centered policies of attack. In fact, the shuffling of Captain Atom in favor of Colbert is a movement in favor of good diplomacy since that was her job within the team to begin with. It can be argued, then, that while the Justice League must be led by an iconically masculine figure such as Batman the European branch needs good diplomats as chairwoman. For example, in issue #26 (May 1991), when the JLE is relocated in England, one of the first measures of the League under Cobert's command will be to increase the diplomatic relations with the country of residence allowing inspector Camus, a man from Scotland Yard to live within the team's headquarters to smooth the communications within police, the U.K. government and the team. Within this framework, America refers to military and economic actions, and Europe (with all its feminized connotations) refers to public diplomacy.

In issue #37 (April 1992), another non-superpowered woman, Sue Dibny, is charged with the conducting the affairs of the JLE. Still, as she is quickly to establish, she is coordinator and liaison, since the team does not have a leader. This way, the team is still gendered and, at the same time, leaderless. In a genre typified by hyper-masculinity, while a female-centered team is a necessary breath of fresh air, there are tropes and stereotypes that would place such an organization as secondary to a more assertive traditionally masculine team, such as the original Justice League.

Dealing with Russia

In the 1980s the Soviet position changed radically, mainly because of Mikhail Gorbachev. In the 1985–86 period, the new Soviet leadership for the first time accepted the enormity of its economic problems and wanted a global solution. Gorbachev called for a policy based on ethical principles to solve global problems rather than on Marxist-Leninist concepts of irreconcilable conflict between capitalism and communism. These policies resulted in a resumption of dialogue between the Americans and the Soviets for first time in many years.

Still, European relations with Russia "have not been easy, with its combination of unstable politics and an economy lacking a sound legal and administrative framework" (Pinder 140). Through the 1980s, the Soviet Union failed to recognize European Integration in any fashion. The uneasy relationship with the Soviets is illustrated in the pages of the *Justice League Europe*. On one hand, there is a Soviet hero within the ranks of the team, Dmitri who is also the only European member. Even so, Russia is depicted as a shadowy country still plotting against America.

Although Russia's integration into the Western world was desirable and inevitable for Gorbachev, the rest of the Soviet leadership still hated and/or feared the idea. Gorbachev's "New Thinking" was applied both in foreign and domestic policy under three programs whose names became household words: *perestroika* (rebuilding), *glasnost* (transparency, openness), and *uskorenie* (acceleration). It is clear that the openness proposed by Gorbachev were not fully accepted. As Lara Piccardo explains, Russian's attitude toward Europe was one of a "bipolar logic." They see contemporary Europe as either a competitor or an enemy, not as a friend (124).

The potential menace of Russia coming back to its "old habits" against democracy and capitalism makes one more last come-back when the JLE books are close to the end of its run. "Red winter" is the last arc before the book closing at issue #50 and revolves around Russia going potentially rogue. The reality is that a supervillain, Sonar, has taken control of the brigade of Rocket Reds, soviet soldiers, and unleashed them upon the world. Russia prefers the no intervention of the Justice League Europe in national business, even when the world is threatened. The series illustrated the reality of a post-communist Russia which was looking for a place within the new global map without losing its own identity.

Conclusions

During the period of the Cold War, the U.S and Europe share a powerful common interest in preventing Communist disorder from infecting the world. After the fall of both the Berlin Wall and Communism, Europe faced an uncertain destiny that depended, on its capacity to overcome differences, find common purposes, and carry on. Unity within difference.

The Justice League Europe illustrated some of these issues in its many arcs. The lack of a clear leadership or leading country plagued the series. From issue 1 to 50, the JLE was conducted by Captain Atom and briefly, by Catherine Cobert, Sue Dibny, and Green Lantern, while the league's headquarters were sited in Paris, England and Vienna. The main goal of the JLE was, from the beginning, the same one that pursued Europe after 1989: union within diversity. Unlike the American counterpart, the JLE and Europe were characterized by the recurring searching to fulfill the motto "Together we win."

NOTES

1. Plus five annuals. It must be noted that starting with issue #51 the title was renamed Justice League International.

2. Jack O'Lantern is also a member of the European team Global Guardians. Though that team is composed by superheroes, O'Lantern has gone rogue.

WORKS CITED

Bindi, Federiga. "European Union Foreign Policy: A Historical Overview." In *The Foreign Policy of the European Union: Assessing Europe's Role in the World*. Ed. Federiga Bindi and Irina Angelescu. Washington, D.C.: Brookings Institution Press, 2012, 13–40.

Emara, Khalid. "Is Sarkozy's Union for the Mediterranean Going to Work?" In *The Foreign Policy of the European Union: Assessing Europe's Role in the World*. Ed. Federiga Bindi and Irina Angelescu. Washington, D.C.: Brookings Institution Press, 2012, 197–200.

Giffen, Keith, J.M DeMatteis (w, s), and Bart Sears (a). "Another Fine Mess." *Justice League Europe* #3 (June 1989). New York: DC Comics.

_____. "How Ya Gonna Keep 'Em Down on the Farm After They've Seen Paree." *Justice League Europe* #1 (April 1989). New York: DC Comics.

_____. "Stagg Party!" *Justice League Europe* #5 (August 1989). New York: DC Comics.

Giffen, Keith, Gerard Jones (w, s), and Marshall Rogers (a). "Catnap." *Justice League Europe* # 22 (January 1991). New York: DC Comics.

Giffen, Keith, Gerard Jones (w, s), Bart Sears (a). "Conquest." *Justice League Europe* # 16, July 1990. New York: DC Comics, 1990.

Giffen, Keith, Bill Loebs (w, s), and Art Nichols (a). "Under the Skin." *Justice League Europe* #9 (December 1989). New York: DC Comics.

_____. "Kings of the Dust." *Justice League Europe* #15 (June 1990). New York: DC Comics.

Gordon, Philip, and Jeremy Shapiro. *Allies at War: America, Europe, and the Crisis Over Iraq*. New York: McGraw-Hill, 2004. Ebook.

Hadar, Leon. *Sandstorm: Policy Failure in the Middle East*. New York: Palgrave Macmillan, 2005.

Howorth, Jolyon. "Foreign and Defence Policy Cooperation." In *Europe, America, Bush: Transatlantic Relations in the Twenty-First Century*. Ed. John Peterson and Mark A. Pollack. New York: Routledge, 2003, 13–28.

Jones, Gerard (w), and Ron Randall (a). "Red Winter Part 1: A Wind from the East." *Justice League Europe* #45 (December 1992). New York: DC Comics.

Lemelle, Anthony, Jr. *Black Masculinity and Sexual Politics*. New York: Routledge, 2010.

Leonardi, Robert. *Cohesion Policy in the European Union: The Building of Europe*. New York: Palgrave Macmillan, 2005.

Menéndez Alarcón, Antonio. *The Cultural Realm of European Integration: Social Rep-*

resentations in France, Spain and the United Kingdom. Westport, CT: Greenwood, 2004.

Milton-Edwards, Beverly. *The Israeli-Palestinian Conflict: A People's War*. New York: Routledge, 2005.

Milzow, Katrin. *National Interests and European Integration: Discourse and Politics of Blair, Chirac, and Schroder*. New York: Palgrave Macmillan, 2012.

Moravcsik, Andrew. "U.S.-EU Relations: Putting the Bush Years in Perspective." In *The Foreign Policy of the European Union: Assessing Europe's Role in the World*. Edited by Federiga Bindi and Irina Angelescu, Washington, D.C.: Brookings Institution Press, 2012, 203–08.

Petersen, Spike. "Gendered Identities, Ideologies, and Practices in the Context of War and Militarism." In *Gender, War, and Militarism: Feminist Perspectives*. Ed. Laura Sjoberg and Sandra Via. Santa Barbara, CA: ABC-CLIO, 2010, 17–29.

Piccardo, Lara. "The European Union and Russia: Past, Present, and Future of a Difficult Relationship." In *The Foreign Policy of the European Union: Assessing Europe's Role in the World*. Ed. Federiga Bindi and Irina Angelescu. Washington, D.C.: Brookings Institution Press, 2012, 119–32.

Pinder, John. *The European Union: A Very Short Introduction*. New York: Oxford University Press, 2001.

Redwood, John. *Superpower Struggles: Mighty America, Faltering Europe, Rising Asia*. New York: Palgrave McMillan, 2005.

Soeters, Joseph. *Ethnic Conflict and Terrorism: The Origins and Dynamics of Civil Wars*. New York: Routledge, 2005.

Yuval-Davis, Nira. *Gender and Nation*. London: Sage, 1997.

Extreme Transitions
Trends and Trepidations from 1992 to 1996

D.R. HAMMONTREE

It is an imbalanced time in Justice League history: a transitional period in the superhero zeitgeist. This is the era "of reiteration" (Duncan and Smith 77), what can be seen as the "extreme" era in comics, is one of oversaturation, and gimmicks that lead to high sales figures. From 1993 to 1996 superhero comics were in a transitional interval dominated by extreme artistic styles out of proportion muscled bodies, splash pages, an oversaturation of purples and yellows. The biggest influence on style and content were the Marvel (later Image) artists like Rob Liefeld, Todd McFarland, and Jim Lee. Writing and narrative became secondary, compared to the previous "era of ambition" (Duncan and Smith 71) that ran from 1986 to 1992. As well, market flux motivated the business side to overreach in the pursuit to both maintain and recruit readers.

The Justice League books published during this time fall between the 1987 and 1992, J. M. DeMatteis and Keith Giffen's run and Grant Morrison's 1996 revamp. These issues are rarely cited, in little demand, and seldom reprinted in collections or trade paperbacks. As cultural artifacts, these books reveal an industry in some flux. Some issues reveal good intentions and ancillary characters reveal potential. But there are no lasting impacts here. Any new characters don't get off the ground and the established ones see small changes that are later ignored. This essay focuses on how this period of Justice League books embody an attempt to engage in this extreme style of the time. These trends are also revealing of the larger socio-cultural and rhetorical landscape of the times.

The 1990s

In politics, ideas of reform were overall illusionary in an atmosphere that saw the entrenchment and stabilization of the Regan era, neoliberal "backlash" politics. Overall "the powerful contradictions between unreal images of the amusement culture and the reality of diminishing economic prospects would become the basis of great fear and uncertainty for much of Generation X"[1] (Sacks 157). This emergence of the so-called angst, grunge or "Gen X" culture lead the popular press to convey that the youth were apathetic, ambivalent, or just cynical. To some extent, this Gen X culture served as a distraction from rather than a critique of the emergent "trickle-down" realities (job loss, lack of security, mass privatization and deregulation) faced in the United States.

Within this mix of the popular and political culture, these Justice League books are situated in a market downturn. The comic industry by 1992 also saw the aftereffects of bombastic post–Cold War rhetoric in mainstream popular culture, leaning toward the extreme, oddly the very extreme styles from the 1980s that Gen X culture was rejecting. Out of the 1980s came the Schwarzenegger-esque power genre. Perhaps in a response to the "wimpy" grunge culture that was itself reaction to these excessive 1980s attitudes, the use of anabolic steroids in professional sports (and wrestling entertainment) satisfied such desire to power, so comic heroes "bulked up." Meanwhile, video games were influencing the design and layout of comic panels, as the 2-D fighting games of the 16- and 32-bit variety (*Mortal Kombat, Double Dragon*, etc.) and first-person shooter games (*Doom*) were finding their styles emulated in the four-color world.

Editorial decisions in the comic industry seemed drawn to the extreme over the reflective, ambition era books which had already imploded with too many derivate storylines. Top tier, non-mutant properties (Superman, Batman, Wonder Woman and Spider-man) would go through a bit of an identity crisis to reach (or lose) readers and the same with the second-tier characters (Green Lantern). Meanwhile Marvel's various X-Men books were achieving great success, to be followed, albeit briefly, by the Image books.

The Run

For these Justice League books, this time is best understood if divided into three stages: traditional, transitional, and extreme.

First, the "traditional" period looks to get the Justice League back to their starting points, harkening back to the Silver Age, reintroducing a membership of first-string and second-string characters like Superman and Green

Lantern (Hal Jordan). This traditional period encompasses the Dan Jurgens run of *Justice League America* (*JLA*), sees the return of the Maritain Manhunter, and rebrands *Justice League Europe* (*JLE*) to *Justice League International* (*JLI*). Next, the "transitional" period sees more of the same tone of the previous runs, but introduces *Justice League Taskforce* (*JLTF*). This period ends with the death of Ice during the company-wide *Zero Hour* event. Finally, the "extreme" era draws from the popularity of Marvel X-Men books and Image Comics, intensifying conflict or dark characters, epitomized by the art and style of *Extreme Justice* (*EJ*). These books, *JLA,JLTF,* and *EJ*, focus on internal conflicts among team members setting up longer narrative and plots that are largely abandoned by 1996. As the summary shows, in this era so many different styles were employed to try and delight audiences. In other words, what works for one may not work for all. In turn, an unsuccessful series is published, surviving on its own inertia and brand recognition. Styles are mismatched and creative energies misdirected, all because of a lack of clear understanding as to the reason behind these extreme trends of the day.

Traditional

This traditional phase generally encompasses issues from April 1992 (*JLE* #37, *JLA* #61) to between May 1993 (with *JLE* #50) and late July 1993 (with the end of the Dan Jurgens run of the *JLA*, issue #77). Writers during the majority of this time were Dan Jurgens (*JLA*) and Gerard Jones (*JLE*).

Under the editorship of Brian Augustyn and Ruben Diaz these two books took different paths with Jurgens linking his JLA stories with his writing on *Superman* and Jones given the thankless task of combining both the tone of the DeMatteis and Giffen run. Both writers also seem to be under a mandate to harken back to the early 1980s style of the Conway stories. The inclusion of Silver Age members of the team (including Batman, Superman, Wonder Woman, Hal Jordan, and Aquaman) seems to be an attempt to move these books away from the dynamic established in the Giffen and DeMatteis years. Unfortunately, by bringing first-string characters (with their own titles) into a serialized team book makes it difficult for character development, as the iconic characters overwhelm minor characters and the more character-driven stories take place in their own titles.

In *Justice League Europe*, the narrative picks up right from the last run ended, with the same lineup and setting. This team is initially comprised of Flash (Wally West), Elongated Man, Sue Dibny, Aquaman, Crimson Fox, Power Girl, Dr. Light, and Metamorpho. Yet the attempts to duplicate the lighthearted tone of the previous run in *JLE* are disjointed. Jones writes with more slapstick as opposed to the satirical bent of DeMatteis and Giffen.

An underpinning theme here is the lack of leadership for the *JLE* that may parallel a lack of direction for the books at this time. Issues #37–39 see Batman help a disjointed, leaderless team to take on "Deconstructo," a disenfranchised deconstructionist visual artist with a reality-bending devise. The leadership gap is filled with the inclusion of Hal Jordan (requested via a fan vote) that gives the JLE its leadership. Unfortunately, this leadership would be short lived, as a Green Lantern reboot was in the works after the return of Superman. Most of the *JLE/JLI* seldom gain any coherent lack of identity of its own, with its core characters in a state of confusion. Seldom do individuals take on any unique personalities, and the narrative remains fragmented, at the mercy of other editors working on other books.

The most compelling arc in this run would be the lead up to the villain Sonar taking over the recently collapsed Soviet Union by brainwashing the Rocket Reds and several *JLE* members. This time of transitions is hardly confined to the Justice League. With the apparent end of the Soviet Union, many writers would need to transition away from the comfortable Cold War conflicts. Such early post–Cold War stories are of note in that they give some insights into the cultural impact of such a geopolitical shift.

A *JLE* character with some potential was Maya (Chandi Gupta), a teenager with elemental abilities that initially believed she was a reincarnation of Shiva. Maya seems to be an ambitious attempt to bring a uniqueness to the run, an original character for Jones to use in expanding the group chemistry. Maya could also be an attempt to draw in new readers, an alternative to the many more testosterone driven books and styles. However, this character did not get to develop beyond her role as a plot device in the Overmaster arc, after which the *JLE* disbands. It is of some comfort that Maya was not rebooted as yet another hyper-sexualized female heroine, as was the trend of the day.

In the *Justice League America* much of the team rosters were inherited form the previous editorial team. Booster Gold, Blue Beetle, Fire, Ice, and Guy Gardner (the DeMatteis and Giffen roll call) were joined by Superman and Maxmia. Also joining the team is Bloodwynd (later revealed to be Martian Manhunter). Dan Jurgens also integrates the JLA with his Superman books. Most notable is issue #69 (December 1992), a chapter in the "Death of Superman" crossover featuring a rampaging Doomsday decimating the team. The aftereffects downgraded the humor quotient dramatically, if not altogether, specifically between Blue Beetle and Booster Gold. After the death of Superman the roster expanded with Wonder Woman leading a team that also included the Ray, Agent Liberty, and Black Kondor.

It is Jurgens' last storyline in JLA that is most engaging. The "Destiny's Hand" arc (*Justice League America* # 72 [March 1993]–75 [June 1993]) evokes the Conway JLA of the late 70s and early 80s while also drawing from Mark

Gruenwald's *Squadron Supreme* (1985–86) plot concerning heroes and the potential to abuse their power. Dr. Destiny finds within the doubts and subconscious of the Atom (Ray Palmer) the idea of a "Justice league Gone Bad— a world gone to Hell" (Jurgens #75, 15) and creates a dark version of the Conway era JLA that then threatens overtake the present reality. The overall theme touches on the problem with misplaced nostalgia and romanticism of the past as well as the potential dangers of two-dimensional view of Silver Age heroes and villains. Many threads along this line would come again, such as *Kingdom Come* (1996) and *Identity Crisis* (2004). The arc was a departure from Jurgens' reputation as a "no thrills" and steady storyteller.

Looking at the Jurgens and Jones run now draws us closer to the cultural and rhetorical underpinnings reflecting the attitudes and trends of the time. Here comic fandom is the discourse community (Porter 106) that, by 1992, seemed too oversaturated with so-called realism: a counter to the realism of the time was the Giffen and DeMattes *JLI* books. By 1992 the run had gone a bit long and editors seemed up in the air as to how to best continue a core group of titles. This mix of traditional combined with elements from Giffen and DeMatteis led to a hit-and-miss attempt in the first period of these books. The problem in the early 1990s was more that the industry was not responding to need so much as generating need with dramatic changes to its core characters, in hopes of competing with styles and trends found in other series like Marvel's *X-Men* books.

Transitional

This next stage in its editorial development runs from June 1993 until August 1994, up to the *Zero Hour* crossover. In this period, *Justice League Europe* becomes *Justice League International* with issue #51 (June 1993) and runs until issue #67 (August 1994). *JLA* issues comprise #78 (early August 1993) to issue # 91 (August 1994). As well, a new series, *Justice League Task Force* featuring the Martian Manhunter (J'onn J'onzz), begins in June 1993 as a "special ops" series with guest appearances up until issue #15 (August 1994) where it then changes editorial direction. The end of this stage cumulates in the "Judgment Day" storyline and a fracturing between teams. Most significantly, departure of Dan Jurgens leads to a shift in the tone and direction of these three books. The inclusion of *Justice League Task Force* is also a noteworthy marker as the tone and intention of is unique from the editorial course the books would take during the next, "extreme" stage.

Although a short span comprising around 15 issues for each book, this lull can best be seen as, indeed, a "transitional" period situated within a specific "social formation" (Charland 464) expressed by the wider industry and cultural expectations. After the fallout from the first wave of superhero shifts (like the "Death of Superman" arc) this run would attempt to bridge the gaps between those heroes with their own books (Green Lantern, Guy Gardner, Wonder Woman) while still looking for its own editorial direction. The plots here also set the stage for the extreme stage.

Justice League Task Force begins as a covert espionage team working under a United Nations mandate. Martian Manhunter, along with Gypsy, lead selected teams of underused DC characters. A notable appearance includes Nightwing (Dick Grayson), whose tendency to lead frustrates J'onn J'onzz. Indeed throughout the run J'onn J'onzz becomes easily frustrated by his inability to hold any iteration of his team together. These early issues feature various writers including Dennis O'Neil, Jeph Loeb, Michael Jan Freeman, and Peter David. Although action oriented, it is a series driven by character conflicts, notably between Gypsy and J'onn J'onzz.

Meanwhile, the *Justice League International* storyline continued much as it did before with Gerard Jones writing. During this period, Hal Jordan departs from the *JLI* with issue #61 (February 1994). It is Dr. Light who takes on a leadership role and gradually gains confidence, as opposed to her earlier characterization that was hesitant and uncertain about her role on the team. The comedic tone would also disappear with the exit of the slapstick Elongated Man. These decisions finish the title's transition to a run-of-the-mill team book with very little character development or group chemistry.

Dan Vado takes over writing in *Justice League America*. The lineup now includes Wonder Woman, Maxmia, the Ray, the Flash (Jay Garrick), and the real Bloodwynd along with Booster Gold, Blue Beetle, Fire, and Ice. Capitan Atom also returns to the team, causing friction with Wonder Woman that will lead into the death of Ice in the "Judgment Day" crossover. "Judgment Day" also introduces a new Amazing Man and sets the stage for the "Extreme" era, the split of Justice League teams.

These stories, or their editorial direction, are left in a bit of a hodgepodge at this point, leaving little lasting impression compared to the Giffen and DeMattes era. It seems that larger company-wide events, like *Zero Hour*, took any steam away from this title. Indeed, this is why Justice League books suffer when mainline characters (with their own books are included).

By the end of this phase, it seems apparent that a change in tone was needed. This transitional period sees much more conflict, but without strong characterization to propel such conflict. Motivations are lost on readers. Wonder Woman, for example, already had a book of her own, so her own characterization remains static and at the mercy of another editorial team. The foundation for a successful team book is not here. Market forces are also seeing bi-monthly issues published: too much space is given to very little. By this time, core readers may be buying out of habit, out of a need for a complete, monthly run rather than the quality of the product. At the end of the day, the Justice League brand alone could be what is selling the books, rather than the content of the books themselves.

Extreme

In 1994 DC Comics published a series called *Zero Hour* that crossed over with every title they published. Most titles had changes in tone and direction following *Zero Hour*. These post–*Zero Hour* books represent the final stage of this four-year "wilderness" period for the Justice League franchise. Ruben Diaz takes over editorial duties at this time. Now Wonder Woman leads the Justice League America, Martian Manhunter a Justice League Task Force "rookie" team, and Captain Atom a separate Justice League team in *Extreme Justice*.

Gerard Jones' *JLI* plots transfer to *Justice League America* beginning with issue #93 (November 1994) until issue #113 (August 1996). The new roster includes Nuklon, Obsidian, Fire and (a new) Ice remain with this team. Also on the roster are Wonder Woman (serving as team leader), Metamorpho, Silver Fox, Power Girl, and Hawkman. The team is also partially space bound, choosing the Overmaster's former satellite headquarters as their base of operations. Various lingering plotlines are quickly resolved, setting the stage for the new direction.

Jones' writing is lighthearted but not overtly comedic while artists Randy Green and Chuck Wojtkiewicz compose in an artistic style akin to an animated cartoon style rather than that of the extreme Image-era characters. These pencilers work best with Jones' writing and develop an upbeat tone to contrast with *Justice League Task Force* and *Extreme Justice*.

As for the other Justice League books, on the surface it may appear that *Extreme Justice* is the culmination of 90s era style but this honor may go to *Justice League Task Force*. The team, led by the Martian Manhunter, comprises Gypsy, Triumph, the Ray, and L-Ron. This new team iteration, complete with team uniforms, seems an attempt to capture the ethos of Image Comics' *WildC.A.T.S.* or *Youngblood* (two series that were in turn heavily influenced by the 80s era *X-Men* and *New Teen Titans*). Christopher Priest (with early assistance from Mark Waid) served as writer for the reminder of the run with art duties going to various pencilers. This iteration of *Justice League Task Force* had the potential for original storytelling without the hampering of characters under the editorial control of others, but this was short lived as the Ray and Triumph would soon have their own series.

In the end, the *Justice League Task Force* is an example of early 1990s "extreme" action and art without solid character development or storytelling. As a stand along book, *Justice League Task Force* was disjointed.

The eighteen issues of *Extreme Justice* from January 1995 to July 1996 have the distinction of combining the "extreme" era elements while developing coherent plots, character development, and action. Indeed, the *Extreme Justice*, despite its name, may be the strongest of the run of these Justice League books. This book is notable for character development more than all previous books since the Giffen and DeMatteis era. The characters are free to grow without editorial constraints imposed by other books. The lineup includes Captain Atom, Maxima, Amazing Man, Booster Gold, Blue Beetle, and later Firestorm. Plastique, a former Firestorm villain, also plays a support role as Captain Atom's fiancée.

Early *Extreme Justice* issues are typical of the style of the day. Marc Campos' artistic decisions are derivative of Mike Deodato, Todd McFarland and Rob Liefeld, all popular "splash page" at the time. It would be safe to describe the paneling as busy. Long hair is a feature with many characters, and the physique of some characters is very much out of proportion.

The writing, however, reintroduces plotlines from the late 1980s and early 1990s to sketch out a coherent, character-driven narrative. Character related developments in this series, seldom featured in the other Justice League books, include a relationship between Maxima and Amazing Man, the introduction of the Wonder Twins, and a resolution between Ronnie Raymond and Martin Stein (the two Firestorms).

By 1996, Image Comics, which had codified a style that permeated early 1990s comic books, was facing a backlash as critiques of style over substance began to take a toll. The mood was changing, demonstrating a shift in values and attitudes that, from a rhetorical lens, "lays bare for critique the expectations or prejudices of a discursively constituted audience" (Charland 467). An example of this change of attitudes and direction, a retreat from the extreme into the mythic, is demonstrated with Grant Morrison's *JLA*, the new direction the franchise would take after this extreme era.

The influences of the marketplace serve as a means of understanding the various trends of the time and the editorial balances made before the superhero genre reset itself once again. The machismo bulk and the oversexed fetishism of the 1990s never quite went away but were challenged by the anti-consumer apathy and resistance of the grunge style. These Justice League books lose their core pathos and serve as a rhetorical misreading of an audience, attempting to do too much in terms of keeping up with trends, leading to uneven storytelling and lack of character development resulting in a loss of reader interest.

Audiences must be given time to know and care for characters. The success of the 90s era X-Men franchise was not due to their artists (as many of the Image artists would like to believe) but in the development of their characters, along with a balance of action (art) and soap opera. Chris Claremont's

Uncanny X-Men and Marv Wolfman and George Perez's *New Teen Titans* are examples of 80s team books that were successful in achieving this balance and thus appealing to the audience. With the end of DeMatteis and Giffen run, the Justice League books were left empty, not to be re-energized until a new foundational framework could be achieved. Before a successful new focus could be found there were the misdirections and missed opportunities.

NOTE

1. Peter Sack's account and argument draw more toward a frustration with a so-called entitlement culture. Nevertheless, he does get at the realities of economic insecurities in the "Gen-X" 1990s.

WORKS CITED

Charland, Maurice. "Rehabilitating Rhetoric: Confronting Blindspots in Discourse and Social Theory." In *Contemporary Rhetorical Theory*. Ed. John Louis Lucaites, Celeste Michelle Condit, and Sally Caudill. New York: Guilford, 1999.
Duncan, Randy, and Matthew J. Smith. *The Power of Comics: History, Form & Culture*. New York: Continuum, 2009. Print.
Harvey, David. *A Brief History of Neoliberalism*. Oxford: Oxford University Press, 2005. Print.
Jurgens, Dan (w, a). "Destiny's Hand: Finale." *Justice League America* #75 (June 1993).
Porter, James E. *Audience and Rhetoric: An Archaeological Composition of the Discourse Community*. Englewood Cliffs, NJ: Prentice Hall, 1992. Print.
Rosteck, Thomas, ed. *At the Intersection: Cultural Studies and Rhetorical Studies*. New York: Guilford, 1999. Print.
Sacks, Peter. *Generation X Goes to College: An Eye-Opening Account of Teaching in Postmodern America*. Chicago: Open Court, 1996. Print.

What We've Got Here Is Failure to Communicate

Trust, Technology and Fear in "The Tower of Babel"

NICOLE FREIM

A re-imagined version of a classic Golden Age superteam, the Justice League has been quite popular since its inception, mainly due to its use of the company's most popular characters. The initial line-up featured Aquaman, Flash, Green Lantern, Martian Manhunter, and Wonder Woman, with occasional visits from Batman and Superman. Launched in 1960, the *Justice League of America* was born in the Silver Age of comic books, a period dominated by the restrictive Comics Code and a myriad of campy plot lines.

The group survived through the Silver and Bronze Ages and a variety of roster changes, and in the Iron Age (some people call this the "modern" age, but I prefer "iron" for the symmetry) it became Justice League International. There were several spin-off titles, like *Extreme Justice* and *Justice League Quarterly*, but all titles were cancelled in 1996 as the comics market collapsed under the weight of the ill-fated investment boom of the 1990s—strangely, comics were not worth as much when there were a million of them available.

DC decided to overhaul many of its titles, and in 1997, the company launched *JLA*, written by Grant Morrison and drawn by Howard Porter. The starting membership included Batman, The Flash (Wally West), Green Lantern (Kyle Rayner), Martian Manhunter, Plastic Man, Superman, and Wonder Woman. Their base of operations was a tower on the moon, allowing them to be above the Earth and all its inhabitants. Morrison specifically wanted to explore the idea of the characters as a modern pantheon of gods, examining how their various powers fit together and what their responsibilities should be. Over the first few years, he added several characters to the roster (some called "reserve" members), like Oracle, Huntress, Steel, and Zauriel.

The idea of stories centering around a group of powerful individuals is not new. Pantheons of gods can be found in multiple ancient religions, with each god overseeing his or her own domain. This concept of uniting people who can complement each other's strengths and weaknesses would later be adopted by gamers everywhere to assign roles for maximum effectiveness. Morrison's use of the most powerful members of the DC universe meant that the threats the team dealt with had to be epic in scale. His approach worked, and *JLA* was one of DC's best selling titles for several years.

Mark Waid, who had previously worked on *Justice League Quarterly* and *Justice League Task Force*, took over writing the series with *JLA* #43 (July 2000). His four-part story, "Tower of Babel," signaled a shift in both the focus of the book and the team dynamics. The villain of the storyline is Ra's al Ghul, a man (mostly immortal and slightly insane, but a man nonetheless) as opposed to more powerful, otherworldly forces like White Martians, rebellious angels, or Darkseid.

Part one of the story is called "Survival of the Fittest." The issue opens with Ra's Al Ghul ordering one of his men to be (ostensibly) put to death for his failure to care correctly for a Javan tiger cub; according to Ra's, this failure means that the species will be extinct because there are no more males to mate with the female he also has. He complains to his daughter Talia about the fact that so many species are now only preserved in conservatories while "six billion shortsighted parasites" thrive and pillage the planet. The plan he is about to set in motion will cause mankind to "pare the human race to a manageable size" (Waid, "Part 1...," 2). And Ra's is confident that Batman will be distracted; in fact, Ra's says the method is so obvious, that he is surprised it never occurred to him before. The distraction is stealing the coffins of Thomas and Martha Wayne.

The first Leaguer to be attacked is the Martian Manhunter, prioritized due to the telepathic link he maintains between the League members when necessary. Talia hits J'onn with a missile that does not carry an explosive but rather a cloud of nanites. Leaving J'onn, the story picks up with Flash and Wonder Woman working on containing a wildfire in Germany's Black Forest. They do not know how the fire was started, and J'onn—the nearest leaguer when the fire began—has been out of communication. When Wally and Diana spy a man on fire (presumably the cause of the blaze), they create a vortex to pull the air away from him and put him out. At this point, they discover the man is J'onn.

The scene shifts to the United Nations, where the warring countries of Rhapastan and Turkey are sitting down to peace talks with Atlantis mediating.

The king, Aquaman, is late for the meeting as he and Plastic Man are being chased by assassins. The armed men follow the heroes into the chamber and use a grenade on Plastic Man, which freezes him solid. Aquaman intercepts the next missile, thinking it will shatter the brittle Plastic Man, but that missile was actually meant for Aquaman, breaking open and releasing a gas which makes the king of the seas fear water. The attackers report, "JLA target two gassed, target three flash-frozen" and they depart—after using a hammer to break Plastic Man into pieces (Waid, "Part 1…," 12).

Up in the Watchtower, Superman has concluded that the nanites which hit J'onn were formulated to bond with his skin. The nanites were "engineered to transmute trace elements into magnesium—an element that bursts into flame in the open air" (Waid, "Part 1…," 13). J'onn is submerged in a tank of water to prevent himself from burning. Meanwhile, Flash is reassembling Plastic Man (commenting that he is trying "not to throw up" while watching himself do this). Aquaman reported what the assassins said about the JLA targets, and Diana points out that all the members are probably being hunted.

Superman checks in with Batman, but Bruce has little time for talk; he is in the middle of fighting the crew of a helicopter. He asks Clark if anyone is dead and if it's something they can't handle without him. Clark says no and tries to explain more, but Batman cuts him off and closes the channel. Superman leaves to work on finding out the villain's plan, and Wally and Diana go to check on Green Lantern, who is not responding to their signals.

Ra's is contemplating his success, and considering disciplining his daughter for letting J'onn burn a forest, when the next stage of his plan is ready to take effect. Dr. Kant confirms that "shielding earpieces are being provided to all workers as we speak." Ra's offers the observation that "whoever said a picture was worth a thousand words … is about to see just how badly he miscounted" (Waid, "Part 1…," 17). As the countdown begins, Clark arrives at the *Daily Planet* to find that the newspaper is filled with random letters instead of words. Looking outside, he realizes that this is not a technical glitch but a widespread problem as all street signs have also turned to "babble."

Flash and Wonder Woman are having a hard time finding Green Lantern's apartment since all the numbers have changed. Getting no answer to a knock but hearing something inside, Wally breaks the lock and they enter to find that Green Lantern has gone blind.

JLA #44 (August 2000) features Batman on the cover holding up other members of the JLA as marionettes and continues with part two of the story "Seven Little Indians"—which should really be "Eight Little Indians" since in the original story the perpetrator was one of the victims. The opening narration discusses various problems the world is experiencing, from a gangland riot prompted by the loss of markers delineating the edges of territories to the looming collapse of the world's economy.

During this, Ra's "patiently awaits the arrival of the one man most likely to oppose him" and "he arrives slightly ahead of schedule" (Waid, "Part 2…," 1). Batman is demanding the return of his parents' bodies, while Ra's is apologizing for being consumed by other matters like "anarchy. Riots. A world panicked by a sudden, global dyslexia engineered by my scientists" (Waid, "Part 2…," 2). Batman tries to say that the League is no doubt already defending the Earth, but Ra's explains the rest of the team is occupied. He then turns Bruce's attention to the coffins hovering over the Lazarus Pit that Ra's uses to extend his life span, offering to bring Thomas and Martha back to life.

Superman and Oracle have discovered that there is a sine wave which is "broadcasting a signal straight to the language centers of our brain—creating a universal aphasia that makes the written word incomprehensible" (Waid, "Part 2…," 7.). As they ponder the problem, the panels show potential catastrophes like two jets barely missing each other in the sky and hospitals having trouble with administering medications and performing operations. Clark remembers a giant force field once used by Brainiac; after a quick rewire, he uses it to counteract the signal in Metropolis, protecting one city on the planet.

In New York City, Diana and Wally are trying to reason with Kyle by explaining that his blindness must be part of the overall attack on the League. While they are discussing it, Arthur realizes that the enemy must be using their signal devices to track each member. He warns the others, but he is too late to prevent an attack at Kyle's apartment. Flash and Wonder Woman are both targeted with individual nanites.

Wonder Woman finds herself in mortal combat with a soldier who is her "equal in every way" and cannot be beaten (Waid, "Part 2…," 9). The fighting rages for hours, but we see that it only feels like hours to Diana; she is locked in a virtual world. The enemy tells Kyle, "The man who designed this trap realized that Wonder Woman's competitive nature can be a great weakness. In battle, all that could make her surrender is a heart attack" (Waid, "Part 2…," 10). The projectile aimed at The Flash lodges in his spinal column, giving him "epileptic seizures at lightspeed" (Waid, "Part 2…," 11). Enraged that Talia refers to him as "no longer of any consequence" (Waid, "Part 2…," 13), Kyle tries to fight the hit squad, but he cannot see to shape his power ring's creations.

As Talia rounds up the team to leave, she calls the whole thing "madness" and comments that she finds no honor in fighting the League in this manner. She has had her fill of her father's manipulations and really only longs for peace for herself and the man she loves, Batman (Waid, "Part 2…," 14). While she may be helping her father, Talia is not certain that he has taken the right course. The team's exit is blocked, however, by the arrival of the Martian Manhunter in an Atlantean protective suit, aided by Superman.

While this fight is going on, Ra's is trying to convince Batman that bringing his parents back to life would be a good thing, asking how often he's dreamed of hearing his father's voice or feeling his mother's touch (Waid, "Part 2...," 15). Batman responds that he dreams of "being worthy of their memory" and asks why Ra's has gone to so much trouble to use the Waynes as bait. Ra's claims his goal is the same as always: "to winnow the ranks of mankind before they finish laying ecological waste to my planet" (Waid, "Part 2...," 16). Between Ra's confidence in his victory and the sight of a glowing stone in his hands, Batman realizes what has happened. He begins trying to warn his team, although Ra's claims the signal will not reach through the compound walls. All of Ra's men pile on Batman, trying to stop him from getting outside, but they are (of course) unsuccessful.

Batman breaks out to warn the League just as Talia produces a glowing stone of her own: a piece of kryptonite which has been experimented on to "accelerate its half-life" making it "less lethal but still crippling to the Kryptonian physiology." It is not necessarily going to kill Superman, but it will produce "unpredictable changes" in his "cellular structure" (Waid, "Part 2...," 20). Batman comes over the communication channel, urging the team to retreat and admitting "all the plans, the traps, the signal trackers—they were mine! Superman—I did this to you!" (Waid, "Part 2...," 21).

Part three, "Protected by the Cold," begins with still more potential catastrophes of a bomb scare and a military reaction to a border being crossed. Most of the League is suffering varying degrees of incapacitation. Batman is the only one unhampered, but he is running from Ra's' minions. As he tries to explain the situation to Superman, Ra's initiates the next phase of his plan which scrambles the ability to understand spoken language in addition to the written word. Batman fakes a fall off a cliff to elude the enemy while the rest of the League starts to pull themselves together back at the Watchtower.

J'onn tricks Arthur's mind into believing he is in a desert and directs Plastic Man into Diana's ear canal to remove the nanite. Clark uses his laser vision to remove the device on Wally's spine. Wally is relieved, saying "there were whole days I prayed just to die" only to learn he was out for a mere 22 minutes (Waid, "Part 3...," 6). After Diana has a hunch, J'onn confirms that he sees a post-hypnotic suggestion in Kyle's mind (Waid, "Part 3...," 7). Since the ring is powered by Kyle's will, his own will was making him blind. He removes the ring and tells himself he is not blind, and his sight returns.

What he sees is Superman, whose skin has turned transparent, allowing him to absorb more solar energy and overcharging him with power. Not only is it incredibly painful, but he can see and hear everything happening on Earth. He is shown crying, presumably over the frantic state of the world (rather than his own physical pain).

Talia questions her father about his actions, where all this will end. Ra's maintains that it will end where it should: "with a healthy planet no longer abused by the human race" (Waid, "Part 2...," 10). He envisions the population reducing themselves—survival of the fittest—and then being able to rule those who are left. He considers this to be a "gift" for Talia. As they are talking, a soldier comes to inform Ra's that Batman is dead. Talia refuses to believe this, insisting that without a body, Batman must have survived (clearly she has read a number of his comics). She is frustrated that Ra's has had her betray Batman's plans and turned her into an assassin. Ra's orders a search for Batman, and the reader sees that the soldier is Bruce in disguise.

While the Leaguers recover, they begin to question why Batman would construct these plans and wonder what else he has done that they don't know about. J'onn references the files he once kept on various members of the team, but he says they were "information only. No schemes, no plans." At this point a message comes from Batman claiming he has found the source of Ra's transmissions which are affecting people. The Leaguers begin to head for the door when Superman interrupts with a quiet "unless it's another trap" (Waid, "Part 2...," 12).

Clark pauses for a moment and then takes off quickly to intercept Bruce. The rest of the group follows, rendezvousing in Antarctica. The other Leaguers are reluctant to work with Batman but agree because, as Batman points out, "ambulance drivers can't read street signs" (Waid, "Part 2...," 16). Superman is still overcharged, and so he decides to take out the structure by himself once everyone is clear. He emerges from the burning building and confronts Batman with a simple "tell me why" (Waid, "Part 2...," 20.). Batman claims he had his reasons, but the conversation is cut short by a transmission from Talia. She explains that Ra's had a fail safe in a biochemical attack on Turkey by its neighbor Rhapastan; she is sharing the information because she has "had enough of being a pawn in my father's endless schemes" (Waid, "Part 2...," 21). She is shot, however, before she can give the League the full details.

The conclusion to the story arc is called "Harsh Words," and begins with J'onn realizing he has shed enough skin cells and hence nanites that he can function without bursting into flame. He turns his mental powers to helping Aquaman defeat the lingering effects of the fear toxin, mainly by encouraging him to turn the fear into anger: "Remember who did this to you! Think about who betrayed your trust!" (Waid, "Part 4...," 2). Meanwhile, Batman suggests splitting up to deal with Ra's and the biochemical attack.

Superman carries Batman with him as they fly toward Ra's. He again asks Bruce for an explanation. Batman explains that the incident a few years ago with Agamemno prompted this. In that miniseries, the villain organized a group of criminals (which became the Injustice Gang) and used his powers to swap their minds and bodies with the JLA's (Penguin in Batman's body, Lex Luthor in Superman's body, etc.). Batman decided, "there ought to be fail-safes designed in the event something similar ever happened again" (Waid, "Part 4...," 5). Superman is less than impressed with Bruce's decision.

Ra's is disciplining the soldier who shot Talia (he thought he would be rewarded because she was betraying Ra's—but why expect sanity from a man willing to have most of the Earth's population fight each other to the death?) when Superman and Batman arrive. Ra's distracts the heroes by releasing some of his caged animals, knowing that Superman will capture them rather than kill them to get to Ra's.

The Flash is stuck on the beach beside a dead soldier and an open bio-chemical weapon; if he moves, the wind of his passing would disperse the toxin. So he must stay put and let Green Lantern contain the area in a dome. Plastic Man and Wonder Woman head off to search for the other canister. One of the soldiers carrying it is concerned that their gas masks may also be defective like their fallen compatriot. One soldier attempts to divert the heroes' attention and the other climbs for higher ground to release the weapon.

Batman asks Superman to "recover the coffins," and Superman is shocked that Ra's has done this. When they catch up with Ra's, he is lamenting that the JLA will "continue to blight the world with their presence. God-powerful aliens. A child with a magic ring. So much wasted potential. So much they could do to remake an endangered planet" (Waid, "Part 4...," 11). Superman thinks the best way to start changing the planet is to remove Ra's. He cannot get the coffins, however, as Ra's has trapped them with kryptonite. Fortunately, Martian Manhunter and Aquaman show up in the nick of time to assist. Aquaman takes down Ra's henchman, Dr. Kant, saying that he con-quered his fear thanks to J'onn who "gave me strength by standing with me. That's the way the League works ... in theory" (Waid, "Part 4...," 15). The last is delivered with a sidelong glance at Batman. They discover that Ra's has managed to escape, and Dr. Kant assures them that the biochemical weapons have most certainly been deployed by now.

Wonder Woman has other ideas, though. The soldier with the canister hesitated in releasing the chemical, and she uses that to convince him that he is not ready to die today. The golden lasso holds him while she points out that there is no honor in serving Ra's—"there is only the suffering you bring upon the innocent" (Waid, "Part 4...," 17). She convinces him to deactivate the canister and let himself be taken in. Plastic Man is wildly impressed. Clark clears Wally of any germs and helps Kyle heave the dome of contami-nated land into the sun.

Crisis averted, the scene shifts to the Watchtower where the team is debating Batman's fate as he awaits the decision in the other room. Superman says, "You've heard his reasoning. We are the most powerful beings on this planet ... but even we're not above being manipulated. The people we help

... do they worry about that? Should they worry about that?" (Waid, "Part 4...," 18). This seems to be a fair question for a group as powerful as the JLA.

The Flash comments that he does not like Batman right now, but he does not think expulsion is the answer. In fact, he wonders, "Who am I to argue with Batman? What if there should be strategies against us?" Martian Manhunter feels for Batman because J'onn once kept a set of files on his team members which fell into the wrong hands, a fact which still tortures him. J'onn says he has never forgiven himself, though Aquaman says the rest of the team has forgiven him. But J'onn does not want to be a hypocrite and votes for keeping Batman. Green Lantern first tries to abstain, but when prompted says, "Then while he and I need to have a talk.... I say he stays." Kyle is angry, but he admits that he got the ring through dumb luck when it could have gone to "some sicko. And the thought of that happening makes me respect why someone would want to figure out its fail safe ... even not tell us so we couldn't devise an end-run" (Waid, "Part 4...," 20).

Aquaman, Wonder Woman, and Plastic Man vote to have Batman removed, mainly focusing on their inability to trust him now. Arthur says that the team has earned trust, if not from the world then certainly from each other. Diana says that while she believes that "Batman never meant his contingency plans to be abused ... but he could have told us they existed without detailing them" (Waid, "Part 4...," 20). Plastic Man is very direct, saying only, "Get him out of here" as he remembers being shattered into a thousand pieces.

With the vote tied, Superman is left as the deciding vote. Wally asks, "You're the closest thing he has to a friend on this team. How well do you really know him? Or, I guess, more to the point ... how well does he know you? Well enough to know better than any of us how you'll vote?" (Waid, "Part 4...," 21). As they open the door into the conference room to see that Batman is gone, Superman says, "Yes."

On the surface, the story is about a villain who once again has plans for world domination. However, this storyline reflects a growing number of concerns in our world and presents some interesting questions about society's dependence on technology and the way it is changing the world.

Ra's' motivations are repeatedly stated as stemming from concern for the planet. His attempts to save and breed a number of threatened or extinct species does lend his argument a certain weight. His method may be twisted and cruel, but his logic that the planet is being abused by the human race has a kernel of truth in it. We've long had groups concerned with protecting the environment. The Sierra Club was founded in 1892, and World Wildlife Fund has been around (in one form or another) since 1947. In the 1990s, WWF came up with a new mission statement that stated its goal was to "stop the degradation of the planet's natural environment and to build a future in which humans live in harmony with nature" and it planned to do this through preserving biological diversity in plants and animals, moving toward the use of renewable resources, and trying to reduce pollution and waste.

Although his plan includes ruling over whoever is left, Ra's' goal of thinning the population to reduce humanity's impact on the planet is actually a somewhat benevolent goal. This motivation sets him apart from other villains like Luthor, who seek power, or villains like the Joker, who seek destruction. While prompting the population to slaughter one another is reprehensible, there are probably extreme environmental activists who would say the ends would not be a bad result.

Another key element of the story is the fear of the power of technology. To enact this plan, Ra's must utilize technology in two ways. The first is the use of sophisticated technology in order to defeat the JLA. While the post-hypnotic suggestion Green Lantern received or the freezing of Plastic Man was not dependent on advances in technology, most of the other Leaguers are taken down with new methods. Yes, this is a work of fiction, and so the creators could create whatever technology they deem necessary. Yet as often happens with science fiction, there seems to be an element of foreshadowing here.

Superman is not defeated merely by a chunk of green kryptonite which weakens him (or by any of the other colors which have varying effects); he is defeated by an irradiated kryptonite, one that has been tinkered with to produce unforeseen results. Wonder Woman is not defeated by an opponent who is her match; she is defeated through a virtual opponent who can never be beaten because she's created by technology. The nanites which attack J'onn or the technology which gives the Flash endless seizures are new methods of fighting the heroes, methods which reflect the growing surge in technology which our society was experiencing at the time. Even 15 years later, nanites are still in the experimental phase, but they are something that is being actively worked on by scientists.

This story came hard on the heels of the Y2K scare, which was rooted in fears of technology failing. The human flaw in the design of computers was threatening to leave us all vulnerable to the collapse of the system. People everywhere worried about what might happen if the computers—which were increasingly relied upon—shut down. The problem turned out not to be a worldwide catastrophe, but perhaps some of the fear remained in people's minds. Computers and technology had been developing at a rapid pace, and we seemed to suddenly pause to realize that our growing dependence on it could be a problem.

The use of technology to block communication is the extension of that fear. The growth of the internet was connecting all the world, and yet people can drown in that much information. Neil Postman discusses this in his book *Technopoly*. "Like the Sorcerer's Apprentice, we are awash in information.

And all the sorcerer has left is a broom. Information has become a form of garbage, not only incapable of answering the most fundamental human questions but barely useful in providing coherent direction to the solution of even mundane problems" (69–70). We had a new stream of information, but it was growing faster than we could keep up with it.

This tied in to another fear that had developed around technology: it would isolate us from others. The story takes this idea to the extreme by using technology to make communication impossible. In this case, it really is technology that is to blame for our conflicts. The problems dramatized in *The Net* (1995 film and 1998–99 television series) outlined our worries about what can be done to us with technology. The fear of losing control of our own information, our own lives, partly hinged on being unable to connect with anyone else. The lack of human connection was what does the lead character in.

In *JLA*, not only did they lose the ability to speak and understand, but the written word was also taken away. Communication by any means was impossible. In the *Buffy the Vampire Slayer* episode "Hush," which aired in December 1999, when the residents could not speak, at least they could still write and read. Ra's took that away, too, knowing that people could not deal with the complete isolation it would engender. Society was being pushed apart due to technology making it hard to communicate. Many people fear that we may lose our ability to interact in person due to an overreliance on technology; this story twists that fear and pushes it to the extreme.

At the core of the story is the betrayal the League members feel over Batman's role in the events. The Justice League has traditionally been a group of the elite. Indeed, Danny Fingeroth points out that unlike some teams which are thrown together by circumstance (such as the X-Men), the Justice League is a "meritocracy" and a person is invited to join because he or she is "deemed by the other members of the team to be the best" (103). Because this group is considered the cream of the crop, a betrayal by one of their own is more devastating.

Wonder Woman and Aquaman object to not being informed—claiming that if Batman had really felt these plans were necessary, he should have trusted the group to agree. They didn't need details, but they should have been aware of the existence of his plans because the group is so elite (and hence trustworthy) and must be able to trust one another in order to function effectively. One might argue that informing them of the existence of the plans would not be a simple matter. It is difficult to envision Batman telling this characterization of Aquaman, "I have a plan to stop you should the need arise," and Aquaman simply nodding and letting it rest there. Could anyone resist trying to find out what plans are in place to stop them if they were to go rogue?

It also reflects on the motivation of the group. When creating the team, Julius Schwartz chose the word "league" over "society" (which had been used before) because "he felt that *society* only implies a loose association of individuals, whereas *league* implies a team of superheroes contributing their individual abilities to a common purpose" (Wright 185). The JLA must pool their abilities and work together to achieve their ends. This plan of Batman's feels like he is standing outside the group and making judgments, as when Superman points out that Batman acted alone in deciding these contingencies were necessary.

While Morrison's exploration of the group as modern day gods was intriguing, this grounding of the team in concerns of the world—like fears of technology and environmental issues—is an interesting direction. Bringing the conflict out in the group, when Batman's fears are certainly well founded because the JLA's powers and abilities had been used against their will before, shines a new light on the team as more than a collection of powered individuals. It does make the reader pause to think how should these "gods" be policed? Who would have to do it? And should these "gods" be concerned about such things as protecting the environment? As we journey farther into the 21st century, what do we expect from our heroes?

WORKS CITED

Fingeroth, Danny. *Superman on the Couch: What Superheroes Really Tell Us about Ourselves and Our Society.* New York: Continuum, 2004.

Postman, Neil. *Technopoly.* New York: Vintage, 1993.

Waid, Mark (w), and Howard Porter (a). *JLA.* Issues 43–46. New York: DC Comics, 2000.

Wright, Bradford W. *Comic Book Nation: The Transformation of Youth Culture in America.* Baltimore: Johns Hopkins University Press, 2001.

"Whether we fear we do too much—or not enough"
JLA/Avengers *and the Cross-Universe Causes of Conflict*

JOSEPH J. DAROWSKI

History of Intercompany Crossovers

The comic book industry has a long history that has seen many different companies change names, rise and fall in prominence, declare bankruptcy, and buy the rights to characters previously owned by their competitors. Companies can explode into prominence then disappear, or establish a core identity with fans and subsequently be forced to redefine themselves to retain any relevance. But, within all of that convoluted chaos, which has seen companies such as Dell Comics, EC Comics, Dark Horse Comics, Image Comics, and many others impact the history of popular culture, it is DC Comics and Marvel Comics that have dominated the comic book industry for the last half century.

Sometimes referred to as "The Big Two," DC and Marvel have the largest market shares of the American comic book publishing industry, and the intellectual property of the two companies has been frequently mined for television and film adaptations, novels, video games, and too much merchandise to begin to number. And, as would be expected for companies with such long histories in the same industry, there have been times of jovial competition, times when creators from one company have fired cheap shots at the others' expense in fan publications, and also times of collaboration.

In the early Golden Age of comic books, National Periodicals, the company that would become DC Comics, codified the superhero genre with the publication of the first Superman comic book adventure in *Action Comics* #1 in 1938. Not long after the company that would become Marvel Comics started publishing the adventures of characters that fit that mold, most famously Captain America, who first appeared in 1941. The superhero genre lost popularity after the end of World War II, and while Superman, Batman, and Wonder Woman comic books continued to sell, publishers also began to put out more diversified content, finding success with horror, crime, romance, and science fiction comic books. DC Comics would reignite interest in superhero comic books at the dawn of the Silver Age when it reintroduced the Flash in 1956. The inescapable connection between the superhero genre and comic books would be cemented when, after DC Comics had success with a superhero team in the Justice League, Atlas Comics shifted the focus of their comic book line to superheroes, beginning with the release of *The Fantastic Four* #1 in 1961. Soon both publishers—Atlas having rebranded their company as Marvel Comics—were putting out more superhero adventures than any other genre, a trend that continues to the present day.

As two narrative universes were formed, many comic book fans declared affinities for one over the other, and a rivalry of sorts naturally developed. But, even self-declared DC fanboys or card carrying members of The Merry Marvel Marching Society—a real fan club for which you could receive a membership card—knew about the other companies stable of characters. Naturally, debates would spring up: Who is stronger, Superman or the Hulk? Who would win in a fight, Batman or Captain America? But because the characters belonged to different companies, these conversations could only ever exist in fans' heads, not on the comic book page. Except when they didn't.

There are a handful of times that comic books featuring characters from both companies' rosters have been published. These are certainly the exception to the publishing practices of DC and Marvel, not the rule. Oddly, the first crossover between the two companies was not with superheroes. In 1975 Marvel was planning to publish an adaptation of *The Wizard of Oz* novels while DC Comics was planning to publish an adaptation of the MGM musical. While details are scarce as to how the collaboration was brokered, the two companies joint-released a mini-series of *The Wizard of Oz*, making this the first DC/Marvel crossover. Because the next crossover was only a year later, it is likely that *The Wizard of Oz* is the reason that fans saw Superman battle Spider-Man in 1976 (Cronin).

After the Superman/Spider-Man meet-up there were sporadic intercompany crossovers through 1982, including Batman meeting the Hulk and the X-Men meeting the Teen Titans. After this, Marvel and DC don't crossover their narrative universes until the mid–1990s. They had begun work on a Justice League/Avengers crossover—written by Roy Thomas based on a plot by Gerry Conway with art by George Pérez—but editorial disputes caused the project to fall apart.

In 1995 whatever editorial frostiness had halted the Justice League/
Avengers team up had abated (likely with subsequent changes in company
personnel) and a Spider-Man/Batman team up was published. But this was
just a teaser for what was looming. In 1996 *DC vs. Marvel/Marvel vs. DC*[1] was
published, promising a crossover of all the mainstays of the two companies,
would meet each other, battle, and (of course) eventually team up. But, this
crossover was unlike any other, because between the third and fourth issues
of the mini-series the two comic book universes merged. Not as in Wonder
Woman and Storm now inhabited the same universe, but as in Wonder
Woman and Storm merged into one being, called Amazon. The two companies created a new imprint, Amalgam Comics, which published twelve issues
of the adventures of merged versions of their most popular characters, before
the characters unmerged in the finale of the mini-series.[2] A year later, the
publishers revisited the Amalgam universe and published twelve more issues
featuring a blend of DC and Marvel properties. A few other crossovers followed, none with the promotion nor impact of the DC vs. Marvel mini-series,
until 2003's *JLA/Avengers-Avengers/JLA*[3] crossover. Since 2003 the two companies have not allowed their respective characters to meet up, making this
story both the last inter-company crossover to date, and also the only
crossover that has occurred in a post–9/11 environment. It is easy to dismiss
these kinds of crossovers as simple promotional stunts where the interest is
more in the news and sales that will be generated when characters from
opposing companies meet, but that does not mean that creators are not trying
to tell the best story possible. In this instance, there are clearly identifiable
themes present in the story that is told in *JLA/Avengers* that reflect the fears
and concerns present in the post–9/11 America in which the creators and
consumers were living.

JLA/Avengers

In the early 1980s it was announced that George Pérez would be the
artist on a Justice League/Avengers story. Twenty years later, he was able to
fulfill that goal, as the iconic penciller was the artist the companies agreed
on for *JLA/Avengers*. Kurt Busiek, a writer who had worked for both companies and who had an in-depth familiarity with both universes' long continuities, was selected as the writer for the series.

A simplified version of the plot will leave out several of the twists and
turns of the series, but provide enough context for this analysis. The story
involves a being called Krona who travels from universe to universe, destroying them in search of "the ultimate truth" (Busiek, "A Journey"). In subsequent
issues readers learn that Krona considers himself a "scientist. A seeker of

knowledge" who was banished from his own universe when his attempts to study the creation of his universe were deemed unsafe (Busiek, "A Contest… "). But his "quest to learn the truth of all creation" is dangerous and he "tear[s] apart the fabric of universes" through his investigations and now he "wanders the multiverse, leaving destruction in his wake" (Busiek, "Strange…"). A foe who can cross between dimensions creates the opportunity for the Justice League and the Avengers to meet. But one supreme cosmic being is not enough to bring together the greatest heroes of two universes. The Grandmaster wishes to protect his universe, the Marvel universe, from Krona's attack, and challenges Krona to a game. If Krona wins, Grandmaster will lead him to Galactus, a cosmic being who predates the Big Bang and therefore knows the origin of creation. If Krona loses, he is to leave the Marvel universe forever. The game involves the Justice League and the Avengers racing to gather 12 items of power, six from the DC universe and six from the Marvel universe.

Members of the Justice League travel to the Avengers' Earth and vice-versa, as each team tries to lay claim to all twelve objects. Batman and Captain America figure out what is really going on, and prevent Krona from winning the contest, but Krona reneges on his agreement with Grandmaster. Grandmaster unites all the objects as a weapon and merges the two universes, creating one where the Justice League and Avengers are allies. But the two universes are incompatible and cannot survive and the heroes turn their attention to battling Grandmaster and Krona, the pawns turning on the chess masters. With alternate versions characters from all throughout the history of the Justice League and Avengers appearing and disappearing, the two teams assault Krona's interdimensional headquarters and destroy his machines, causing the universes to revert to their original states and stopping the threat of Krona. The heroes return and the status quo from before the mini-series began carries on.

Before beginning a thematic analysis of the series, George Pérez's art must be acknowledged. Pérez has a long a storied career for multiple comic book publishers and has become particularly known for his images of large groups of characters. Every character is distinctive and easily identified because of the details that he includes on every face, costume, and characters. This made him an ideal choice for this series. At the time this series was produced Pérez had an exclusive contract with another publisher, Crossgen, but had a clause written into his contract that if a JLA/Avengers crossover were to happen he would be allowed to complete art for that project (Lawrence).

The entire book is extremely well-drawn, with dynamic images, complex action, and easy-to-follow panel layouts. But the covers are particularly noteworthy, providing a balance of iconic timelessness for these classic characters and specific, thematic relationships with the individual issues. All four covers have art that extends across the front and back covers, that can be viewed when holding the comic completely open.

The first issue has the most iconic characters from both teams on the front cover—Superman, Batman, and Wonder Woman as well as Captain America, Thor, and Iron Man (and a tiny Atom and Wasp)—all staring off into the distance. On the back of the cover 14 more characters, evenly divided between the two companies' rosters, also stare off at an unseen threat, while behind them cosmic beings loom. This lines up with the first issue, which sees the two teams encountering cosmic threats and villains from each other's universes.

The second cover has a fantastic fight taking place with the characters from each universe battling one another. Front and center Thor and Superman square off, but the image as a whole is simultaneously chaotic and intricately laid out with lines guiding the eyes from one conflict to another. The speed waves from the Flash cross from left to right on the bottom of the image while a streak of light from Photon crosses the upper portion of the image. In the middle portion a blast from Green Lantern's ring intersects with the elongated neck of Plastic Man which interstects with a focused windstorm created by Red Tornado which leads the reader's eye past Wonder Woman grappling with Hercules and so on. In this issue, the teams battle each other as they race for the twelve most powerful objects on the two Earths.

The third issue's cover is the most visually arresting of the series, as it includes literally every character to have appeared as an Avenger or a member of the Justice League all coming forward towards the reader. Two hundred and eight characters, each with enough detail that fans can recognize them, take up the entirety of the front and back covers (Mayo). It is impressive how intricately placed each of the hundreds of characters are to ensure clarity of the entire image but also each distinct character. The third issue is the point in the story when the teams try to work together to unravel the mystery of what is happening. On the cover, the Justice League and Avengers characters are interspersed as though they were part of one massive collective.

The fourth and final cover is the simplest, featuring Superman holding Captain America's shield and Thor's hammer on the front, and two Earths merging together on the back, their intersecting outlines forming an infinity symbol, indicative of the number of universes available to the comic book companies. This image, perhaps more than even covers featuring Batman and Captain America in the same image, feels transgressive of the established order of the comic book industry. As Roz Kaveney notes, this image is "genuinely iconic because [it is] so deeply wrong at important levels. It is magnificent and it is also in a real sense contrary to nature"[4] (30). Fittingly, this is the last such image that has been produced in cooperation between the two companies, an image that carries weight but feels wrong to the reader.

Sources of Conflict

Returning to the narrative, this pattern is a fairly common trope of superhero team-ups, even when contained within the Marvel and DC universes. It has become a common trope of the superhero genre that when heroes first meet for a team-up, there is an initial battle before issues are sorted out and they work together. The cause of the fight could be a misunderstanding, that one of them is being manipulated and can't reveal it to the other, that they have the same goal and view the other as an obstacle, or any other reason the creators devise to ensure a half-issue of fighting between characters that are really on the same side. This trope, which seems to serve the interests of fans and creators alike, is absolutely going to be employed for something as rare as a company crossover that affords readers the chance to see Batman fight Captain America or Thor test the strength of Mjolnir against Superman's invulnerability. If *JLA/Avengers* had hinged on the Justice League and Avengers fighting solely because cosmic beings manipulated them into pursuing the same twelve objects, the series would be entertaining, but lack resonance with the post–9/11 world when it was produced.

In *Super-History: Comic Book Superheroes and American Society*, Jeffrey K. Johnson notes that the first decade of this century could be termed the "Decade of Fear," both in terms of reactions to the turn of the millennium and the tragic events of 9/11, but also in how the comic book industry reflected America's attitudes in the pages of their publications. Johnson notes that it took some time for the major comic book companies to fully reflect the complex response shifting landscape of American culture following 9/11. While later series, such DC Comics' *Identity Crisis* and Marvel Comics' *Civil War* have clear post 9/11 themes, the short-term response from the companies included "safe" comics, such as *Batman: Hush*, *Marvel: 1602*, and *JLA/Avengers* (175). While it is completely true that the later series are undeniably exploring issues and concerns of a post–9/11 world, even *JLA/Avengers*, published in 2003, contains elements that appear to be a reaction to the changing world of the new century.

The most significant evidence that this is a post–9/11 story comes from the motivation for the conflict between the two teams. There are actually two reasons provided for the Justice League to fight the Avengers, one which exists solely for this story, and one that highlights the differences between the traditions of DC and Marvel Comics while simultaneously reflecting larger cultural debates of the era. As the heroes cross over and see the other team's Earth, both groups are dismayed. Superman is disgusted that the Avengers have not done more to improve the world he finds. With their powers, he seems to conclude, they should have been able to improve the world more than what he sees in a gritty world that openly questions its heroes. He even comments that perhaps the heroes and citizens of this Earth "are just backward" and later concluding that "it's clear [the Avengers are] not fighting hard enough" to enforce their will (Busiek, "A Contest..."). Captain America, conversely, seems put off by the "sleek and elegant" heroes of the DC Universe, preferring the rougher heroes from his world (Busiek, "A Contest..."). He even protests, after visiting Metropolis, that "this is [the hero's] city, it wasn't built by men. They must own this world, like little tin Gods—demanding the public's adoration instead of protecting its freedoms!" and he goes on to refer to the Justice League as "fascist overlords" and "high and mighty stormtroopers" (Busiek, "A Journey...").

In short, years before this debate would be made explicit in Marvel's *Civil War*, Busiek and Perez are using superheroes to comment on many of the debates that arose in American following 9/11. The way in which this is presented allows the long histories of both companies to naturally inform the positions taken. DC Comics has often been described as a universe of gods who inhabit mythic cites like Metropolis and Gotham City. Marvel Comics, conversely, has been identified with flawed heroes who live in a fictionalized version of the real world. The Avengers have a home base in New York City, not a watchtower on the moon.

But, beyond that difference in the styles of stories told, the debate Captain American and Superman are giving voice to is one that America has been wrestling with since the passage of the PATRIOT Act in 2001, very shortly after the infamous 9/11 attacks. Security versus freedom. The reach of the government versus the rights of its citizens. Protection versus potential violence. Individual rights versus the good of the larger society. Captain America accuses the Justice League of having gone to far in ensuring their vision of a better world exists in the DC Universe. Superman accuses the Avengers of not having done enough to protect the citizens of their Earth. As Travis Langley points out,

> When motivated by losses in either freedom or security, people often relinquish the other. Feeling vulnerable in the wake of the attacks of September 11, 2001, many American citizens accepted a lessening of liberties in the form of wire tapping, e-mail monitoring, lengthier airplane boarding procedures, broadened government ability to engage in search and seizure, expanded regulation of financial transactions, and easing of restrictions on foreign intelligence gathering on United States soil [70–71].

In this narrative Captain America believes the Justice League have sacrificed the freedom of the citizens of their Earth for greater security, while Superman argues that the Avengers have enforced too little security while allowing their citizens too much freedom. In the brief visits they have on each other's Earth, Captain America sees museums and awards honoring the Justice League, while the Justice League sees destruction and violence on the Avenger's Earth.

Addressing such a serious and recent subject as 9/11 in a crossover event featuring a man in a bat suit and a woman who can shrink and grow wings in her back may seem like a thematic mismatch, but superhero comic books have always reflected the issues of their times. From the covers depicting heroes battling Nazis in World War II to Captain America giving up his costume and name in the wake of the Watergate scandal, comic books have always addressed adult, real-world issues while trying to provide entertainment. Both Marvel and DC have seen shifts and changes in the roles of their superheroes and the themes of their stories following 9/11. A few examples highlight how the narratives of the two companies have adapted to changing times. The entire Marvel universe was embroiled in a *Civil War* that seemed driven more by differing post–9/11 ideologies than any other conflict. Within the series it has been argued that Iron Man's role in the series is "more a response to the challenge of traditional ideal of the superhero in a post–9/11 world" (Darowski 182). Jeffrey K. Johnson argues that DC Comics' *Infinite Crisis* in part hinges on the simple morality of the Golden Age Superman running up against the complexity and shades of gray of a post–9/11 world view (199–208). The Incredible Hulk explored the blurred lines between heroes and monsters that resulted in the aftermath of 9/11 and America's response to the attacks (Southgate 197). Undoubtedly numerous other examples could be identified for not only 9/11, but for other significant events in American history such as the rise of the feminist movement or the end of the Cold War.

It is the presence of these complex real-world issues which elevates *JLA/Avengers* from a simple cash-grab by the companies or a What if...? tale that services fan curiosity. But what is the conclusion the series draws, after raising these issues? For one thing, it seems to point out that much of the infighting that has plagued American politics, the finger-pointing, name-calling, and increasingly partisan bickering, is pointless. The two teams fight and argue amongst themselves when there is a bigger threat to their continued safety and well-being looming beyond their self-limiting scope of vision.

Perhaps more significantly the series seems to acknowledge that the spectrum on which the heroes found each other fighting does not have a definitive right or wrong. Clearly being too far on either end—allowing complete freedom of the individuals and thus allowing them to harm the larger society or ensuring safety through constant surveillance and enforcement of even thought—is in the wrong. But there can be legitimate differences of opinion about what the correct amount of government protection is without turning anyone who thinks differently into a villain. When the two teams are departing to return to their respective Earth's, Superman salutes Captain America and says, "Whether we fear we do too much—or not enough..." Captain America then returns the salute and finishes the thought, "We keep trying" (Busiek, "The Brave..."). Scarlet Witch acknowledges that the most important part of this adventure is that the two sides "have come together" and "overcome our differences" (Busiek, "The Brave..."). Though their styles may be different, the goal is the same. Instead of demonizing anyone who approaches an issue with a different methodology, working together can lead to positive results. And that's a message that certainly resonates beyond the comic book page and into the world of the readers.

NOTES

1. It was a four-part mini-series, with each company publishing two of the issues. The issues published by DC Comics were titled *DC vs. Marvel*, while the issues published by Marvel were called *Marvel vs. DC*. Inter-company cooperation can only go so far.

2. Among the merged characters included Batman/Wolverine as Dark Claw, Doctor Strange/Doctor Fate as Doctor Strangefate, Justice League/X-Men as JLX, Superman/Captain America as Super Soldier, Bruce Wayne/Nick Fury as Bruce Wayne: Agent of S.H.I.E.L.D., and Spider-Man/Superboy as Spider-Boy.

3. Similar reasoning discussed for *DC vs. Marvel/Marvel vs. DC* applies for the swapped positions of the two teams in this four issues mini-series. Though in this case, *JLA/Avengers* was published by Marvel while *Avengers/JLA* was published by DC. For simplicity I will refer to the series as JLA/Avengers for the remainder of this essay.

4. A brief anecdotal bit of evidence regarding this idea, while reading this series for research my seven-year-old daughter saw this cover and, as a child familiar with superheroes but by no means an avid reader, seemed legitimately upset about it because, as she said, "he's a DC guy holding Marvel stuff! That can't happen!"

WORKS CITED

Busiek, Kurt (w), and George Perez (a). "A Journey into Mystery." *JLA/Avengers* #1. New York: Marvel Comics, 2003.
_____. "A Contest of Champions." *Avengers/JLA* #2. New York: DC Comics, 2003.
_____. "Strange Adventures." *JLA/Avengers* #2. New York: Marvel, Comics, 2003.
_____. "The Brave and the Bold." *Avengers/JLA* #4. NY: DC Comics, 2003.
Cronin, Brian. "Comic Book Urban Legends Revealed #17." ComicBookResources. com. 22 September 2005. Web. 27 April 2016. http://goodcomics.comicbook resources.com/2005/09/22/comic-book-urban-legends-revealed-17/.
Darowski, John. "'I would be the bad guy': Tony Stark as Villain of Marvel's *Civil War*." In *The Ages of Iron Man: Essays on the Armored Avenger in Changing Times*. Ed. Joseph J. Darowski. Jefferson, NC: McFarland, 2015.
Johnson, Jeffrey K. *Super-History: Comic Book Superheroes and American Society*. Jefferson, NC: McFarland, 2012.
_____. "This Isn't Your Grandfather's Comic Book Universe: The Return of the Golden Age Superman." In *The Ages of Superman: Essays on the Man of Steel in Changing Times*. Ed. Joseph J. Darowski. Jefferson, NC: McFarland, 2012.

Kaveny, Roz. *Superheroes! Capes and Crusaders in Comics and Films.* New York: I.B. Tauris, 2008.

Langley, Travis. "Freedom versus Security: The Basic Human Dilemma from 9/11 to Marvel's *Civil War.*" In *Marvel Comics' Civil War and the Age of Terror: Critical Essays on the Comic Saga.* Ed. Kevin Michael Scott. Jefferson, NC: McFarland, 2015.

Lawrence, Christopher. *George Pérez Storyteller.* Mt. Laurel, NJ: Dynamite Entertainment, 2006.

Mayo, John. "JLA/Avengers Key." ComicBookPage.com 2016. Web. 27 April 2016. http://www.comicbookpage.com/Comics/JLA_Avengers/JLAAvengers3Cover. php?Image=Cover3Key.

Southgate, Brooke. "'I didn't come here for a whisper': Monsters, Violence, and Heroes in *World War Hulk* and Post-9/11 America." In *The Ages of the Incredible Hulk: Essays on the Green Goliath in Changing Times.* Ed. Joseph J. Darowski. Jefferson, NC: McFarland, 2015.

Madwomen
Sexism as Nostalgia, or Feminism
in The New Frontier

JENNIFER SWARTZ-LEVINE

The Way Things Weren't

Nostalgia suffuses the pages of *The New Frontier* (cover dated March–November 2004), a DC Comics mini-series that was written and drawn by Darwyn Cooke. The plot is set in the Eisenhower and Kennedy years and the art style is highly evocative of a silver age *Justice League* comic book. But the hazy-washed nostalgia of yesteryear is not truly the order of the day, as we learn early on. We quickly discover that the shiny space-age was much more menacing than one might assume from viewing the Mamie Eisenhower pink bathrooms and Formica counter-topped kitchens that dominated suburban middle-America homes in the 1950s.

It is against that backdrop of "the way things weren't" that we discover that most of the superheroes have disappeared. One of the major plot points engages governmental oppression, as our Justice Society heroes disband in the face of McCarthy-like hearings in order to refrain from unmasking, registering with the government, and swearing a loyalty oath. Most of them choose to exercise a maneuver that is reminiscent of John Galt's choice in Ayn Rand's *Atlas Shrugged* (1957), where he, and other of society's leaders and industrialists, disappears from public life.[1] In a newspaper article appearing in *The New Frontier*, Iris West writes, "The JSA … simply vanished … they refused to recognize Congress' authority, but as patriotic Americans they refuse to break Federal law. Henceforth, they were retiring" (Cooke, "Book 1").[2] The only two exceptions to this are Superman and Wonder Woman, who sign the oath and become sanctioned representatives of the government (Cooke, "Book 1"). Their initial charge, as we also gather from

Iris West's article, is to "round up the remaining Masked Men who refused to turn themselves in or retire" (Cooke, "Book 1"). Superman in particular is vigilant in fulfilling his duties in this regard, thereby marking him in the American consciousness as their most patriotic adopted son. Yet this is a world that needs all its heroes, even the ones who don't fall in line with American domestic and foreign policy, for there is a coming menace that hovers— at one point, literally—above them. As the six issue mini-series unfolds, the plot pushes toward exploring the individual stories of members of what would become the Justice League of America as they wage war against the ominous sentient island, the Centre.

This island, which writhes with dinosaurs and pterodactyls, ultimately takes flight, perching over the Atlantic Ocean near Cape Canaveral, Florida. It serves as a stand-in for the hovering menaces of discrimination—both of racism and sexism—that suffused the American experience at the time, even as they were often ignored by the larger culture.[3] Comic books, however, are an excellent means by which to explore complex issues, for as Kelli E. Stanley observes, "they expose the collective psyche of a nation or culture because they embody the fantasies that fuel our national identity" (143). In the case of *The New Frontier*, difference was seen as threatening, a concept J'onn J'onzz, who eventually becomes the Martian Manhunter, discovers when he goes to a movie about Martians (Cooke, "Book 3"). He senses that his fellow theater patrons fear that which they don't understand, and that to stay safe, he must continue to masquerade as human. In a parallel story arc, John Henry, whose wife and daughter are burned to death when his home is set on fire by the Ku Klux Klan, becomes a vigilante to avenge their deaths. He pays with his life when his location is betrayed by a little girl who already has absorbed the racist beliefs of the adults (Cooke, "Book 4"). An Edward R. Murrow broadcast exposes the horror of what happens to John Henry; sadly, the only one who seems to be affected in the pages of the comic is J'onn J'onzz, who sees John Henry's murder as a sign that he must return to Mars.

One of the other ways in which Darwyn Cooke explores the social challenges of 1950s society is an examination of the ways in which women are treated. While *The New Frontier* has an astonishingly large cast of characters, many of whom are female and play important roles, the most important female superhero, Wonder Woman, is at turns held up as an ambassador for American values, decried for defending the powerless, silenced when she attempts to voice her opinion, and forced into retirement when her beliefs differ from those of the President and Vice President. She is both celebrated and ignored, shifting back and forth between empowered warrior and marginalized woman.

Wonder Woman's plight is not immediately obvious, though, for it is obscured by the nostalgia that suggested that the 1950s was wholly idyllic.

The same mindset that ignored J'onn J'onzz and John Henry insisted that the era was a softer, safer time. World War II was over, the Korean Conflict had ended, soldiers had returned home, and families were settling down in Levittown-like developments in suburbs all across America. Yet, as Stephanie Coontz reminds us, "the reality of these families was far more painful and complex than the situation-comedy reruns or the expurgated memories of the nostalgic would suggest" (29). The reality of being a woman in the 1950s was often to be defined solely by the roles of wife and mother. In *The Feminine Mystique* (1963), Betty Friedan contends, "The feminine mystique permits, even encourages, women to ignore the question of their identity" (126). And while she is neither wife nor mother, Wonder Woman is not immune to this problem, which becomes increasingly evident as she struggles to make her way in the brave new world of *The New Frontier*.

"There's the door, Spaceman"

In keeping with the times, Wonder Woman and her female superhero compatriots are secondary characters, willing to stand ever-so-slightly behind their dominant male counterparts. Laura Mattoon D'Amore writes, "Super-heroines have always been the aside, the marginalized, the coda" (1234), and, mindful of that precedent, superheroines in *The New Frontier* make only very brief appearances (or are referred to off-hand) in the first book. As the series progresses, however, Darwyn Cooke undercuts that expected norm with Wonder Woman's first major entrance. Wonder Woman appears on a splash page, where she is standing on a table, clutching a wine goblet in one hand and a bottle in the other, surrounded by Vietnamese women who are holding weapons (Cooke, "Book 2"). There is clearly a celebration happening, and Superman, who has come to check on Wonder Woman and find out why she has not reported her whereabouts to the government for two weeks, is hor-rified to discover the cause. Wonder Woman defeated the rapists who were holding these women captive and released them, but then she put the weapons on the ground and stood by while the women killed their jailors. This Wonder Woman is a far cry from the one who was the secretary of the Justice Society of America in the 1940s (Daniels 57, Hanley 109). She completes her assigned mission, but then creates one of her own, in which she sanctions revenge and revels in the outcome. This Wonder Woman is subversion writ large as she defies every stereotypical trope about what it means to be female. It is espe-cially shocking to witness this bloodthirsty Princess Diana since she is drawn in the Silver Age style and the story takes place in an era where nice girls were supposed to think nice thoughts, as opposed to encouraging female prisoners to rise up against their oppressors and exact vengeance.

Her actions and rationale for encouraging the women shock Superman. He asks her why she has disappeared and her reply is that she is "over here winning the hearts and minds of the disenfranchised" (Cooke, "Book 2"). But the way she does it is antithetical to everything that was American foreign policy at the time. She says to Superman, "Did they tell you why I'm here, Kal? I had been sent into Cambodia to retrieve a crashed C-47 transport that had an American crew. This of course *never officially happened*, because there aren't any Americans over here" (Cooke, "Book 2"). She fulfills her charge as emissary of the United States government by sticking to her mandate, even though that mission is a covert one (at this point, America was not yet officially involved in South Indochina and what would eventually become the Vietnam War). But she then emphasizes that she is "only involved in humanitarian efforts" (Cooke, "Book 2"), which she interprets differently than the American government. They want her to rescue American military transport planes, and she wants to rescue powerless Vietnamese rape victims whose families have been massacred and who can do nothing to further the American agenda. She believes saving these disenfranchised souls who have been subjected to unimaginable horror is just as humanitarian as reclaiming the soldiers from the downed C-47.

But the way she rescues these women is a subversion of every concept of an American feminine ideal. Nice girls aren't supposed to sanction killing, no matter how badly treated the victims are. Yet in this instance, Princess Diana is Wonder Woman at her most warrior-like, a far cry from the silver age Wonder Woman, who was most enchanted by the idea of marrying Steve Trevor and finding her happily ever after. This Wonder Woman liberates the victims, enables the downtrodden to avenge themselves, and rejoices with them afterward. She tells Superman:

> On our way back to Laos, I noticed a small camp at the mouth of the river. It was a rebel base in territory that had belonged to the South last month, but what made my blood race was the *tiger cages* I saw in the paddy. Like a good soldier, I completed my mission. That evening I returned to the camp. I didn't *hurt* them. I simply *disarmed* them. And then I opened the tiger cages. These women had been living like this for weeks. Nothing more than animals ... sexual cattle. They stood in silence, facing their tormentors. I had placed the weapons in the clearing. *The choice* was theirs [Cooke, "Book 2"].

It is this moment, of providing the women choice and refusing to interfere with their revenge, that she believes is as freeing as letting them out of the cages. She has given them back the ability to shape their own destiny without the interference of outside forces. The decision they make to kill their captors is, in the eyes of many, an act that is as equally horrific as the torture to which they were subjected. However, Wonder Woman and the Vietnamese villagers see this act as empowering. They have wreaked vengeance on their rapists, thereby reasserting their autonomy over both their bodies and their existences.

Clearly, though, from the bodies Superman finds and the party going on in the hut, their decision stuns Superman to his core. He both is horrified that murder has happened and that the act was committed by women. He says, "These women did that? And ... and you stood by and watched? Diana ... how could you?" (Cooke, "Book 2"). He is repulsed by three things—that it happened at all, that Wonder Woman stood back and allowed it to happen, and that the people who did this are women. While he is deeply disturbed by the act itself, his horror is further informed by their gender, as it eclipses his comprehension that the ones who might have vengeful impulses are women. This disgust is predicated by the fact that cultural expectations for women at the time were that they fulfill their duties to home and to family. Of this era, Kelli E. Stanley observes, "Popular culture in the 1950s continually reinforced the concept of women as decorative but useless.... Female sexuality was dangerous but exaggerated, controlled, shaped, and yet enhanced by the bras and girdles of the period" (151). Female power, such as the kind Wonder Woman exhibits, is dangerous, too. She is unfettered vengeance, treacherous in both her skills and her willingness to teach other women to rise up and defend themselves, as well.

Her actions run counter to everything presented in the 1950s, especially in popular culture: magazine articles lectured women on how to be better spouses and television shows depicted women only in their roles as loving wives and mothers. After all, June Cleaver would not have found herself wreaking revenge in *Leave It to Beaver*, nor would Lucy Ricardo, for all her zaniness in *I Love Lucy*, have had any clue about the ravages these women had endured. This was par for the pop culture course, though, as Stanley further writes: "Women were either wives and mothers (loveable and maternal or emasculating and bitchy) or sexual objects (dangerous femme fatales who controlled their own allure, bubble-headed playthings who remained unaware of it, or childlike waifs who needed a much older Pygmalion to waken their sexuality)" (151). So to expect Superman, the poster boy for small-town Americana, to endorse these women's revenge is misguided.

This divide drives a wedge between Superman and Wonder Woman, in that each is disappointed in the response of the other, and both make choices that they see through the lens of gender. At the end of *The New Frontier: The Deluxe Edition*, Darwyn Cooke writes of this scene, "How can two people of such common virtue be so far apart ideologically? That is part of what I believe made *New Frontier* an interesting read; forcing these fictional characters to take stands on impossibly complex, real situations" (n.p.). There is no question that both Wonder Woman and Superman are creatures of infinite morality, but they deploy that morality differently. Wonder Woman is most horrified at the treatment of these women. Superman is shaken by the women's treatment of the men. Both realize that atrocities have occurred in this Vietnamese village, but they fundamentally disagree on how to handle them. Superman values human life above all, even the lives of those who have betrayed every basic tenet of humanity. Wonder Woman, however, values the women's lives above the lives of their captors. In her view, the men forfeited their right to life the second they forced the women into those cages and inflicted their will on the captives. To Wonder Woman and the women she rescues, it is the choices one makes that determine if one gets to live. The rapists have failed this test, and Wonder Woman and her crew are avenging angels of retribution.

Superman reiterates his dismay when he says, "But to allow cold-blooded murder ... and then to celebrate. You're supposed to set an example!" (Cooke, "Book 2"). One doesn't quite know if the example she's supposed to set is that of a superhero or that of a woman, or, if in Superman's mind, it's one and the same thing. In any case, she has, in his view, failed mightily. These women might no longer be confined to tiger cages, but the fact that that Wonder Woman has sanctioned murder and is now training these women "to survive the coming war" (Cooke, "Book 2"), is well over the line of what she was charged with doing. But to Wonder Woman, her actions fall within the mandate she has been given. She responds to Superman's assertion that she should set an example with derision: "What, hand them a smile and a box of flags? Their families, their mates ... their children were murdered before their eyes. This is civil war. I've given them their freedom and a chance for justice.... The American way!" (Cooke, "Book 2"). For it to be something other than cheap jingoism, Wonder Woman sees her charge as giving these women their freedom and the skills they need to ensure that they never again will be victimized and powerless. Yet Superman wants her to leave things at the "smile and a box of flags" stage, if the article he wrote as Clark Kent is to be believed. Just a few pages before this scene, a newspaper article, headlined "Superman and Wonder Woman Ease Suffering for Indochina: America Offers Relief to War-Torn Region" (Cooke, "Book 2"), is accompanied by a photo of Wonder Woman, smiling at a child who smiles back while waving an American flag. The caption underneath is the same phrase with which she taunted him when he first shows up in the Vietnamese hut: "Wonder Woman: winning the hearts and minds of the disenfranchised" (Cooke, "Book 2"). The accompanying article also quotes a representative of the Eisenhower administration: "Superman and Wonder Woman are involved in relief efforts in Indo-China. This administration would like to stress that their mission is humanitarian, not military in nature" (Cooke, "Book 2"). This is, however, a lie, in every conceivable way. Wonder Woman is there on a military rescue mission. Other than in the photo, there are no smiling children with American flags to be found. And the government is most definitely involved in military activities in Indo-China. Clark Kent, it would seem, is just as much a government agent as Superman is in this story, as he whitewashes reality and attempts to make Wonder Woman complicit in his actions. In his guise as Superman, he tells Wonder Woman that he will have to report her since "what you've done is in strict violation of our protocol" (Cooke, "Book 2").

What Superman forgets, as we all so often do, is that Wonder Woman is a warrior. She is not the kind, caring representative of female domesticity in the way that she often is portrayed (and definitely was portrayed in her own title in the silver age comics), but rather a dispenser of justice that comes straight from the Greek gods that are her heritage. Wonder Woman's "capacity for violence is linked to her Amazonian otherness, a violence and power existing outside the domain of civilization" (Stanley 161). She's not like Superman at all, who is, at his heart, a good boy who was adopted by Midwestern parents. He might be from another planet, but his very being is informed by the "Midwestern nice" philosophy, and he projects that on those around him. His "role as the champion of the 'American Way' is made possible by his normalized Midwest upbringing in Kansas. Though god-like, his humanity is bourgeois, conservative, and reassuring" (Stanley 161). Wonder Woman, however, is an entirely different creature. William Moulton Marston, Wonder Woman's creator, wanted her to be a role model for young girls and that he believed in that women, by using loving dominance, would tame the combative natures of men (Daniels 19, 22–23). Her aim is to bring peace, but she often does this through war, which makes her dual-edged nature one that is hard to untangle. Marc Edward DiPaolo notes, "A warrior pacifist, a feminist sex symbol, a foreign-royal-turned-American-immigrant, and a devout pagan living in a secular age, Wonder Woman is a heroic figure who embodies a set of seemingly contradictory character traits" (151). Yet at her very core, Wonder Woman is committed to administering justice, which, given her belief system, often meant fiercely avenging wrongs. As an immortal Amazon, hers is not the God of the Judeo-Christian faith, but rather she follows a pantheon of gods and goddesses who are capricious, violent, and, above-all, vengeful. This has always been an elemental part of her history, but the implications of her faith are infrequently explored in the post–World War II and silver age eras. Instead, she often is depicted as occasionally timid and frequently love-sick (especially in her secret identity of Diana Prince), when her origin story indicates she is nothing of the sort. Darwyn Cooke resurrects her origin by bringing her warrior nature to the fore and explores how the values that are inculcated in both Wonder Woman and Superman shape their reactions to what happens in Vietnam. Of their confrontation, Cooke writes, "I also thought it was high time that we saw a Wonder Woman that was true to her heritage, an Amazon with Mediterranean beauty, enormous passion and … taller than Superman" (n.p.).

Her passion for freeing these women is evident as she climbs off the table, towers over Superman, and kicks him out of the hut. She says to him disparagingly, "Take a good look around. There are no rules here. Just suffering and madness. I want you to go back to the undersecretary and tell him that" and then dismisses him: "there's the door, Spaceman" (Cooke, "Book 2"). Superman should not be surprised, at either her passions or her actions. She sees her charge as helping these women become as Amazonian and warrior-like as she. He expects her to behave like an American woman would have at the time, and he is mistaken. He might have taken on the folkways of his adopted country, but she has not. In fact, at this point in the text, she is not an American, even though she acts on its behalf. No, Wonder Woman's first affiliation is that of Amazon warrior, who might live on Paradise Island, but who believes that sometimes waging war is the only way to bring peace.

The next time we see her is at a reception at the White House, where she is being recognized for her work. At a ceremony awarding her American citizenship, President Eisenhower makes a statement in which he praises Superman and Wonder Woman for their service: "These modern-day Olympians come from faraway lands, but they have chosen this great nation as their home. They have given selflessly in the name of America" (Cooke, "Book 3"). At first, Wonder Woman thinks this ceremony is a validation of the work she has done on behalf of America, but she doesn't realize that it actually is a brush off. Eisenhower and his Vice President, Richard Nixon, acknowledge her work, but intend to shuffle her off the national stage. When she went rogue in order to save the women and teach them to defend themselves, she did not conform to American foreign policy. She has thus become a liability. Matthew J. Costello writes that President Eisenhower "saw the United States as the moral force for good in promoting the global progress of freedom against tyranny" (49) and that America "must also support an expansive foreign policy, to serve as a beacon of light to those who seek freedom from the oppressor's yoke" (49). And this is Wonder Woman's problem: it all depends on who gets to define the identity of the oppressor. As she takes the podium, she thinks that being granted American citizenship is an endorsement of the choices she made in Vietnam, but it is a ceremony meant to silence her before she reveals the atrocities she witnessed: "My heart is filled with joy today to be ... American. I can imagine no greater honor. But this appointment is also a sacred responsibility. I want to talk today about our future. I want to talk to you about love, a better tomorrow. My time in Vietnam has opened my eyes to the futility of—" (Cooke, "Book 3"). But since America is not yet militarily involved, the opinions of this freshly minted American citizen about what she saw in the Vietnamese village cannot be communicated, either to the press corps or to the nation. Her smiling visage, surrounded by American flags, is another photo op in which she is an unwitting participant. She doesn't realize that this moment, just like the Clark Kent article, is propaganda.

Neither Eisenhower nor Nixon is interested in her take on American foreign policy or who she believes is wielding the "oppressor's yoke," and they are even less invested in letting her share those opinions with the press. She is rushed off the stage by Vice President Nixon, who says, "Thank you, my dear. Stirring thoughts, indeed. Folks, we are running short on time, but please enjoy this afternoon's celebration" (Cooke, "Book 3"). Not only does he silence her at the podium, he infantilizes her by calling her "my dear." She is reduced to an ornament, a pretty bauble who decorates the pressroom, and whose main duty is to fall in line. When she fails to do so, she is no longer useful, and therefore must be stripped of her autonomy and her public voice.

In a final attempt to communicate her concerns, she speaks to President Eisenhower in the Oval Office, where he tells her that she "deserve[s] a vacation, some time to relax and enjoy [her]self" (Cooke, "Book 3"). She doesn't realize that he, too, plans to retire her in order to neutralize her perceived instability. She tells him that she has "too much to do. I'm sure when I share my experiences in Asia with you—" (Cooke, "Book 3"), only to be cut off, as he reaches up and pats her on the cheek. He tells her, "I really must get back. Lovely seeing you. Remember what they say: 'Old soldiers never die ... they just fade away'" (Cooke, "Book 3"). Much like his vice president, he dismisses her. Nixon ran her off the stage and called her "my dear," and Eisenhower pats her on the cheek and cuts her off mid-sentence. This is the moment when Wonder Woman realizes that her beliefs about rescuing the Vietnamese women and providing her version of humanitarian aid in Vietnam is all for naught. Justice doesn't prevail, at least not the kind that she wants to dispense. Instead, American foreign policy marches ahead, and Diana, the new citizen and "old solider," is put out to pasture.

Superman doesn't understand why Wonder Woman has left, and flies over Paradise Island to meet with her. He finds her reading a book and clutching a goblet of wine, which serves as a visual link to when he spied her through the window of the Vietnamese hut. He is puzzled by her absence, and wonders if it was "that oaf Nixon at the press conference" (Cooke, "Book 4") that led to her leaving public life. She retorts, "I didn't retire. I was forced out because of my beliefs" (Cooke, "Book 4"). Superman cannot believe that Eisenhower and Nixon want Wonder Woman off the national stage, and he continues to place his faith in the government: "But Diana, why would they do that? You're a champion of the people" (Cooke, "Book 4"). Unwittingly, he has captured the central issue. She might be a champion of the disenfranchised and victimized, but she seeks justice for the wrong players in this particular setting. Thus, she must be disempowered, lest she change the national discussion about what is happening in Vietnam. She retorts, "So they bought me off with a medal and sent me on holiday. Because what I have to say doesn't line up with their agenda. They don't want me if they can't use me. That's not the

America I fought for. My America—our America—is an ideal, not an administration. During World War 2, we knew we were right and we've always just assumed we were right ever since" (Cooke, "Book 4"). Disenchanted by American foreign policy, she realizes that she has fallen victim to nostalgia, as well. Her actions on behalf of the Eisenhower administration are a result of her loyalty to the United States during World War II, when America's mission was clear. The Eisenhower and Nixon of Darwyn Cooke's world play on Wonder Woman's sense of obligation to America because of the justness of America's mandate in World War II. She was blinded by past allegiance and now that she has been marginalized by Nixon and Eisenhower, realizes that she was exploited for public relations purposes. Her mission now is to pull Superman out of the thrall of the government by recalibrating his moral barometer to align with her views. She says, "Kal, your real power lies not in your strength, but in your values and compassionate spirit. That is what America needs right now, not another administration. It needs a leader" (Cooke, "Book 4"). America's fate depends on its adopted son understanding that he has been used just as much as she and that he needs to divorce himself from blind adherence to governmental authority.

Wonder Woman's words to Superman are prescient—events are about to transpire that will definitely need his leadership. Shortly after this discussion, Wonder Woman arrives in the invisible plane, whose form can be seen since it is outlined with her spilled blood. The Centre has attacked Paradise Island (Cooke, "Book 5") and she flies to Cape Canaveral, where the other superheroes are gathering. She crash lands and is rescued by Superman. This moment is depicted in a splash page that highlights her weakness, as Superman flies with her inert form, calling for a "medic!" (Cooke, "Book 5"). This splash page serves as a bookend to the first one in the Vietnamese hut which highlighted her might. That Wonder Woman has been vanquished, for the warrior Diana now is beyond her own strength. Her power has been sacrificed in an attempt both to save her sisters and get to Cape Canaveral in order to warn the others. When she recovers, she tells Superman of the atrocities that happened on Paradise Island. The Centre has destroyed much of it, and is now on its way to South Florida: "It was gone as quickly as it came. Our idyllic southlands had been destroyed as nothing but a distraction. The monstrosity has a far greater destination. It's on its way here" (Cooke, "Book 5"). She knows this is no longer her fight, but one which requires both Superman's leadership and the rest of the superheroes, since, "it's too big to stop alone. To defeat this, you'll all have to come together … for the greater good" (Cooke, "Book 5"). As she sends him out the door to lead the troops into battle, she repeats what she said to him in Vietnam: "there's the door … Spaceman" (Cooke, "Book 5"). This time, however, it is said in a much different way. Then, she was angry at his inability to understand the women's suffering and point of view. Now, she is proud that he is about to take on the dangerous Centre and lead their fellow superheroes into battle. Yet she still is marginalized, and not simply because of her injuries. She kisses Superman goodbye, almost like a good wife sending her husband off to work. There is a war to be won, and one of the superheroes mightiest combatants has been sidelined by her wounds; as she lies on the table and kisses Superman goodbye, her warrior Amazon self is completely abnegated and she disappears from the comic for all but a few more brief appearances.

However, Darwyn Cooke isn't done turning tropes on their head. In a romantic movie script, Superman would command the troops and defeat the Centre, returning to adulation from Lois Lane and Wonder Woman. But just when we think it's going that way, Superman is defeated. He goes down in the ocean, where his body cannot be found and he is believed to be dead. It is left to the other superheroes to win the day, and it is the second-stringers, the ones who are not Superman, Batman, and Wonder Woman, who come to the fore. Adam Strange brings Ray Palmer, who has not yet become the Atom, to the group of scientists and military experts who are working with the superheroes to defeat the Centre. Ray Palmer's ability to shrink matter is harnessed, attached to a backpack worn by the Flash, and it is he and the others who take down the Centre. He is aided in this by the Blackhawks, Ace Morgan, Hal Jordan (who only recently has obtained his Green Lantern powers), and the Green Arrow, but Superman, Wonder Woman, and Batman are mostly absent from the narrative's climax. True, Wonder Woman recovers enough that she is able to join the battle, enjoining the others to "fight on! To the last breath, fight on!" (Cooke, "Book 6"), but the heroes here are the Flash and Green Lantern. Much of this is done to adhere to Darwyn Cooke's self-imposed mandate not to conflict with established continuity for the Justice League (Cooke n.p.), but it is interesting that the big three are jettisoned, for the most part, as they often were during the *Justice Society* comics in the 1940s.[4]

After the Centre has been defeated, Aquaman returns a still-recovering Superman to the surface, to the relief of many, but most especially Lois Lane. Our narrator intones, "It's the kind of moment you dream about. A moment so perfect, it makes you want to cry. Because you know that whatever comes our way ... it'll never feel this good again" (Cooke, "Book 6"). The final splash page is a picture taken by Jimmy Olsen that has the heroes, including Superman and Wonder Woman, celebrating their victory. The accompanying headline trumpets an article by Lois Lane, "HEROES! Exclusive Coverage of Earth's Finest Hour" (Cooke, "Book 6"). The black and white image and the headline, combined with the caption that "it'll never feel this good again," immerses the heroes' shared victory in nostalgia. Because what else is nostalgia, other than the belief that things never will be as good as they once were? A hearkening back to a supposedly simpler time, a time where good was more clearly defined, and our heroes always were triumphant? Yet the real story, the one that hides behind Jimmy Olsen's picture, is one where Superman was defeated and nearly destroyed, J'onn J'onzz and John Henry were discriminated against, female superheroes other than Wonder Woman largely were absent from the text, Wonder Woman herself faced significant inequality, and life was not the simple, pastoral place the picture would suggest.

The New Frontier?

The Epilogue continues to evoke this nostalgia, as it is set against "The New Frontier" speech delivered by John F. Kennedy during his acceptance of the Presidential nomination at the Democratic National Committee's 1960 convention (Web). Matt Yockey writes, "In retro-actively writing [the Justice League's] genesis, Cooke celebrates the Silver Age as, like the Kennedy era, a period of hope in stark contrast to the present" (365). But the reality Darwyn Cooke depicts is much more complicated and darker than the accompanying text from Kennedy would suggest. As Kennedy's speech unrolls, we follow our superheroes into the future. Nostalgia might make us long for a simpler time, but The New Frontier—both the comic and the speech—indicates that very little has changed, especially for women. Wonder Woman is depicted reading to a group of children. The portion of Kennedy's speech assigned to this panel is "Today our concern must be with the future. For the world is changing. The old era is ending. The old ways will not do" (Cooke, "Book 6"). And yet, the old ways are still with us, at least for Wonder Woman. Laura Mattoon D'Amore writes that "the body of the superheroine becomes contested terrain, simultaneously embodying progressive ideas about women's roles while remaining staunchly characterized as nurturing and maternal" (1227). So it is for Wonder Woman, at least in this scene. While she is mentoring a group of children in this new era, she herself is left in the past, still trapped in the newspaper article that Clark Kent wrote long ago. She might be "winning [the] hearts and minds" of these children, but she's not getting to be her warrior self. The Wonder Woman who stood back and let the Vietnamese women avenge themselves and then trained them for the upcoming war has given way to a Wonder Woman whose previous unruliness and violence has been tamed into motherly domestication.

Yet there is some hope. Further in Kennedy's speech, there is a panel depicting female superheroes, including Supergirl, Wonder Girl, and Black Canary. Their appearance indicates that women will have a more prominent place in the future (although it should be noted that two of these female characters are girls and not women). The next generation of heroes is forming, since in addition to Supergirl, Wonder Girl, and Black Canary, the rest of the Teen Titans are there—we also see Robin, Kid Flash, Speedy, and Aqualad (Cooke, "Book 6"). The newly formed Justice League of America is present, too, with characters that have been integral parts of *The New Frontier*: Wonder Woman, Aquaman, Green Lantern, the Flash, and Martian Manhunter (Cooke, "Book 6"). The final image of the text is Darwyn Cooke's faithful interpretation of the cover of *Brave and the Bold #28*, where the JLA is formally introduced. He ended, quite deliberately, where the JLA begins, and says, "as promised, we end where it began—the first public appearance of the Justice League of America" (Cooke n.p.). This era may be over, but the JLA's work is just beginning; however, it too will be a place where female superheroes have just as complicated a time navigating issues of gender as they did in *The New Frontier*.

NOTES

1. Cooke notes that the idea of the superheroes being driven away by McCarthy-like hearings was originated by Paul Levitz (n.p.). Levitz mentions this as well in the Special Features to the *New Frontier* animated movie and Cooke also says that James Robinson's *The Golden Age* was an influence ("Superheroes United").

2. *The New Frontier* also uses media in fascinating ways to advance the story. Important details are often communicated through the newspaper, the television, and movies. By using mass media in ways that would have been accessible to every American, Darwyn Cooke further cements *The New Frontier* as part of the center of American life.

3. Darwyn Cooke notes that the island is based on Dinosaur Island, which has a rich history in DC Comics ("Commentary") and that when he was writing *The New Frontier*, he saw the island as representative of Communism ("Legion of Doom").

4. Cooke mentions that characters who had their own books frequently were named "honorary members" of the Justice Society and only made rare appearances in the *Justice Society of America* comic (n.p.).

WORKS CITED

"Comic Book Commentary: Homage to *The New Frontier*." *Justice League: The New Frontier*. Dir. David Bullock. Warner Bros., 2008. Blu-Ray.

Cooke, Darwyn. "Annotations." *DC: The New Frontier: The Deluxe Edition*. New York: DC Comics, 2015. Print.

Cooke, Darwyn (w, a). *DC: The New Frontier #1* (March 2004). New York: DC Comics.

_____. *DC: The New Frontier #2* (April 2004). New York: DC Comics.

_____. *DC: The New Frontier #3* (May 2004). New York: DC Comics.

_____. *DC: The New Frontier #4* (July 2004). New York: DC Comics.

_____. *DC: The New Frontier #5* (September 2004). New York: DC Comics.

_____. *DC: The New Frontier#6* (November 2004). New York: DC Comics.

Coontz, Stephanie. *The Way We Never Were: American Families and the Nostalgia Trap*. New York: Basic Books, 1992. Print.

Costello, Matthew J. *Secret Identity Crisis: Comic Books and the Unmasking of Cold War America*. New York: Continuum, 2009. Print.

D'Amore, Laura Mattoon. "The Accidental Supermom: Superheroines and Maternal

Performativity, 1963–1980." *The Journal of Popular Culture* 45.6 (2012): 1226–48. Print.

Daniels, Les. *Wonder Woman: The Complete History.* San Francisco: Chronicle Books, 2000. Print.

DiPaolo, Marc Edward. "Wonder Woman as World War II Veteran, Camp Feminist Icon, and Male Sex Fantasy." *The Amazing Transforming Superhero!* Ed. Terrence R. Wandtke. Jefferson, NC: McFarland, 2007, 151–73. Print.

Friedan, Betty. *The Feminine Mystique.* New York: W. W. Norton, 1963. Print.

Hanley, Tim. *Wonder Woman Unbound: The Curious History of the World's Most Famous Heroine.* Chicago: Chicago Review Press, 2014. Print.

Kennedy, John Fitzgerald. "1960 Democratic National Convention, 15 July 1960." John F. Kennedy Presidential Library and Museum. n.d. Web. 19 January 2016.

"Legion of Doom: The Pathology of the Super Villain." *Justice League: The New Frontier.* Dir. David Bullock. Warner Bros., 2008. Blu-Ray.

Rand, Ayn. *Atlas Shrugged.* New York: Penguin, 2007. Print.

Stanley, Kelli E. "'Suffering Sappho!' Wonder Woman and the (Re)Invention of the Feminine Ideal." *Helios* 32.2 (2005): 143–71. Print.

"Super Heroes United! The Complete Justice League History." *Justice League: The New Frontier.* Dir. David Bullock. Warner Bros., 2008. Blu-Ray.

Yockey, Matt. "Retopia: The Dialectics of the Superhero Comic Book." *Studies in Comics* 3.2 (2012): 349–70. Print.

Absolute Secrets Kept Absolutely

Public Memory and Forgetting *in* Identity Crisis

Daniel J. O'Rourke

The DC Comics mini-series *Identity Crisis*—written by Brad Meltzer with pencils by Rags Morales—opens with a series of personal interactions between superheroes and their families or colleagues. Elongated Man (Ralph Dibny) and Firehawk (Lorraine Riley) are on a stakeout when the younger woman asks, "So how'd you meet your wife? Dibny responds, "Can I say one thing?—And not be too sexist?… But when you're on a stakeout with Batman, he **never** asks that" (Meltzer 8). Clark Kent (Superman) is seen having breakfast with his parents, Jonathan and Martha Kent, at their family farm in Smallville. Finally, a frame depicts Nightwing (Dick Grayson) standing before the grave of his parents, John and Mary Grayson. His thoughts are illustrated in word balloons: "I hate coming here. But it was the first lesson Bruce taught me. Never Forget" (Meltzer 6). His former lover and Teen Titans teammate, Starfire, descends into the scene. Nightwing mentally responds: "Bruce was wrong about one thing. You don't have to do everything alone" (Meltzer 6).

Communities and Crisis

The opening pages of a comic book; a superhero, family, friends, and memories; in the superhero genre these are usually the context for a conflict about to happen. According to the tropes, a warning is sounded and the hero must respond alone. She puts a on a costume to signal the transformation from citizen to superhero. A part of this uniform is often a mask. To those

186

unfamiliar with the narrative form of comics, it seems a bit silly that a simple piece of cloth covering one's eyes could ever disguise a well-muscled, athletic form. Hair color, height, weight, and vocal patterns all betray the identity of the hero. But the reader of comics knows that there is something magical in the mask that represents much more. The mask is the symbol of the secret identity. Peter Coogan has noted that the secret identity is one of the defining characteristics of the superhero genre (24–42). Early pulp fictions portrayed heroes in a romantic vein; detectives and cowboys dressed and acted like other humans and operated in the same environment (Coogan 49). Superheroes adopted a mythic genre in which they stood apart from humans and their environment. A costume, chevron, and codename defined the superhuman actor and drew singular attention to their deeds (Coogan 49). Readers of comics realize that the mask does little to shield the physical identity of the hero. The mask is a symbolic, generic device that stands as a promise to protect the significant people in the life of the hero. Oliver Queen (Green Arrow) explains to the younger Wally West (Flash): "You don't just wear the mask for yourself. It's for your wife ... your parents ... even for—one day— your children. There are animals out there Wally. And when it comes to family, we can't always be there to defend them. But the mask will" (Meltzer 208).

Villains rarely stand a chance against the amazing powers and will of the superhero. Amoral criminals thus strike at a hero's non-super family and friends as a means of weakening the resolve of the superhero or to gain revenge for a past defeat. Day-to-day heroes such as police, firefighters, and nurses should be seen as romantic figures that toil in the real world and do not wear masks. They are public servants who quietly put their lives on the line to serve their communities and make the world a better place. But when the stakes are much larger and often more ambiguous, there are times when only the inspiration of a superhero will do.

The Justice League creates a community of superheroes. As *Identity Crisis* reveals, trusted family members and friends extend this community far beyond those wearing capes. In the field of Communication Studies, theorists have suggested that "public memory" is what defines and holds a group together (Hume). Initially, primitive humans formed tribes to increase their chances of physical survival in a harsh world. Over time, their actions were symbolically defined as words and stories to teach future generations the survival lessons of their ancestors. It was the collective memory of shared experiences and values that turned these individuals into a community. Communities strengthen their bonds by recalling their shared history in rituals, ceremonial speeches, and recorded volumes. What a community chooses to remember and celebrate defines who they are and what they hold dear.

An interesting extension of this theory suggests that just as a community may choose to remember, it may also elect to forget or redefine some painful or embarrassing memories. In the United States, issues such as slavery, the internment of Japanese Americans, or denying women the right to vote were actions that tested the highest democratic ideals of its citizens. Bradford Vivian notes that such memories will never be forgotten but there may come a time when they must be reframed to encompass a new vision for the future. After a bloody Civil War, Lincoln was challenged at Gettysburg to find a way to unite a divided nation. Recalling the founding of the country and the principles that had been tested in a civil war, Lincoln was able to speak of a new democracy of all the people. More close to the period of *Identity Crisis*'s production, the United States of America had been attacked and faced the trauma of 9/11 less than three years before the first issue was published. Trauma, memory, and identity were very explicit topics of discussion in the post–9/11 American culture.

In the comic book *Identity Crisis*, the community of superheroes is tested by a series of tragic events and must explore their history, survive their present, and prepare for their future. As a community that literally has generations of members at the time *Identity Crisis* takes place (with the costumed identity of heroes such as the Flash and Green Lantern having been passed down to new characters), what is remembered and shared with newer members changes the identity of the group as a whole.

Legend has it that in the Silver Age of comics, editors teamed superheroes as a way to increase sales (Wright 182–84). The theory was, that a devoted reader of Superman might plunk down 12 more cents if the Man of Steel appeared in a *Justice League of America* comic book. The hope was that this might not only extend the economic reach of Superman, but it could also introduce the reader to other less-popular characters such as the Green Arrow or Green Lantern, and readers might choose to go pick up the individual adventures of those characters. Of course, the concept of superhero teams extends earlier than the comic book Silver Age. During World War II, the comic book industry had published the adventures of teams of superheroes such as the Justice Society of America, the All-Star Squadron and the Sentinels of Liberty.

Narratively, the interplay of superheroes in a team such as the Justice League offers interesting plot opportunities for creative writers. All superheroes are not created equal. To send a man who stretches or an archer into battle with a team that includes a goddess or an alien who can move planets can present some narrative challenges but also opportunities unique to the superhero genre. In the hands of a most capable writer, such as Brad Meltzer, the question of character moves to the forefront. In the introduction to the collected *Identity Crisis*, filmmaker Joss Whedon writes of Meltzer: "He humanizes. He sees the smallest quirks, the deepest passions, the matter-of fact absurdity that is inevitable in the life of a super-powered person…. What follows is a story so genuinely tragic that it **does** change the universe—at least for a few characters" (iv).

In rhetorical theory, the term "Crisis" comes from the combination of the Chinese characters for "threat" and "opportunity" (Bostdorff 5–6). Once a threat is defined, a heightened state of apprehension is created in an audience that builds a sense of anticipation. Leaders may fail to meet the challenge and be deemed ineffective. Great leaders (or heroes) see opportunities for new solutions that move a community forward. The story of *Identity Crisis* is a relational tale of a community dealing with an issue that threatens its very existence. Their heroic solution may not be available to its readers, but the lesson of dealing with a crisis can inform us all. In analyzing *Identity Crisis* there are valuable lessons offered to its "nonsuper" readers.

Identity Crisis

The aforementioned opening scene with Elongated Man and Firehawk soon reveals that this stakeout is merely an elaborate ruse to get Ralph Dibny out of the house. Sue Dibny, Ralph's wife, is planning a surprise anniversary party. Unfortunately, the heroes discover some criminals purchasing weapons and are about to intervene when Ralph receives an emergency call from Sue. There is an intruder in their home. Ralph rushes to the scene but arrives too late. Sue has been murdered and the house set ablaze to destroy the evidence of the crime.

The murder of an innocent family member within the community of heroes sparks a dramatic response. Superhero teams as diverse as the Teen Titans, the Outsiders, the Justice Society, and the Justice League International all pledge their support and stake claims to villains who use fire or heat as a weapon. It is here, however, that the story takes a turn. A small group of Justice League members, including Ralph Dibny, congregate to begin a search of their own. Their target is Dr. Light. Two second-generation heroes, Wally West (The Flash) and Kyle Rayner (Green Lantern), notice the absence of their colleagues and question why they have set out on a private mission. Secrets of the Justice League begin to unfold.

The threat of disclosure to the full Justice League warrants an explanation to the new members. The first thread of a dark chapter in team history is unraveled. Dibny recounts a time when Dr. Light invaded the Justice League satellite and found Sue Dibny alone, staring at the stars. She sounded a distress signal but, before help could arrive, Light attacked and raped her. Heroes soon answered the call. The Flash (Barry Allen), Elongated Man, Green Lantern (Hal Jordan), Hawkman, Black Canary, Green Arrow, and Zatanna quickly subdued Light but he taunted the heroes and threatened to attack their loved ones as well. Zatanna used her magic to put Light to sleep and disarm him but Hawkman questioned if that would enough to eliminate the threat to their loved ones. He proposed that the memory of the attack be wiped from Dr. Light's mind to reduce the threat to other family and friends. A heated discussion ensued about the ethics of the suggestion but a majority of shaken team members voted with Hawkman. The delicate mind wipe not only eliminated the memory of the rape, it also damaged the mind of Dr. Light. The fears of the minority had been realized.

Dibny's account of the attack explains why the League members believe Dr. Light to be a suspect, so Wally (Flash) and Kyle (Green Lantern) agree to join the search party. The case becomes more complicated, however, as other family members of heroes are threatened and attacked. In response to the increased pressure from superheroes searching for a perpetrator, villains also begin to team-up and fortify their defenses. Everyone, on both sides of the law, is worried for themselves, their families, and their loved ones. In the course of the story, a dialogue is established between two generations of the Justice League. The younger Flash (Wally) pressures the older Green Arrow to know if this was the only incident of memory wipes. Oliver admits that it was not. On one occasion a group of supervillains switched bodies with the heroes and learned their secret identites, the memories of the heroes' true selves was magically removed from the villains.

It is here that Green Arrow offers his eloquent definition of "the mask" and expresses the need to preserve the community of heroes over the desires of individuals. Later, Green Arrow reveals that Batman saw the League removing Dr. Light's memory of the attack and was violently opposed to that course of action. The League restrained Batman and Zatanna magically made Batman forget the event as well. Wally is shocked. He wonders how Oliver could treat fellow heroes so badly. Oliver reasons that they might have done the same to him and that one cannot really keep secrets from great detectives. "People aren't stupid, Wally," Oliver explains. "They believe what they want to believe." The panel then zooms in the supersensitive ears of Superman. Oliver concludes, "And hear what they want to hear" (Meltzer 103). The Green Arrow acknowledges the power of forgetting, rationalization, and the need for secrets even in a community of superheroes. Absolute secrets must be kept absolutely.

To solve the crime of *Identity Crisis* Batman asks the question: "Who benefits?" This is the key to unraveling a murder mystery that unveils deeper secrets at every turn. To evaluate the worth of *Identity Crisis* to its readers, we must ask: "How do they benefit?" *Identity Crisis* is more than the traditional physical battle of superhero versus super villain, this time the "enemy" comes from within the community. The death of Sue Dibny is an "accidental tragedy." The villain of this story is not Darkseid or an alien armada, but a lonely, deranged former member of the Justice League's inner circle. It was, in fact, Jean Loring, estranged wife of superhero The Atom. By threatening the loved ones of superheroes, she hoped the Atom would return to her to protect her, as most heroes did with their loved ones after Sue Dibny died. She attempted to used trauma to reintegrate herself into the community, but caused deeper explorations of earlier trauma and nearly destroyed the community.

Meltzer, Morales, and Bair offer a nuanced portrait of a community in crisis. Members of the Justice League and their families have died before and likely will die again. The deeper threat in this story is the forced mind wipes employed by Zatanna to preserve the secrets of the Justice League. This threat to the public memory of the community threatens division and dissolution. Fortunately, in this case, absolute secrets are kept absolutely through magic.

Once again, we are reminded that human readers are not blessed (or cursed) with superpowers. In our communities, we cannot simply speak backwards—"*Tegrof*"—to erase painful memories. Legislators in Oklahoma recently attempted such "magical denial" when they voted to ban AP U.S. history in high schools because it stressed "what is bad about America" rather than "American exceptionalism." The advanced course content included discussions about the racial prejudices of the Founding Fathers, the internment of Americans of Japanese descent during World War II, and the ethics of dropping the atomic bomb (Hartmann). "*Tegrof.*" Unfortunately, even if young Oklahomans are spared the painful public memories of their ancestors, their fellow citizens in the larger national community will remember.

Poet George Santayana once said: "Those who forget the past are condemned to repeat it." As imperfect beings, the challenge of humanity is to remember the mistakes of the past and find new ways to improve our collective future. The concept of public memory and forgetting suggests that our memories define who we are and why we have chosen to belong to a community. Our communities, like the people in them, will be imperfect. We do not possess the magic to expunge our collective sins. Yet this does not mean that we are not worthy of redemption. One must recognize his errors before he can correct them. However, the redefinition is delicate and difficult to achieve.

Because of the nature of the story in *Identity Crisis*, the example of Sue Dibny, a victim of a vicious sexual assault, is appropriate to consider the nature of memory and identity. Obviously, the imaginary narrative from a superhero story cannot offer a direct relation to any real-world survivor of rape, but the issues surrounding memory and trauma raised in *Identity Crisis* can serve as a starting point for this conversation. A victim of rape will never forget the horror of the experience. Guilt, doubt, mistrust, fear, and a host of other emotions can overwhelm the victim. If the woman is trapped in that moment and lives the experience over and over again, recovery will be difficult to achieve. However, if the victim seeks counseling and group support, she might be able to reframe the experience in a larger context. The strength of surviving, the courage to report the crime, and the knowledge that she is not alone can allow the woman to redefine the narrative in a larger frame that will enable her to move forward. This would be an example of public memory/forgetting/redefinition that emphasizes healing rather than suffering. In turn, her new narrative may help other rape victims in the future.

The existence of the Justice League was threatened by the inability of its members to deal with their public memories in *Identity Crisis*. Erasing past mistakes by magical incantation necessitated the continuation of the practice to ensure the preservation of the community. No hero is more defined by his tragic past that Bruce Wayne/Batman. Had such a magical solution existed, many adults would have been tempted to use it to spare a ten-year-old boy the devastating memory of witnessing the murder of his parents. Yet it was that tragic act that created the Batman. There is no doubt that Bruce Wayne/Batman could not remain in a community that publically acknowledged its wiping of memories. Still, near the conclusion of *Identity Crises*, the Green Arrow suggests that "the World's Greatest Detective" must have deduced the truth about the actions of Zatanna, including the use of her powers on Batman himself. As readers, we are left to make up our own minds. We know that our memories define us, but it is equally true that rationalization, forgetting, and redefinition are powerful tools for human survival.

Identity Crisis is a meaningful story exploring the personalities and relationships of the superheroes in the Justice League. The mystery and tragedy of the narrative allow us new insights into the people behind the masks and their extended relationships with family and friends. On another level, *Identity Crisis* may be critically understood as a story about community. Any community, be it superhero or human, is built upon the collective experiences and memories of its members. Jeffrey K. Johnson asserts that *Identity Crisis* is a clear move towards darker stories embraced by comic book companies in a morally ambiguous post–9/11 world. Much as Americans felt heightened distrust, fear, and paranoia in their communities as tragedy forced them to reconsider their larger identities and to view the world with more distrust, the same happens in the Justice League.

Numerous superheroes trade their morals and their values for safety and violate the rights of other heroes and villains that disagree. No one is safe and no one can be trusted. Our heroes and their families are not who or what we thought they were and now everyone must be seen with fear and suspicion. As many Americans began to distrust those around them, so did their heroes (Johnson 176).

With this reading, all of the issues of collective memory, identity, and trust that are played out on comic book pages with heroes in spandex are reflective of the issues present in the country where this entertainment was being produced and consumed.

To grow and evolve, communities must define their past, celebrate their traditions, and find ways to address their past mistakes in future challenges. Every community will face crisis. Superheroes may deal with it through time travel or magic, humans must employ the more mundane tools of honesty, compassion, and communication. To move forward, we must speak forward. Imperfect communities must address their public memories and redefine them in a new larger context to address the "sins" of the past. Redemption is possible, if we are considerate and honest in our desire to improve. As Ralph Dibny reminds us in the conclusion of *Identity Crisis*, tragedy may befall us, but the conversation continues.

Works Cited

Bostdorff, Denise. *The Presidency and the Rhetoric of Foreign Crisis*. Columbia: University of South Carolina Press, 1994.

Coogan, Peter. *Superhero: The Secret Origin of a Genre*. Austin: MonkeyBrain Books Publication, 2006.

Hartmann, Margaret. "Why Oklahoma Lawmakers Voted to Ban AP U.S. History." *New York Magazine* 18 February 2015. www.nymag.com. Retrieved 16 September 2015.

Hume, Janice. "Memory Matters: The Evolution of Scholarship in Collective Memory and Mass Communication." *The Review of Communication* 10, no. 3 (July 2010): 181–96.

Johnson, Jeffrey K. *Super-History: Comic Book Superheroes and American Society*. Jefferson, NC: McFarland, 2012.

Meltzer, Brad (w), Rags Morales (p), Michael Bair (i), Ken Lopez (l), and Alex Sinclair (c). *Identity Crisis*. New York: DC Comics, 2005.

Vivian, Bradford T. "Up from Memory: Epideictic Forgetting in Booker T. Washington's Cotton States Exposition Address." *Philosophy and Rhetoric* 45, no. 2 (2012): 189–212.

Whedon, Joss. "Introduction." In *Identity Crisis*. Ed. Brad Meltzer, et al. New York: DC Comics, 2005.

Wright, Bradford W. *Comic Book Nation: The Transformation of Youth Culture in America*. Baltimore: Johns Hopkins University Press, 2001.

The Good, the Bad and the Reboot

Justice League *in the* New 52

CATHY LEOGRANDE

Reboot. It may not be as upsetting a term as retcon (short for retroactive continuity) but it can strike a sense of dread into fans' hearts. In 2011, DC Comics announced it would cancel all of its superhero comics and began a do-over. It was not a relaunch, which introduces a clean starting point for new audiences, but generally continues previous continuity. It was not a retcon, which changes previously established facts and events. This was a major overhaul. This was pushing the reset button and wiping away everything fans knew about Superman, Batman and other beloved characters. This was goodbye to previous history, hello to new origin stories, and transformation of some or all of what was canon in order to allow a new audience to begin at the same point as fans who have been immersed in the stories for years. The promise was exciting creativity. The fear was a disastrous mess. New and old fans waited to see what happened.

The *Justice League* was front and center in the plan, and became one of the first renumbered issues with *Justice League* #1 on August 31, 2011. Many fans feel this group rivals Marvel's *Avengers* for great characters, storylines, and fresh feel. This essay is focused on the Justice League from the period of the launch of the *New 52* until *Convergence*. This particular period (August 2011–June 2015) was a time in United States history when a number of issues were reshaping American culture. There was tension between tradition and future thinking, between corporate control and individuals, and within populations regarding race and gender. This essay reviews the context for the *New 52* relaunch, the impact on JL, and the critical hot spots that garnered the most attention from critics and fans.

It's Just Business: Rationale for the New 52

The *New 52* was planned at a time of change and uncertainty in the comic industry. With factors including the ease of access online access to digital media growing, and the dominance of Marvel on the big screen, DC decision-makers knew they needed to evolve. The economic downturn after 2008 left people with less money to spend on items like comics. New leadership personnel knew that they had to make changes. Among the many possibilities, the *New 52* emerged as a risky but admirable revamp on a bigger scale than what had been previously done.

In recent years, the comic book industry has been servicing a different audience. Some credit this to the rise of graphic novels. In 1986, the first six chapters of *Maus* by Art Spiegelman were published as a book and distributed in bookstores rather than comic stores. Notable comic book creators Alison Bechdal and Marjane Satrapi are among those that cite *Maus* as an influence on their work (Chute). The term graphic novel had emerged earlier and gained popularity to describe this thing that was different from a collection of single-issue comics. *Maus* brought adults to a form of writing that had been seen as low-status and primarily for children. Manga has also entered that space, and brought in readers who may not have been drawn to traditional superhero comics in the past. Heidi MacDonald summed up this problem:

> The methods and product mixes that were formulated to deal with a readership that grew up when comics were a niche product for nerds have to be reevaluated when new readers are coming in from the top properties in every form of entertainment, from graphic novels that they were taught in school, from webcomics, from creators with strong social media, from every which way. There is no well marked four lane highway to comics any more, just a delightful variety of roads, interstates and worn down dirt paths.

In February 2010, Dan DiDio and Jim Lee became co-publishers of DC Comics, along with Geoff Johns as chief creative officer. They understood the problems facing DC and the industry itself. Some fans came to comics from movies, rather than the reverse. Unlike Marvel, DC had not figured out best to manage the connections between that aspect of their fictional world. DC knew that it had to do something different to capture this varied audience.

The *New 52* as a wholesale overhaul was designed to clear obstacles so that new fans could enter and not lack insights based on convoluted backstories from 20 years ago. DC had used a variety of strategies to explain events and characters across storylines, including a number of Earths, each with parallel versions of the same characters. The complexities made it difficult for any new reader. The crossover *Crisis on Infinite Earth* in 1985 had been an attempt to reset the continuities and bring some consistency to the multiverses that delighted and confused DC fans. There are mixed opinions on how well that was accomplished. In *Reboot or Die: The New Life of DC Comics*, Zachary Sniderman noted that *Crisis* helped, but left a "better-organized mess" that still made it almost impossible to keep characters and storylines straight. He stated, "All that mumbo-jumbo is driving away the casual fan that just wants to see their favorite superhero punch a bad guy and save the day without getting bogged down in continuity errors. Not every current comic book is an intellectual maze but it's still a trick to figure out why Robin is a girl in one series, a boy in another, and non-existent in a third." The hope for the *New 52* was that it would modernize some of the lore that was leftover from different eras. The stated goal was to stay true to the core parts of each character and story, and build from that foundation.

Technology was also behind the *New 52*. Back in 1994, the Voyager Company released a CD-ROM with the complete version of *Maus* along with interviews and other materials (Horowitz 403). Over 20 years later, some entire comics were born and lived on the internet. Digital versions of stories were changing the way companies did business and fans gained access to material. Decisions about how many new issues to release at once, when and in what format were critical. For years, comic book publishers had freedom over this. Wednesday was generally New Comic Book Day in America. Release dates were announced for publications, but delays could result in postponement or even cancellation. Then came the Internet, and tablets. Many comic shops had a difficult time competing when an app could let readers download a high quality electronic version of print titles that made it easier to take along and allowed adults to mask their love of superheroes on daily commutes. When the *New 52* was released, DC also launched Same Day Digital. Fans could buy the digital version of comics the same day as they were released in stores. It seemed that sales and readers were more important than format.

The *New 52* was DC's attempt to regain primacy over Marvel in terms of sales and popularity. Creative factors related to stories, characters and continuity were given as the main reasons for the massive changes. However, most fans and industry leaders recognized the business factors were at least equal in degree to artistic ones. While some hardcore fans object to any changes in their beloved comics, others call for adaptations that allow characters and stories to adjust with changes in the real world.

Ten Years After the Towers

Comic book creators and publishers released special issues to raise money to benefit victims after the events of September 11, 2001. After that, there was a general business-as-usual stance for the next few years. Comic creators, like many Americans, weren't sure of their role and identity in this new world of terrorism and fear that had invaded our reality and our country for what seemed like the first time. The post–9/11 world was closer to the turbulent 1960s that the previous Reagan years. Politicians like George W. Bush, seeking reelection, maintained this sense of fear to keep people on guard and worried about what might come next. Comics soon caught up.

By September 2003, DC was ready to try to be reflective of society. Qurac was a previously established fictional country in the Middle East. A superpowered mercenary terrorist group originally called the *Jihad* (changed in 1987 to *Onslaught*) made their home there. Storylines prior to 2001 had included Israeli superhero team the Hayoth, as well as enemies from China and Russia, and nuclear weaponry. In 2003, *JLA* #83 (September 2003) titled *American Nightmare*, began with a chemical attack in London. Then-president Lex Luthor claims it was perpetrated by the Qurac (thinly-veiled Iraq), but is hounded by a crowd of shouting protestors. He uses the London attack to call for an invasion of Qurac. As Superman debates him in private, he says, "It's unbecoming to question your president during times of international unrest." In an interesting visual, the "A" in the JLA logo on a meeting table begins to transforms and become a horrible mess. It was all a dream, brought about by a "Transconscious Simulator." The issue closes with some pointed dialogue by Superman:

> We exist ... because those with the power to stop injustice simply must.... With clarity, compassion and truth as their most powerful weapons. We can show them a better way. I know we can. Armed conflict may be an option, and I will support it... if the truth is clear, and the cause is just. But I will know the truth, and I will not be ashamed or be called un–American for demanding it.... This dream ... things spun completely out of my grasp. Luthor took the U.S. to war, despite our protests, the U.N.'s.... He killed everything we stand for. And I let it happen because I couldn't make up my mind.

Superman and the Justice League mirrored Americans' fears and insecurity. Some authors saw this as Leftist, pacifist, Anti-American, and hypocritical of the DC characters. Others saw it as reflective of the confusion and distrust of Bush's policies that was reflective of many Americans (Bozell; Elder; Mayakis).

Later issues would continue to bring the unsettling nature of reality into the stories. Kahndaq was another fictional Middle Eastern country, ruled for a time by Asim Muhunnad (a Saddam Hussein type character). One of the main languages spoken there is Arabic. Kahndaq also becomes part of the Freedom of Power Treaty, a group that includes China, North Korea, and Myanmar. Scientists activate some of the Four Horsemen of Apokolips, reminiscent of the fear among some Americans that end times are here. Bialya, another fictional Middle Eastern country, experiences genocide. The country's president refuses humanitarian aid, and there is a discussion of a food stealing ring similar to the real problems in some African nations. Reese Taylor is a corrupt employee of WayneTech who sells food shipments meant for refugee camps. Story lines address corrupt big businesses as well as good one (like WayneTech and S.T.A.R. Labs). The villain *Chemo* is born from failed chemical experiments and uses toxic waste as a weapon. These are some examples of how comics took on the changes of the post 9/11 world. This was the context for the *New 52* reboot.

Overall Reception

When passionate fans are asked to accept changes, there is generally a mix of responses. When a comic book company that began in the 1930s reboots its entire catalog of characters and stories, the spectrum of reactions is guaranteed to span from admiration and affection to vitriol and hate. Announcements of the goals and plans for the *New 52* brought high expectations and anticipation along with worries and fears. It is no wonder that one could find fans who demonstrated acceptance, resignation, anger, wonder, irritation, surprise, and every other possible emotion during the period the *New 52* began, took shape, and ended.

Most fans were willing to go along for the ride. They recognized that times were changing and that their beloved characters would have to change along or risk death by attrition. The promised goal of streamlined continuities, greater diversity to reflect the real world, and accessibility for new fans sounded laudable. It was not that fans were resistant; they wanted to embrace new stories and revamped characters. In September 2011, hundreds of fans (some in costume) lined up in Times Square for the midnight launch and a chance to get Jim Lee and Geoff Johns to sign their comics. *Justice League* #1 presold the entire first print run of 200,000 copies (Sniderman). The troubling fear that the results could be dumbed down versions of complexly layered stories was a concern. Lee and Johns reiterated that well told stories with the essential traits that made characters interesting would appeal to new and veteran fans.

Starting a massive company-wide relaunch with *Justice League* was brilliant. It was bound to garner disparate feelings from fans, and getting people talking about the reboot was good for business. With the return of the iconic DC superhero team in "Origins," both fans and industry critics were off and running. Chris Sims, senior writer at ComicsAlliance, was not impressed (2011). He said,

> The short version is that this comic is just flat-out not very good. And the thing is, it should be. A comic book with this much riding on it, this much promotion, the two cre-

ators who are meant to be the top guys in the industry working with the genuinely exciting premise of doing a bold new unshackled story of some of the greatest fictional characters ever? There's no reason it shouldn't be amazing. And yet, what we have here is, as Curt Franklin put it, a comic that reads like it came with an action figure. It's not that there aren't good parts to it, but it's a C- book at best, and as an introduction to the New DC Universe, that doesn't cut it.... This is their shot. This is the issue that they had to make their case, the one they promoted, with the goal being to get people back into stores to buy single issues. And as a 20-page story, it's a complete failure in that respect. What *actually happens* in this issue? [Sims].

In the same article, editor Caleb Gollner disagreed. While he agreed that some points were problematic, he enjoyed the initial offering: "I think I just enjoyed the overall energy. The comic felt modern to me in a way that a lot of other DC titles didn't, or never have." After the first story arc concluded in six issues, Sims remained unimpressed. He saw two-dimensional characters, lackluster dialogue, and horrifying violence without heroic redemption. David Uzemeri saw the exact opposite. In his counterpoint article, it was the character development that earned his praise:

On a microscale, though, what it's really about is how these seven people relate to each other, and why they work well together. That's why Johns introduces them one-by-one rather than bringing the whole team together at the beginning.... The characters are ricocheting and reflecting off each other in new and interesting patterns, and it's this chaotic froth of relationships that makes the core of the book.... Justice League is a book where the external conflicts exist to facilitate the character work, rather than the other way around, a book that dispenses with Johnsian literalism in favor of humanism. In short, Justice League is a totally new direction for Geoff Johns, and I can't wait to see where it takes one of the biggest writers in the business and his comics [Uzemeri].

Perhaps this ability for different readers to see different things in the same comics was intended, or perhaps it was an unplanned byproduct. Whichever is more accurate, the fans started talking about Justice League characters and followed them individually and as a team throughout the *New 52*.

As time went on, the New 52 Justice League-related titles helped redefine the team. Additional members were added, such as Firestorm and Element Woman. *Justice League Dark* saw a team of characters with more supernatural and mystical powers. *Justice League International* was launched, then cancelled after twelve issues leading to the formation of a new, separate *Justice League of America*. The *Trinity War* mystery-based story arc brought all three teams together for eleven issues with information that affected later stories and characters. By August 2013, the teams were veering into different directions. By June 2015, the *New 52* ended. Most people agreed that the relaunch was not successful, although some felt that *Justice League* titles were among those that had worked.

Specific Concerns

In addition to fans who were unhappy about issues with the continuity, the *New 52* brought out critics regarding specific issues. Among these, race and gender changes sparked particularly bitter responses. Some saw the changes especially problematic given the fact that the reboot was an opportunity to rectify lingering complications that had been created in different eras when attention was not always paid to the impact of such choices. By not using the *New 52* to include more progressive stories and characters, some fans saw DC executives as intentionally exclusionary to certain groups.

One of the first complaints was regarding the portrayal of women. Laura Sneddon foreshadowed the concern when she wrote about the fiasco at the DC panel at San Diego ComicCon:

> This was the time for DC to win over the fans, attract new readers, and leave us enthused and eager for what September will bring. Instead, women who have attended the panels or listened to the podcasts have described the experience as uncomfortable at best, offensive at worst. When women pushed their questions about women in comics to the panel, the audience turned against them and the panel responses were flippant or off the mark. Two women have told me they feel like DC sees them as second class readers, and why would an unwanted reader possibly want to spend her money on those comics? Some of the reporting has been sensationalist, and there were a lot of positive announcements from DC at SDCC too, but the overwhelming feeling for female fans is that this was a missed opportunity and a bit of a PR disaster.

Sneddon held out hope that the reality would be better, but was forced to rethink that when she saw the cover of *Justice League #1 Origins*. Amid the new costumes, including Superman's collared blue top and missing red briefs was an even more scantily clad and buxom Wonder Woman. Sneddon's caption read, "One of these costumes is not like the others."

Even as the *New 52* continued, gender issues remained a concern for many. Diana Darcy writes regularly about Helena Bertinelli as the Huntress. In her 2014 article "Five Reasons Helena Bertinelli as a Woman of Colour Matters and More," she praised some aspects of and potential in the change for that character in the New 52. However, she also addressed the problems with this change, including those for Lois Lane, Catwoman, and Wonder Woman:

> Despite their vocal commitment to diversity, DC's track record with women in the *New 52* has been incredibly piss poor, and deeply rooted in a system of unchecked misogyny to boot. Since the start of the *New 52*, three of their most iconic women alone have been both brutalised for pure shock value and even repurposed in such a way that has caused them to lose their power as icons.... Wonder Woman had her feminist foundation severely undercut in order to incorporate men into her narrative in a way that reinforced the sexist idea that women are weak. In the *New 52*, the Amazons also went from being a peaceful, loving, all female society to a misandrist society that rapes and murders men, which rein-

forces the patriarchal myth of feminists as man-haters. Wonder Woman herself is less an ambassador for peace who embraces femininity, and is more of a masculinised, blood-thirsty warrior who swings her sword first, asks questions later. To add further insult to injury, she was even repurposed to function as the iconic girlfriend of Superman in the *New 52*, a role that she was never EVER intended to fulfill by her creator, Charles Moulton Marston [Darcy].

The changes in Wonder Woman were particularly upsetting for many, as attested by the reactions of other fans and reviewers.

Trevor Gentry-Birnbaum agreed that the depiction of women in the *New 52* was problematic. In his article "5 Things Wrong with DC's New 52 Comic Reboot," he includes a section humorously called "There Are Girls Here, Too!" in which he points out concerns:

Even Wonder Woman, the supposed paragon of feminism in the DCU doesn't escape unscathed. In the first issue of her series, she is seen naked for no reason. It literally con-tributes nothing to the plot…. I've always thought that when a male creator writes a story for a girl character that he should formulate it the same way he would a comic about a man. And rest assured, these scantily clad, brain dead females only show up in books penned by men. It's a kind of invisible sexism that allows DC to say they have titles devoted to female characters, but still parade them around as trollops for fanboys' amuse-ment. They say their goal is to increase readership, yet they insult half of their prospective audience with women that look and act like a sixteen year old boy's wet dream.

Gentry-Birnbaum identified one of the roots of the problem: the dearth of female creators and editors at DC. Laura Hudson built on this and extended it to the other main criticism: racism. DC had famously been called out when the map provided for an alternate universe in the *Flashpoint* mini-series labeled Africa as "ape-controlled." Hudson makes a sound argument for how ignorance can easily lead to cringe-worthy moments in comics, and why real diversity behind the scenes is critical:

Including different types of people on a staff of creative people who are building a world together isn't important just because it makes for more PR-friendly staff photographs, but because these are the people entrusted with the god-like power of controlling the actions of these characters, putting words in their mouths, dressing them, representing their expe-riences in the world, not to mention showing the audience how to look at them and telling what they should value about them. Whether you're a racial minority, or a woman, or someone with something other than straight sexuality, or someone with a physical disabil-ity to name only a few examples, you're going to have a different experience of the world. It can be hard to know exactly what that's like if it isn't you—the slights and the everyday indignities that you don't see because that's what privilege means: It means you don't have to deal with them. Often, it means you don't even have to notice that they exist. This also means that you can be a very well-intentioned person and still end up saying and doing—or writing and drawing—accidentally demeaning things simply because you just don't understand. And if you're a creator and you're trying to write and draw characters that are different from you, it can mean that you end up sounding inauthentic, tone-deaf, or worse, actively feeding into stereotypes.

This is a powerful explanation of how and why well-meaning individuals rarely provide authentic results.

Sadly, other attempts to include characters of other races and ethnicities seemed less than successful. Diversity had been one of the stated goals of the *New 52*. However, Gentry-Birnbaum aptly chides DC, calling it "diversity for diversity's sake." He hones in on one of the most visible changes, the inclusion of Cyborg in Justice League:

> The Justice League is a gathering of Earth's most recognizable heroes, each with their own golden age pedigree and status as the DCU's heavy hitters … and Cyborg, who just so happens to be black. Shoehorning Cyborg in to the League feels like superhero affirmative action; as if Superman turned to Batman and said "You know what? We need a black guy." Cyborg can't even carry his own book! While I'm certainly in favor avoiding a fighting force made up of seven white people, it really feels as if it's the Justice League and Black Friend.

Ed Cambro in his article "The Good and Bad of Diversity in Comics" referred to an "interesting bit of irony" in that he has indeed taken over Martian Manhunter's role as "little more than the switchboard operator for the League…. He's now just on promotional posters so DC can say 'We have a black guy on our biggest team!'" This was not the only complaint about race. One that received great attention was Wally West. From Jay Garrick to Barry Allen to Wally West, the *Flash* is one of the most beloved DC superheroes. In 1985, Barry Allen died and Wally West assumed the role. For many readers, Wally West was their Flash. The *New 52* saw Barry Allen return as the character with a new origin story. Another fan complaint was the recreation of Bart Allen/*Kid Flash* as Bar Torr, a foreign-sounding name with a hint of racism. Fans were unhappy that Wally was missing, but it only got worse when he reappeared. Wally had been a redhead with pale skin and freckles, an all-around nice guy. *New 52* Wally was a black street kid who participated in petty crimes. Wally used out-of-date slang, wears a hoodie, and was seen vandalizing by painting graffiti. In the article "Why the New Black Wally West Is Just Offensive," Bobby Joseph writes: "This new 'Black' Wally West kid is devoid of any kind of personality and charm. New Wally West wears a hoodie (as all Black kids do obviously) and is on a downward spiral because he doesn't have a firm family network (yawn) to rely upon."

Both Cambro and Joseph point to the way DC followed Marvel's bad example of creating Black characters, such as Miles Morales, for whom personal connection to crime is seen as necessary in order to give them authenticity.

Cambro shows differences by pointing out a number of cases where minority characters, such as Linda Park, were presented in subtle ways. Their ethnicity was not overstated, merely one more attribute of the character and not a central part of the identity. *New 52* original character Jessica Cruz (an addition to *Green Lantern Corps*) demonstrate this dichotomy. Cruz is a character who experienced an assault, and develops agoraphobia as a response to the incident. Her ethnicity is not central to the character or story in any way. Cambro writes that the Cruz plot "is an example of empowering storytelling … blind to any specific race or gender. Anyone who has dealt with that kind of ordeal can find something true in this portrayal; it just so happens that the character is a minority." He sees authenticity in the feelings generated by the way Cruz's character is drawn as compared to Wally West and Cyborg. He calls out the industry and warns of long term loss of readers:

> It's condescending, hacky, and shows both the creative bankruptcy and how out of touch these companies are. Progress isn't depicting more black criminals, but by having more characters who are treated and act like regular people.... Though meant to be special, these acts often come off as a lazy retroactive progressivism and that obsequiously panders to an audience they might alienate by trying too hard to make them stay.

Like concerns regarding representation of females, these problems seem to originate with the exclusion of talented minority writers, artists and editors within the industry. As Joseph states: "Believe it or not I don't have a problem with White writers writing Black characters. What I do have a problem with is Black characters that are written badly and this new flag of diversity that mainstream comic companies are flying at the moment to fill their demographics quota without using at least some Black writers to tell their tales." Fans and reviewers criticized these efforts as same old gimmicks and tropes that were outdated and out of touch with both sought-after new readers and loyal fans. For many, the Justice League was seen as the premier place to showcase bold new ideas and break new ground. While some innovation was realized, the launch and follow-up seemed at best more of the same, and at worst, insulting and questionable choices.

Summary

Change has been a primary feature of the new century so far. For DC, the reboot of the *New 52* was a major shift, a response to changes in publishing, in comics, as well as the world.

The 2011 announcement of the reboot came with great aspirations. Beyond just streamlining the continuity to appeal to new readers, there was the possibility of real changes, changes that would reflect the reality of the new century. The question of whether the reboot was a success or not, and if the stated goals were achieved differs among fans and critics even five years later. By examining changes to the *Justice League* stories and surrounding characters, readers can see the attempts, successes, near-misses and failures that were DC's way of appealing to new fans and preserving existing readers.

For many fans, the *Justice League* team served as a bridge between events and changes in DC publishing efforts over many years. The seven original members from 1960—Aquaman, Batman, Flash, Green Lantern, Martian Manhunter, Superman and Wonder Woman—have seen additional colleagues come and go. So have the writers, artists and publishers at DC. The *New 52* ended with *Convergence*. As part of that final event, the multiverse was restored, along with every past world. DC co-publisher Dan Didio was quick to point out that this was not another reboot. The continuity reset from *New 52*, including the new origin stories and teams that made up the *Justice League*, were still in effect but the possibilities were greater in this new DC Universe. Characters and worlds from the pre–*New 52* reboot were back in play.

The symbolism of *Justice League* on the first cover of the *New 52* launch seemed to represent the strength of the DC brand, a composite of diverse characters and stories that somehow managed to work together for common purposes. As with the *New 52*, *Justice League* was at the forefront of the next phase with the much-anticipated *Darkseid War*. Despite criticism, the team of superheroes is generally seen as the barometer for the company. The long-time beloved characters are generally the ones that provide the roadmap for whatever journey comes next. These characters seem to say that change may be uncomfortable, but it is a necessary part of growth and continuity. If DC maintains its place with the tumultuous world of comics in the 21st century, it seems certain that they will owe a debt to everyone's favorite team.

WORKS CITED

Bozell, L. Brent, III. "Antiwar Heroes get Superhero Status in Comic-Book Scripts." *Insight on the News* 19.22 (2003): 52. ProQuest. Web. 10 February 2016.

Elder, Joshua. "A Hate-America Superhero?" *FrontPageMag*. David Horowitz Freedom Center, 8 August 2003. Web. 15 February 2016.

Cambro, Ed. "The Good and Bad of Diversity in Comics." *Seqart Organization*. N.p., 5 April 2015. Web. 2 February 2016.

Darcy, Diana. "Five Reasons Helena Bertinelli as a Woman of Colour Matters and More." *Helena Wayne Huntress*. Blogger, 31 May 2014. Web. 10 February 2016.

Gentry-Birnbaum, Trevor. "5 Things Wrong with DC's New 52 Comic Reboot." *WhatCulture*. What Culture Ltd., 30 November 2011. Web. 10 February 2016.

Horowitz, Sarah R. "Art Spiegelman." In *Contemporary Jewish-American Novelists: A Bio-Critical Sourcebook*. Ed. Joel Shatzky and Michael Taub. Westport, CT: Greenwood, 1997, 400–408. Google Books. Web. 15 February 2016.

Hudson, Laura. "Answering Dan Didio: The Problem with Having Only 1% Female Creators at DC Comics." *Comics Alliance*. Townsquare Media, 28 July 2011. Web. 15 February 2016.

Joseph, Bobby. "Why the New Black Wally West Is Just Offensive." *Bleeding Cool*. N.p., 6 May 2014. Web. 15 February 2016.

MacDonald, Heidi. "Are We Seeing the Twilight of the 'Big Two'?" *The Beat*. Wordpress, 19 January 2016. Web. 15 February 2016.

Mayakis, Mike. "Superman vs. The War Party." Antiwar.com. Randolph Bourne Institute, 25 November 2003. Web. 15 February 2016.

Sims, Chris. "'Justice League' #1: Chris Sims and Caleb Goellner Go Head-to-Head On DC's New First Issue." *Comics Alliance*. Townsquare Media, 1 September 2011. Web. 13 February 2016.

Sims, Chris. "Point/Counterpoint: 'Justice League' Is Everything Wrong with Comics." *Comics Alliance*. Townsquare Media, 8 March 2012. Web. 13 February 2016.

Sneddon, Laura. "Women in Comics: The New 52 and the Batgirl of San Diego." *comicbookGRRRL*. Wordpress, 24 July 2011. Web. 15 February 2016.

Sniderman, Zachary. "Reboot or Die: The New Life of DC Comics." *GQ*. Conde Nast, 9 September 2011. Web. 10 February 2016.

Uzemeri, David. "Point/Counterpoint: 'Justice League' Shines with Strong Characters." *Comics Alliance*. Townsquare Media, 8 March 2012. Web. 13 February 2016.

About the Contributors

Leonardo **Acosta Lando** is a lecturer in popular culture at the Universidad de Buenos Aires (UBA)–Facultad de Filosofía y Letras (Argentina). He also teaches psychoanalysis and horror cinema.

W.C. **Bamberger** has published essays on a range of topics including Wonder Woman, Japanese horror films, poet Anne Carson and painter Trevor Winkfield, the death of Kierkegaard, eggs in the writings of Friedrich Nietzsche and Samuel Butler, Argentinian-German composer Mauricio Kagel and bluesman Son House.

Brian **Cogan** has written or co-written and edited or co-edited nine books as well as contributed to academic journals, newspapers, databases, encyclopedias and essay collections on topics including punk music, politics, *Monty Python's Flying Circus*, *South Park* and the baby boomer generation.

John **Darowski** is a PhD candidate in humanities at the University of Louisville. His research is on the superhero Gothic, tracing the impact of the Gothic on the evolution of the superhero and how both genres work together to reflect the cultural context. He has published essays in the previous volumes of the ages of superheroes series.

Joseph J. **Darowski** teaches English at Brigham Young University. He is a member of the editorial review board of *The Journal of Popular Culture* and has previously edited essay collections on the ages of Superman, Wonder Woman, the X-Men, the Avengers, Iron Man, and the Incredible Hulk.

Thomas C. **Donaldson** is a PhD candidate in U.S. cultural history at the University at Albany (SUNY). His primary research focus is on the portrayal of gender in popular media, particularly comic books. His dissertation is "Truth, Justice, and the Status Quo: Antifeminism, the Resurgence of Superhero Comics, and the Remption of Masculine Hegemony as the American Way of Gender, 1955–1990."

Nicole **Freim** has been involved with the Comics and Comic Arts area of the National Popular Culture Association for 18 years, spending more than half that as the area chair. She is on the editorial board of *The International Journal of Comic Arts* and a member of the newly formed Comics Studies Society. She teaches English in Southern California.

D.R. **Hammontree** teaches in the Department of Writing and Rhetoric at Oakland University, where he also serves as an assistant professor and a writing program administrator. He contributed to *The Ages of Wonder Woman* and is a past president of the Michigan Council of Teachers of English.

Charles **Henebry**, a student of emblems—Elizabethan comic books, roughly speaking—has focused his scholarship on the four-color world of superheroes, from the genesis of Superman's costume change to the impact of the 1960s antiwar movement on Iron Man. He has an essay in *The Ages of Iron Man*.

Peter W. **Lee** is a Ph.D. candidate in the History and Culture program at Drew University. His dissertation examines the construction of boyhood in the post–World War II years through American films. He is the editor of *A Galaxy Here and Now: Historical and Cultural Readings of Star Wars* (McFarland, 2016). He has contributed to previous volumes of the Ages of Superheroes series.

Cathy **Leogrande** is a professor in the Teacher Education Department of the Purcell School of Professional Studies at Le Moyne College. Her teaching and research is focused in areas of new literacies, using digital text, media and non-print material as well as comics and graphic novels, manga, and other popular culture to provide K–12 teachers the skills to teach content to students in inclusive classrooms.

Ruth **McClelland-Nugent** is an associate professor of history and director of Women's and Gender Studies at Augusta University. She has published essays in a variety of edited collections, including *The Ages of Wonder Woman*.

Daniel J. **O'Rourke** is an associate professor of communication studies at Ashland University. He has contributed to Ages of the Superheroes volumes on Superman and the X-Men and has also written on Spider-man and the Silver Scorpion.

Fernando Gabriel **Pagnoni Berns** is a graduate teaching assistant in the Facultad de Filosofía y Letras at the Universidad de Buenos Aries (Argentina), where he teaches classes on American horror cinema and Euro horror. He has contributed essays to several books, including to the ages of superheroes series.

Gene **Phillips** has contributed to an assortment of comics fanzines, including *Comics Journal* and *Comics Interpreter*, as well as a handful of essays to other collections on comics. He maintains a blog, *The Archetypal Archive*, which is devoted to critiquing comic books, pop culture, and "canonical literature."

Jason **Sacks** is an independent comics scholar. He is the author or co-editor of several books and numerous essays on a variety of comic topics. He has contributed to the books on the ages of the Incredible Hulk, Iron Man and the Avengers.

Jennifer **Swartz-Levine** is the interim dean of the School of Arts, Humanities, and Social Sciences, an associate professor of English, and the director of the Writing Center at Lake Erie College. She is the faculty leader for Lake Erie College's Arts, Culture, and Humanities Learning Community.

Louie Dean **Valencia-García** is a lecturer in history and literature at Harvard University. He studies modern history, urban space, the history of technology, youth cultural production and queer and subaltern cultures in contemporary history.

Index